RESEARCH IN CHEMISTRY AND CHEMICAL SCIENCES

ENV BOOKS SERIES

RESEARCH IN CHEMISTRY AND CHEMICAL SCIENCES

Editors

Dr. Vijender Singh

Director

Green Consultancy and Research Pvt. Ltd.

3263, Urban Estate, Jind (Haryana)

(India)

&

Dr. Pawan Kumar 'Bharti'

Society for Environment, Health Awareness of Nutrition & Toxicology (SEHAT)

B-225/5D, Top Floor, Subhash Gali, Road No. 7, Block B

Ashok Nagar, Shahdara, Delhi - 110 093

(India)

DPH

DISCOVERY PUBLISHING HOUSE PVT. LTD.

INDIA

Published by:
Namit Wasan
DISCOVERY PUBLISHING HOUSE PVT. LTD.
4383/4B, Ansari Road, Darya Ganj
New Delhi-110 002 (India)
Phone : +91-11-23279245; 23253475; 43596065
E-mail : discoverybooksindia@gmail.com
discoverypublishinghouse@gmail.com
namitwasan9@gmail.com
web : www.discoverypublishinggroup.com

***First Edition:* 2020**

ISBN: 978-93-88854-40-5

Research in Chemistry and Chemical Sciences

Printed at:
Infinity Imaging Systems
Delhi

Preface

Chemistry is the scientific discipline involved with elements and compounds composed of atoms, molecules and ions: their composition, structure, properties, behavior and the changes they undergo during a reaction with other substances.

In the scope of its subject, chemistry occupies an intermediate position between physics and biology. It is sometimes called the central science because it provides a foundation for understanding both basic and applied scientific disciplines at a fundamental level.

Chemistry addresses topics such as how atoms and molecules interact via chemical bonds to form new chemical compounds. There are four types of chemical bonds: covalent bonds, in which compounds share one or more electron(s); ionic bonds, in which a compound donates one or more electrons to another compound to produce ions (cations and anions); hydrogen bonds; and Van der Waals force bonds.

Chemistry is the study of matter, its properties, how and why substances combine or separate to form other substances, and how substances interact with energy. Many people think of chemists as being white-coated scientists mixing strange liquids in a laboratory, but the truth is we are all chemists. Understanding basic chemistry concepts is important for almost every profession. Chemistry is part of everything in our lives.

Every material in existence is made up of matter — even our own bodies. Chemistry is involved in everything we do, from growing and cooking food to cleaning our homes and bodies to launching a space shuttle. Chemistry is one of the physical sciences that help us to describe and explain our world.

The present book updates the subject content on various chemical reactions, metal chemistry, environmental chemistry, bio-chemistry and material science.

Thanks are due to publisher and contributors from various institutions and universities.

The book will be helpful for the researchers, academia working in the field of dynamics and catalytic mechanism, sulphur dioxide oxidation; synthesis and application of transition metal, catalysts for the conversion gases; DNA binding and cleavage study of copper surfactant complexes; thermodynamics, kinetics study of arsenic removal from waste water; activated carbon from saw dust; transport of poly-fluorinated alkyl substances (PFAs) in environment; binding and interaction metal ions with protein; and graphene filler in nano and micro composite.

–Editors

(envbooks@gmail.com)

Contents

Introduction

Chemistry is a branch of science that involves the study of the composition, structure and properties of matter. Often known as the central science, it is a creative discipline chiefly concerned with atomic and molecular structure and its change, for instance through chemical reactions.

Chemistry is the scientific discipline involved with elements and compounds composed of atoms, molecules and ions: their composition, structure, properties, behavior and the changes they undergo during a reaction with other substances.

In the scope of its subject, chemistry occupies an intermediate position between physics and biology. It is sometimes called the central science because it provides a foundation for understanding both basic and applied scientific disciplines at a fundamental level. For example, chemistry explains aspects of plant chemistry (Botany), the formation of igneous rocks (Geology), how atmospheric ozone is formed and how environmental pollutants are degraded (ecology), the properties of the soil on the moon (Astrophysics), how medications work (Pharmacology), and how to collect DNA evidence at a crime scene (Forensics).

Chemistry addresses topics such as how atoms and molecules interact via chemical bonds to form new chemical compounds. There are four types of chemical bonds: covalent bonds, in which compounds share one or more electron(s); ionic bonds, in which a compound donates one or more electrons to another compound to produce ions (cations and anions); hydrogen bonds; and Van der Waals force bonds.

The current model of atomic structure is the quantum mechanical model. Traditional chemistry starts with the study of elementary particles, atoms, molecules, substances, metals, crystals and other aggregates of matter. Matter can be studied in solid, liquid, gas and plasma states, in isolation or in combination. The interactions, reactions and transformations that are studied in chemistry are usually the result of interactions between atoms, leading to rearrangements of the chemical bonds which hold atoms together. Such behaviors are studied in a chemistry laboratory.

The chemistry laboratory stereotypically uses various forms of laboratory glassware. However glassware is not central to chemistry, and a great deal of experimental (as well as applied/industrial) chemistry is done without it.

Solutions of substances in reagent bottles, including ammonium hydroxide and nitric acid, illuminated in different colors.

A chemical reaction is a transformation of some substances into one or more different substances. The basis of such a chemical transformation is the rearrangement of electrons in the chemical bonds between atoms. It can be symbolically depicted through a chemical equation, which usually involves atoms as subjects. The number of atoms on the left and the right in the equation for a chemical transformation is equal. (When the number of atoms on either side is unequal, the transformation is referred to as a nuclear reaction or radioactive decay.) The type of chemical reactions a substance may undergo and the energy changes that may accompany it are constrained by certain basic rules, known as chemical laws.

Energy and entropy considerations are invariably important in almost all chemical studies. Chemical substances are classified in terms of their structure, phase, as well as their chemical compositions. They can be analyzed using the tools of chemical analysis, e.g. spectroscopy and chromatography. Scientists engaged in chemical research are known as chemists. Most chemists specialize in one or more sub-disciplines. Several concepts are essential for the study of chemistry.

Chemistry is the study of matter, its properties, how and why substances combine or separate to form other substances, and how substances interact with energy. Many people think of chemists as being white-coated scientists mixing strange liquids in a laboratory, but the truth is we are all chemists. Understanding basic chemistry concepts is important for almost every profession. Chemistry is part of everything in our lives.

Every material in existence is made up of matter — even our own bodies. Chemistry is involved in everything we do, from growing and cooking food to cleaning our homes and bodies to launching a space shuttle. Chemistry is one of the physical sciences that help us to describe and explain our world.

Branches

There are five main branches of chemistry, each of which has many areas of study.

Analytical chemistry uses qualitative and quantitative observation to identify and measure the physical and chemical properties of substances. In a sense, all chemistry is analytical.

Physical chemistry combines chemistry with physics. Physical chemists study how matter and energy interact. Thermodynamics and quantum mechanics are two of the important branches of physical chemistry.

Organic chemistry specifically studies compounds that contain the element carbon. Carbon has many unique properties that allow it to form complex chemical bonds and very large molecules. Organic chemistry is known as the "Chemistry of Life" because all of the molecules that make up living tissue have carbon as part of their makeup.

Inorganic chemistry studies materials such as metals and gases that do not have carbon as part of their makeup.

Biochemistry is the study of chemical processes that occur within living organisms.

Fields of Study

Within these broad categories are countless fields of study, many of which have important effects on our daily life. Chemists improve many products, from the food we eat and the clothing we wear to the materials with which we build our homes. Chemistry helps to protect our environment and searches for new sources of energy.

Food Chemistry

Food science deals with the three biological components of food — carbohydrates, lipids and proteins. Carbohydrates are sugars and starches, the chemical fuels needed for our cells to function. Lipids are fats and oils and are essential parts of cell membranes and to lubricate and cushion organs within the body. Because fats have 2.25 times the energy per gram than either carbohydrates or proteins, many people try to limit their intake to avoid becoming overweight. Proteins are complex molecules composed of from 100 to 500 or more amino acids that are chained together and folded into three-dimensional shapes necessary for the structure and function of every cell. Our bodies can synthesize some of the amino acids; however eight of them, the essential amino acids, must be taken in as part of our food. Food scientists are also concerned with the inorganic components of food such as its water content, minerals, vitamins and enzymes.

Food chemists improve the quality, safety, storage and taste of our food. Food chemists may work for private industry to develop new products or improve processing. They may also work for government agencies such as the Food and Drug Administration to inspect food products and handlers to protect us from contamination or harmful practices. Food chemists test products to supply information used for the nutrition labels or to determine how packaging and storage affects the safety and quality of the food. Flavorists work with chemicals to change the taste of food. Chemists may also work on other ways to improve sensory appeal, such as enhancing color, odor or texture.

Environmental Chemistry

Environmental chemists study how chemicals interact with the natural environment. Environmental chemistry is an interdisciplinary study that involves both analytical chemistry and an understanding of environmental science. Environmental chemists must first understand the chemicals and chemical reactions present in natural processes in the soil water and air. Sampling and analysis can then determine if human activities have contaminated the environment or caused harmful reactions to affect it.

Water quality is an important area of environmental chemistry. "Pure" water does not exist in nature; it always has some minerals or other substance dissolved in it. Water quality chemists test rivers, lakes and ocean water for characteristics such as dissolved oxygen, salinity, turbidity, suspended sediments, and pH. Water destined for human consumption must be free of harmful contaminants and may be treated with additives like fluoride and chlorine to increase its safety.

Agricultural Chemistry

Agricultural chemistry is concerned with the substances and chemical reactions that are involved with the production, protection and use of crops and livestock. It is a highly interdisciplinary field that relies on ties to many other sciences. Agricultural chemists may work with the Department of Agriculture, the Environmental Protection Agency, the Food and Drug Administration or for private industry. Agricultural chemists develop fertilizers, insecticides and herbicides necessary for large-scale crop production. They must also monitor how these products are used and their impacts on the environment. Nutritional supplements are developed to increase the productivity of meat and dairy herds.

Agricultural biotechnology is a fast-growing focus for many agricultural chemists. Genetically manipulating crops to be resistant to the herbicides used to control weeds in the fields requires detailed understanding of both the plants and the chemicals at the molecular level. Biochemists must understand genetics, chemistry and business needs to develop crops that are easier to transport or that have a longer shelf life.

Chemical Engineering

Chemical engineers research and develop new materials or processes that involve chemical reactions. Chemical engineering combines a background in chemistry with engineering and economics concepts to solve technological problems. Chemical engineering jobs fall into two main groups: industrial applications and development of new products.

Industries require chemical engineers to devise new ways to make the manufacturing of their products easier and more cost effective. Chemical engineers are involved in designing and operating processing plants, develop safety procedures for handling dangerous materials, and supervise the manufacture of nearly every product we use. Chemical engineers work to develop new products and processes in every field from pharmaceuticals to fuels and computer components.

Geochemistry

Geochemists combine chemistry and geology to study the makeup and interaction between substances found in the Earth. Geochemists may spend more time in field studies than other types of chemists. Many work for the U.S. Geological Survey or the Environmental Protection Agency in determining how mining operations and waste can affect water quality and the environment. They may travel to remote abandoned mines to collect samples and perform rough field evaluations, and then follow a stream through its watershed to evaluate how contaminants are moving through the system. Petroleum geochemists are employed by oil and gas companies to help find new energy reserves. They may also work on pipelines and oil rigs to prevent chemical reactions that could cause explosions or spills.

Forensic Chemistry

Forensic chemists capture and analyze the physical evidence left behind at a crime scene to help determine the identities of the people involved as well as to answer other vital questions regarding how and why the crime was carried out. Forensic chemists use a wide variety of analyzation methods, such as chromatography, spectrometry and spectroscopy.

In new research appearing in the Journal of the American Society of Mass Spectrometry, scientists from the department of chemistry at Louisiana State University (LSU) set out to apply laser technology to the field of forensic science.

They developed a system that goes above and beyond the identification of a fingerprint. The technique can capture molecules contained within a fingermark, including lipids, proteins, genetic material, or even trace amounts of explosives, which can be further analyzed. The new tool essentially takes the mystery out of identifying the chemical composition of fingermarks at crime scenes.

The tool focuses a laser — using mirrors and optical fibers — onto a surface containing a fingermark. The laser then heats up any water or moisture on the surface, triggering chemical bonds in the water to stretch and vibrate, according to the LSU College of Science Blog. All of this focused energy causes the water to "explode," turning it into a gas and separating biomolecules such as DNA. This process is called laser ablation.

Next a small vacuum pump system pulls the water and molecules into a tiny filter that captures everything left behind by a person's finger. Forensic scientists can then put the contents into an analysis device such as a mass spectrometer or a gas chromatography-mass spectrometer.

Importantly, this laser ablation technique can easily capture fingermarks on porous surfaces, such as cardboard (on which traditional forensic methods have not been very successful).

To test their new technique, the researchers placed fingermarks on many different surface types, including glass, plastic, aluminum and cardboard. These fingermarks were laced with substances as diverse as caffeine, antiseptic cream, condom lubricants and TNT, according to the LSU College of Science Blog. After each fingermark capture, the chemists were able to identify these substances using mass spectrometry.

REFERENCES

https://en.wikipedia.org/wiki/Chemistry

https://www.nature.com/subjects/chemistry

https://www.livescience.com/45986-what-is-chemistry.html

Pages: 1-26

Research in Chemistry and Chemical Sciences
Edited by: **Dr. Vijender Singh and Dr. Pawan Kumar 'Bharti'**
ISBN: 978-93-88854-40-5
Edition: **2020**
Published by: **Discovery Publishing House Pvt. Ltd., New Delhi (India)**

1

Dynamics and Mechanism of CO_2O_3 Catalyzed and Organics inhibited Sulphur dioxide Oxidation in Environment

Faiyaz Hussain, Sameena Begum, Arun Kumar Sharma*, D.S.N. Prasad

INTRODUCTION

The rapid industrial development on all fronts has led to several environmental pollution phenomena and the chemistry is at the back of all these. Of these, acid rain, stratospheric ozone depletion, green house effect and carbon monoxide pollution are the most prevalent. Here we are concerned mainly with the phenomenon of acid rain which is of common occurrence in several industrially developed countries in northern hemisphere. In our own country, the level of SO_2 in atmospheric environment is increasing and, therefore, the danger of acid rain cannot be simply wished away.

A large number of organic and inorganic chemical species are released in to the atmosphere by anthropogenic and natural sources. The subsequent photochemical and thermal reactions of these species in gas and aqueous phases form the backbone of the atmospheric chemistry.

In atmospheric chemistry, the term precipitation refers to rain, snowfall, fog, mist and dry deposition of particles. The acid precipitations are of two types:

(i) Wet acid precipitations – which include rain, snowfall, fog, mist, etc.

(ii) Dry acid precipitations – which include acid precursor gases like SO_2, nitrogen oxides (NO_x), nitrate and sulphate.

Department of Chemistry, Govt. P.G. College, Jhalawar - 326 001 Rajasthan (India)

The normal pH of unpolluted rain water is estimated to be 5.65, buffered by atmospheric Co_2O_3. Human activity is responsible for lowering the pH of the rain water. The oxides of nitrogen and sulfur, due to their atmospheric oxidation, produce nitric and sulphuric acids respectively and increase the acidity and hence decrease pH. The precipitations which are of pH lower than 5.65 are termed acidic or simply acid rain[1].

The pollutants responsible for acidification of rain are mainly SO_2 and NO_x. Because of the prominent role played by SO_2 in atmospheric acid precipitation, the study of the rate processes involved in SO_2 transformation in to sulphate constitute an important area of research in atmospheric chemistry.

SPECIES OF SO_2 IN AQUEOUS SOLUTION

In aqueous solution SO_2 is present in four forms, viz. SO_2. H_2O, HSO_3^-, SO_3^{2-}, and $S_2O_5^{2-}$ governed by the following equilibria:

$$SO_2\,(g) + H_2O \overset{K_H}{\rightleftharpoons} SO_2.\,H_2O\,(aq) \qquad (1)$$

$$SO_2.H_2O\,(aq) \overset{K_1}{\rightleftharpoons} HSO_3^- + H^+ \qquad (2)$$

$$HSO_3^- \overset{K_2}{\rightleftharpoons} H^+ + SO_3^{2-} \qquad (3)$$

$$2HSO_3^- \overset{K_3}{\rightleftharpoons} S_2O_5^{2-} + H_2O \qquad (4)$$

K_H is Henry's constant and K_1, K_2 are acid dissociation constants. K_3 is the formation constant for $S_2O_5^{2-}$. At 25° C their values are, $K_H^2 = 1.23$ $moll^{-1}$ atm^{-1}, $K_1^2 = 1.4 \times 10^{-2}$, $K_2^2 = 6.24 \times 10^{-8}$ and $K_3^2 = 7.6 \times 10^{-2}$. All these forms of SO_2 are Collectively referred to as sulfur (IV).

Reactivity of aqueous S(IV) strongly depends upon its speciation. In aqueous phase, reactivity pattern is generally: $SO_3^{2-} > HSO_3^- > SO_2.H_2O$ (Ali *et al.*, 1991;[3] Anast and Margerum, 1981;[4] Brandt and van Eldik, 1998;[5] Bhargava and gupta, 1993;[6]). In case of oxidation by H_2O_2 this pattern is reversed (Hoffmann and Edwards, 1975;[7] Martin, 1984;[8])

On the basis of equilibria (1-3), the total concentration of dissolved sulphur dioxide, [S(IV)], can be expressed by the following equation.

$$[S(IV)] = [SO_2 \cdot H_2O]\,(1 + K_{d(1)}\,[H^+]^{-1} + K_{d(1)}\,K_{d(2)}\,[H^+]^{-2}) \qquad (5)$$

Thus it is clear that the nature of the species of S(IV) Present depends on pH. For example in the pH range 4.0 – 5.6, the major species is HSO_3^- and above pH 7.0, SO_3^{2-} is the dominant species. The equation (5) shows that the solubility of SO_2 in water increases with increase in pH

SO_2 OXIDATION PATHWAYS

Sulfur dioxide is oxidized by oxygen in both gas and aqueous phases and different pathways are as follows:

(i) Gas phase oxidation

(ii) Aqueous phase oxidation

In the aqueous phase the major oxidants are H_2O_2, O_3 and O_2. the autoxidation, i. e., is further classified as follows.

(a) Uncatalyzed Autoxidation

Uncatalyzed oxidation (6) has been repeatedly studied. At constant,

$$SO_2 \cdot H_2O + \tfrac{1}{2}O_2 \rightarrow H_2SO_4 \qquad (6)$$

pH, is generally agreed that the rate of the oxidation is given by (7).

$$R = d[SO_4^{2-}]/dt = K[SO_3^{2-}] \qquad (7)$$

Scott and Hobbs (1967),[9] Junge and Ryan (1958),[10] Miller

And De pena (1972),[11] Beilke and Gravenhorst (1978) [12] have on the basis of the dependence of the rate on pH, found the reactive species of S(IV) to be SO_3^{2-}. Based on their studies, Larson *et al.*,1978; [13] haver proposed the rate law (8) for 4-12 pH range.

$$d[SO_4^{2-}]/dt = \{K_1 + K_2[H^+]^{1/2} + K_3[H^+]^{-1}\}[SO_3^{2-}] \qquad (8)$$

On the other hand Beilke *et al.*; 1978 [12]; have proposed the rate law (9)

$$d[SO_4^{2-}]/dt = K[H^+]^{-0.16}[SO_3^{2-}] \qquad (9)$$

In spite of the fact that the uncatalysed reaction has been the subject of several studies, the occurrence of true uncatalysed reaction is doubtful. It maybe a case of trace metal ion catalysis. Brimblecombe and spedding (1974)[14] have pointed out that as little as 5×10^{-8} mol dm^{-3} Fe(III) could account for the observed uncatalysed rates. The experiments of Tsunogai (1971) [15] have shown that a very small concentration of EDTA almost completely stops the reaction. Huss *et al* (1978)[16] have confirmed these findinge and have further shown that the trace amounts of 1, 10 – phenanthroline – a complexing agent for iron(III), too seizes the uncatalysed oxidation.

(b) Catalyzed Autoxidation

This is of two types.

Homogeneous catalysis

The important catalysts are iron, manganese, cobalt, copper and nickel ions.

Heterogeneous catalysis

The important heterogeneous catalysts are metal oxides, flyash, atmospheric dust, rocks & minerals and metal sulfides.

ATMOSPHERIC OXIDANTS AND OXIDATION PATHWAYS

The atmospheric oxidation of SO_2 occurs in both the gas and aqueous phases. The gas phase oxidant is mainly OH radical and aqueous phase oxidants are O_3, H_2O_2 and O_2. The former three are formed by photochemical reactions as shown below.

Formation of OH, HO_2, O_3 and H_2O_2

The photochemical dissociation of NO_2 is the key reaction and responsible for the formation of many radical intermediates and ozone etc. (Calvert and Stockwell, 1984)[17].

$$NO_2 + h\nu\ (\lambda<430nm) \longrightarrow O(^3P) + NO \quad (10)$$

$$O(^3P) + O_2(+M) \longrightarrow O_3(+M) \quad (11)$$

$$O_3 + NO \longrightarrow O_2 + NO_2 \quad (12)$$

$$O_3 + h\nu\ (290\text{-}306\ nm) \longrightarrow O(^1D) + O_2 \quad (13)$$

$$O(^1D) + H_2O \longrightarrow 2OH \quad (14)$$

In atmosphere, hydrogen peroxide is formed as a result of following reactions (Calvert and Stockwell, 1984)[17].

$$HO + CO \longrightarrow H + CO_2 \quad (15)$$

$$H + O_2\ (+M) \longrightarrow HO_2\ (+M) \quad (16)$$

$$2HO_2 \longrightarrow H_2O_2 + O_2 \quad (17)$$

$$HO_2 + H_2O \rightleftharpoons H_2O.HO_2 \quad (18)$$

$$H_2O.HO_2 + HO_2 \longrightarrow H_2O_2 + O_2 + H_2O$$

The oxidation of sulfur(IV) by O_2, known as autoxidation, is very slow, but its oxidation in presence of catalysts such as metal ions is sizable.

Gas phase oxidation

The major gas phase oxidant is OH radical. The atmospheric concentrations of OH radicals is estimated to be ~ $(6 \pm 3)\times10^6$ molecule cm^{-3} (Brandt and van Eldik, 1995;[18] Calvert and Stockwell, 1984; [17]). The reaction of OH with SO_2 is believed to proceed as follows (Calvert and Stockwell, 1984;[17] and references cited therein; Crutzen and Lawrence, 2000;[19]).

$$SO_2 + OH(+M) \longrightarrow HOSO_2\ (+M) \quad (19)$$

$$HOSO_2 + O_2 \longrightarrow SO_3 + HO_2 \quad (20)$$

$$HO_2 + NO \longrightarrow OH + NO_2 \quad (21)$$

Aqueous phase oxidation of by H_2O_2 and O_3

H_2O_2 is also formed as a result of photochemical reactions in the atmosphere. Due to very high value of Henry's law constant (7×10^4 mol $L^{-1}atm^{-1}$ at 25°C), the concentrations of H_2O_2 in aqueous phase is relatively high. The oxidation of sulfur(IV) is catalyzed by hydrogen ions and hence with the increase in the pH, the rate decreases. The following gross mechanism has been proposed (Hoffmann and Edwards, 1975;[7] Halperin and Taube, 1952;[20]).

$$HSO_3^- + H_2O_2 \rightleftharpoons {}^-O_2SOOH + H_2O \quad (22)$$

$${}^-O_2SOOH + HA \longrightarrow H_2SO_4 + A^- \quad (23)$$

where HA is H^+ or some other acid.

In troposphere, ozone is usually found in 30-60 ppbv range and formed as a result of photolytic reaction of NO_2 (Eqs. 6-7). It's solubility in water is much lower than that of H_2O_2 due to the low value of Henry's law constant (1×10^{-2} mol L^{-1} atm^{-1}). A simplified mechanism for the reaction is as follows (Halperin and Taube, 1952; [20] Penkett *et al.*, 1979; [21] Penkett, 1972; [22] Larson *et al.*, 1978;[13] Martin, 1984;[8] and references cited there in).

$$O_3 + HSO_3^- \xrightarrow{H_2O} \text{Intermediate} \longrightarrow SO_4^{2-} + H^+ + O_2 \quad (24)$$

The rate of reaction increases, when pH is increased.

Autoxidation of aqueous SO_2

The oxidation of SO_2(aq.) by O_2 is slow but is strongly catalyzed by

$$S(IV) + 0.5\ O_2 \longrightarrow S(VI) \quad (25)$$

homogenous and heterogeneous catalysts (Martin 1984;[8] Hoffmann and Jacob, 1984;[23] Hoffmann and Boyce; 1983;[24] Kraft and van Eldik, 1989;[25] Brandt and van Eldik, 1995;[18] Kuo *et al.*, 2006;[26]). The uncatalyzed aqueous SO_2 oxidation is believed to be actually catalyzed by trace metal ions present as impurity in water and reagent samples. The transition metal ions in trace concentrations are always present in water. The most important metal ions from atmospheric point of view are Fe(II)/Fe(III), Mn(II), Co(II)/Co(III), Cu(II) and to some extent Ni(II).

KINETICS OF HOMOGENOUS METAL ION CATALYZED AUTOXIDATION REACTIONS

In the atmosphere, the anthropogenic sources and soil are the major contributor of trace metal ions such as iron(II)/(III), copper(II), cobalt(II), and nickel(II). The most important metal ions from atmospheric view are iron and manganese (Penkett *et al.*, 1979;[21] Grgic *et al.*, 1991;[27] Martin 1984;[8]) and to some extent copper.

The major studies on iron(III), manganese(II), copper(II) and cobalt(II) catalyzed autoxidation of SO_2 in aqueous solutions are collected below.

Fe(III)- catalysis- Manoj *et al.*, 2008; [28], Martin, 1984;[8] Fuzzi, 1978;[29] Brimblecombe and Spedding, 1974;[14] Conklin and Hoffmann, 1988;[30] Huss *et al*,1982;[31]

Mn(II) –catalysis –Wilkosz and Mainka,2008;[32] Grgic *et al,2007;*[33] Manoj *et al.*, 2000;[34] Connick and Zhang, 1996;[35] Berglund, *et al.*, 1993;[36] Podkrajsek, *et al.*, 2004;[37] Huss *et al.*, 1982;[38]

Copper(II)- catalysis - Lunak *et al.*, 1978;[39] Fuller and Crist, 1941;[40] Grgic *et al.*,1991.[27]

Cobalt(II)- catalysis - Hobson *et al.*, 1986;[41] Srivastava *et al.*, 1968[42].

Silver(I)-catalysis - Gupta *et al.*, 1999,[43] 2001.[44]

Osmium(VIII)-catalysis - Gupta *et al.*, 2004.[45]

Nickel(II)- catalysis - Linn, Jr. *et al.*, 1990.[46]

Selenium – catalysis – Bronikowski *et al.*, 2000.[47]

GENERAL MECHANISM

For metal ion catalysed autoxidation, two types of the mechanisms, viz. one electron free radical, and two electron polar involving ternary complexes comprised of transition metal, S(IV) and molecular oxygen, have been proposed.

(1) Free Redical Mechanism

Backstron (1934)[48] was first to propose a mechanism for the autoxidation. The free radical mechanism proposed by him is as follows :

Initiation, $M^{1+} + SO_3^{2-} \xrightarrow{K_1} M^{(n-1)+} + SO_3^{-\cdot}$ (26)

Propagation, $SO_3^{-\cdot} + O_2 \xrightarrow{K_2} SO_5^{-\cdot}$ (27)

$SO_5^{-\cdot} + SO_3^{2-} \xrightarrow{K_3} SO_5^{2-} + SO\ 3^{-\cdot}$ (28)

Oxidation, $SO_5^{2-} + SO_3^{2-} \xrightarrow{K_4} 2SO_4^{2-}$ (29)

Termination, $2SO_3^{-\cdot} \xrightarrow{K_5} S_2O_6^{2-}$ (30)

Or $SO_3^{-\cdot} + SO_2^{-\cdot} \xrightarrow{K_6} S_2O_6^{2-} + O_2$ (31)

Or $SO_5^{-\cdot} + SO_5^{-\cdot} \xrightarrow{K_7} S_2O_8^{2-} + O_2$ (32)

For a truly catalytic role, $M^{(n-1)+}$ is oxidised back to M^{n+} through the following propagation steps.

$SO_3^{-\cdot} + M^{(n-1)} + \longrightarrow SO_3^{2-} + M^{n+}$ (33)

$SO_5^{-\cdot} + M^{(n-1)} + \longrightarrow SO_5^{2-} + M^{n+}$ (34)

$SO_5^{2-\cdot} + M^{(n-1)} + \longrightarrow SO_4^{-\cdot} + M^{n+}$ + Other product (35)

The mechanism 26-29 with (30) as chain termination step would lead to the rate expression (36).

$R = k_1[SO_3^{2-}]\,[M^{n+}] + k_2\,(2k_1/k_5)^{0.5}\,[M^{n+}]^{0.5}\,[SO_3^{2-}]^{0.5}\,[O_2]$ (36)

On applying the long chain length approximation, i.e., rate of propagation/rate of initiation >> 1, the equation (36)

Can be written as (37).

$R = K'\,[M^{n+}]^{0.5}\,[SO_3^{2-}]^{0.5}\,[O_2]$ (37)

Different chain termination steps would lead to slightly different rate laws, which can be represented in a general way as follows (38).

$R = K\,[M^{n+}]^a\,[SO_3^{2-}]^b\,[O_2]^c$ (38)

The reaction orders a, b and c vary from 0.5 to 1.5. The reaction order, a, for metal ion is 0.5 for all free radical mechanism, b may be 0.5, 1 or 1.5 depending on the nature of the chain termination step, and c may be 0, 0.5 or 1 again depending on the choice of the chain termination step. The rate law (37) with suitable assumptions reduces to various experimentally observed rate laws.

(2) Inner – sphere complexation mechanism

The following polar Mechanism for metal catalysed autoxidation of S(IV) has been given.

$$Mn + SO_3^{2-} \underset{K-1}{\overset{K_1}{\rightleftharpoons}} MSO_3^{(n-2)+} \quad (39)$$

$$MSO_3^{(n-2)+} + SO_3^{-2} \underset{K-2}{\overset{K_2}{\rightleftharpoons}} M\,(SO_3)_2^{(n-4)+} \quad (40)$$

$$M(SO_3)_2^{(n-4)+} + 0_2 \underset{K-3}{\overset{K_3}{\rightleftharpoons}} M(SO_3)_2^{(n-4)+}.\ O_2 \quad (41)$$

$$M(SO_3)_2^{(n-4).+}\ O_2 \underset{slow}{\overset{K_4}{\rightleftharpoons}} M^{n+} + 2SO_4^{2-} \quad (42)$$

The mechanism involves ternary metal ion-sulfite – O_2 inner sphere complexes. Depending upon the number of inner – sphere complexes formed and the choice of rate determining step, it is possible to derive the rate law. Additional steps involving binuclear metal complexes, if demanded by kinetics results, may be added.

KINETICS OF HETEROGENEOUS PARTICLE SURFACE CATALYZED REACTIONS

The particle surface also acts as a catalyst in the autoxidation of sulfur(IV). The catalytic particulate materials studied and which are of atmospheric importance are as follows: suspended particulate matter-free fall atmospheric dust (Rani *et al.*, 1992),[49] SiO_2 (Prasad *et al.*, 1992),[50] MgO (Bhargava *et al.*, 1993),[51] CdO (Rani *et al.*, 1991),[52] CuO (Prasad *et al.*, 1992),[50] CoO (Gupta *et al.*, 2008;[53]Prasad *et al.*, 1991;[54]), MnO_2 (Gupta *et al.*, 1999;[55]), Ni_2O_3 (Gupta *et al.*, 2008;[53] Bhargava *et al.*, 1992;[56]), Cu_2O (Manoj *et al.*, 1999;[57]), Co_2O_3 (Gupta *et al.*, 2008;[53] Prasad *et al.*, 2003;[58]), CdS (Manoj *et al.*, 2000;[34]), fly ash (Cohen *et al.*, 1981;[59] Madnavat *et al.*, 1993;[60] Saxena *et al.*, 1995;[61]), carbonaceous particles (Brodzinsky *et al.*, 1980;[62]), minerals and rocks (Gupta *et al.*, 1992;[63] Saxena *et al.*, 1993;[64] Prasad *et al.*, 1994;[65]). For autoxidation of aqueous sulfur dioxide by cuprous oxide, Cu_2O, the following rate law has been proposed by Manoj *et al.*, (1999).[57]

$$R_{obs} = k_2\,[Cu_2O]^{0.5}\,[S(IV)]\,[O_2]^{0.5}$$

The detailed mechanisms can be found in cited papers.

NON-RADICAL MECHANISM

A non-radical mechanism generally operates in the catalysis by transition metal oxides and by iron(III) when pH is low. As an example of non-radical mechanism, the mechanism of CuO-catalyzed reaction is given below.

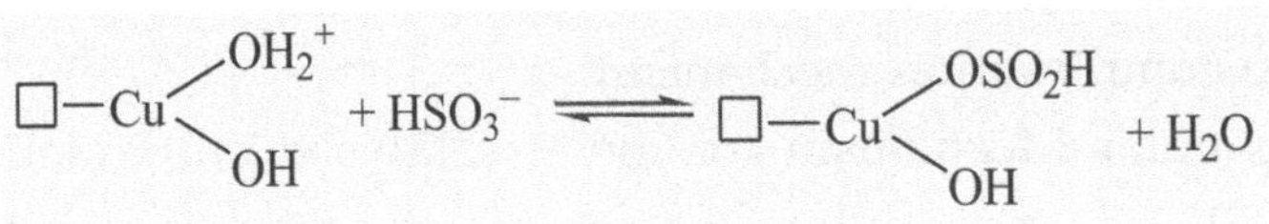
(43)

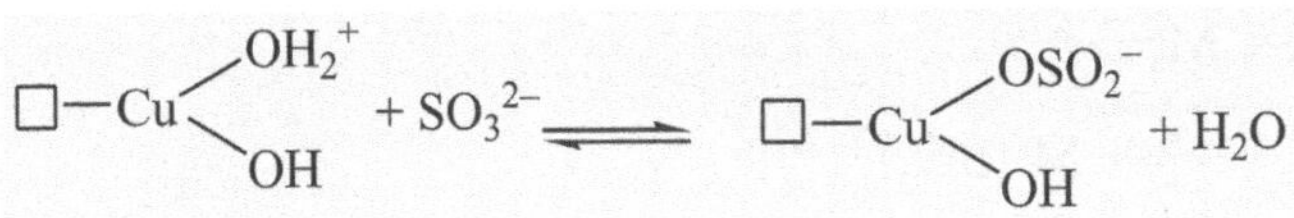
(44)

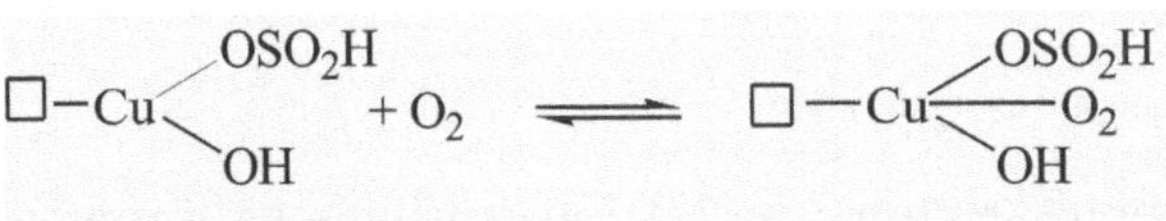
(45)

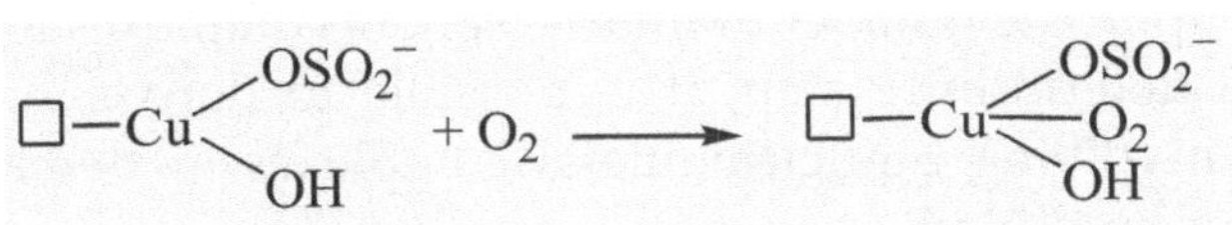
(46)

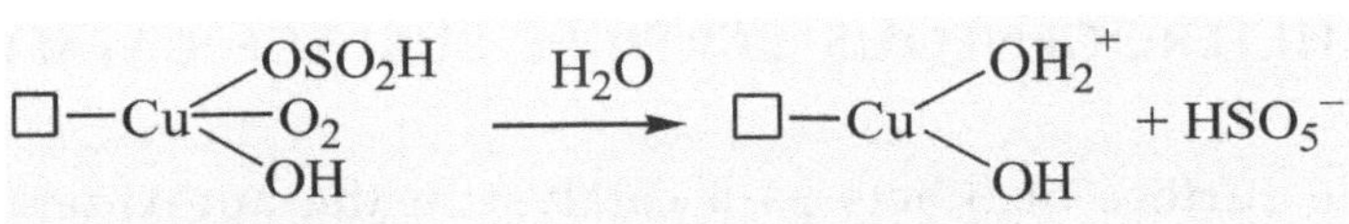
(47)

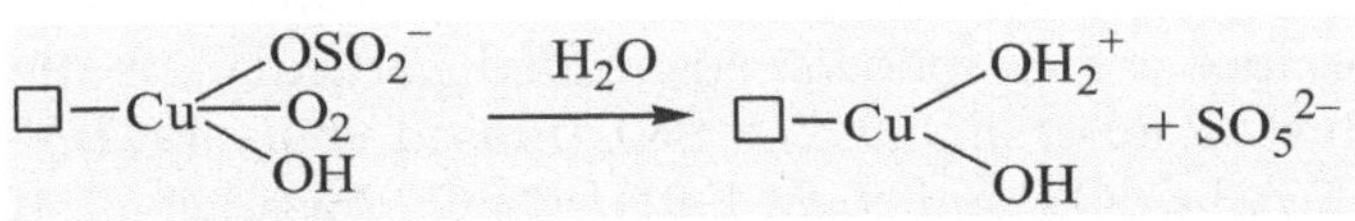
(48)

$SO_5^{2-} + H^+ \longrightarrow HSO_5^-$ (rapid) (49)

$HSO_5^- + S(IV) \longrightarrow 2S(VI)$ (rapid) (50)

The reactivity order for the different transition metal oxides has been found to be: $MnO_2 > CuO > Co_2O_3 > CoO > Ni_2O_3$.

In the autoxidation mechanism, the adsorbed S(IV) transfers its electrons to matrix - M (where M = Cu, Mn, Ni, Co) and S(V) so formed interacts with adjacently adsorbed O_2, takes back an electron from matrix M and leaves off as SO_5^{2-}.

ROLE OF INHIBITORS

There are many organic compounds which act as effective inhibitors for the autoxidation of S(IV). A study of the effect of organic compounds, particularly those found in atmosphere, on the rate of autoxidation of sulfur(IV) is required to unravel the role of such inhibitors in atmospheric chemistry. From atmospheric point of view, ethanol, phenol, benzene etc. are very important. Alcohols are commonly present in both urban and in rural atmospheres. The gas phase concentration of ethanol and phenol have been reported to be 226 and 2.5 ppbv respectively. In addition, aqueous phase concentrations of methanol and ethanol were found 1.8×10^{-6} and 3.1×10^{-7}, respectively in urban atmosphere(Herrmann *et al.*, 2000).[66] The concentration of benzene has been reported to be 1.7 ppb in the atmosphere (Bravo, 2002).[67]

The role of inhibitors on the atmospheric oxidation of sulfur(IV) by O_2 has been examined by a large number of workers. Bigelow, (1898)[68] was the first to observe inhibiting effect on rate of the reaction between sodium sulfite and oxygen. Later on the inhibiting effect of alcohols was investigated by Alyea and Backstrom, (1929) [69] in chain reaction theory based study.

The other inhibitors studied are phenols (Altiwicker, 1980),[70] Alcohols(J. Ziajka, 2003),[71] organic acids (Lee and Rochelle, 1987;[72] Grgic *et al.*, 1998;[73] 2007,[33] Podkrajsek *et al*, 2006; [74] Wilkosz *et al*, 2008;[32] Wolf *et al.*, 2000;[75]), benzene (Ziajka *et al.*, 1994),[76] toluene, naphthalene, paraffin oil (Pasiuk-Bronikowska *et al.*, 1997),[77] α-pinene, cis-verbenol (Ziajka and Pasiuk-Bronikowska, 1998),[78] sobrerol (Pasiuk-Bronikowska *et al.*, 1998,[79] 1999,[80]), myrtenol (Pasiuk-Bronikowska, *et al.*, 2000)[81] and others (Rudzinski and Pasiuk-Bronikowska, 2001; [82] 2003; [83]). The effect of alcohols and ammonia has been studied on catalyezd S(IV) autoxidation (Manoj *et al.*, 1999,[57]Mudgal *et al.*, 2007; Mudgal, 2007;[84]).

Hayon *et al.*, (1972)[85] proposed a radical mechanism involving SO_3^-, SO_4^- and SO_5^- radicals to explain the inhibitory effect through scavenging of radicals as in equations (35).

$$RCH_2OH + SO_5^- \longrightarrow RCHO + SO_4^- + H_2O \qquad (51)$$

Further experiments were conducted for finding the reactivity of oxysulfur radicals with alcohol which proved that these compounds react with SO_4^- rapidly (Ashmore, 1963;[86] Gilbert *et al.*, 1988;[87] Dogliotti and Hayon, 1967;[88] Clifton and Huie, 1989;[89]). The reactions of inhibitors with SO_3^- and SO_5^- were reported to be slow and hence unimportant (Hayon *et al.*, 1972).[85]

Experimental studies on the kinetics and products of sulfate radical-alcohol reactions (Clifton and Huie, 1989;[89] Wine *et al.*, 1989;[90] Ziajka *et al.*, 1996,[91] 2001;[92] Ziajka and Pasiuk-Bronokowska, 1998,[78] 2000,[93] 2003;[71]) have also been carried out. The methanol inhibition of the uncatalyezd autoxidation of HSO_3^- was investigated by Connick *et al*, (1995).[94] The inhibition by methanol in the manganese(II)–catalyezd S(IV)autoxidation has been studied by Connick and Zhang (1996).[35]

Recently Gupta *et al*, 2008;[28] studied the inhibiting effect of ethanol on CoO, Co_2O_3 and Ni_2O_3 catalysed autoxidation of sulfur (IV) in alkaline medium and based on the result a radical mechanism for CoO and Co_2O_3 catalysis in alkaline medium, and a non radical mechanism for Ni_2O_3 in both alkaline and acidic media and for cobalt oxides in acidic media are proposed.

PURPOSE AND SCOPE OF THE PROPOSED WORK

It is fully realized that role of inhibitors owing to their radical scavenging ability is a major diagnostic tool for reaction mechanisms.

Among the inhibitors, the role of Aniline, Iso propyl alcohol, Sodium benzoate, and Benzamide has not been studied in S(IV) autoxidation reaction, although the role of organics and NH_3 are well studied. In view of the fact that inhibitor help in delineating the mechanism of autoxidation, whether radical or non-radical. We have decided to study the effect of iso propyl alcohol, aniline, sodium benzoate, & benzamide on the autoxidation rates and help understand the mechanism.

MATERIALS AND METHODS

CHEMICALS

Sodium sulphite

In aqueous solutions, the dissolved sulfur dioxide, SO_2 is present as $SO_2.H_2O(H_2SO_3)$, HSO_3^-, SO_3^{2-} and $S_2O_5^{2-}$ and all these species have been hereafter referred to as sulfur(IV). In order to obtain an aqueous solution of S(IV), sodium sulfite, Na_2SO_3(E. Merck, 95%) was used as such without any purification. The solution of Na_2SO_3 was prepared daily by dissolving its weighed amount in doubly distilled water. It was standardized iodometrically[1] every time before use. The solution was kept in refrigerator to prevent the autoxidation of S(IV),which is considerably slow at low temperature.

Iodine

Iodine (E. Merck) of 99.8% purity was used. To prepare 0.1 mol L^{-1}, solution of iodine, at first 40 g iodate free potassium iodide(E. Merck 99%) was dissolved in 50 cm^3 of double distilled water. To this, 25.5 g iodine was added. When iodine was fully dissolved, the solution was made up to one liter. The stock solution was kept in cool and dark place. The solution of desired strength was prepared by a suitable dilution of this stock solution.

Di sodium hydrogen phosphate (Anhydrous)

di-sodium hydrogen phosphate (E. Merck, 99.5%) was used. For preparing 1.0 mol L^{-1} stock solution, 178 gm of di-sodium hydrogen phosphate was diluted with double distilled water up to one liter.

Potassium dihydrogen phosphate

Potassium dihydrogen phosphate (E. Merck, 99.5%) was used. For preparing1.0 mol L^{-1} stock solution, 136.09 gm of Potassium dihydrogen phosphate was diluted with double distilled water up to one liter.

Sodium thiosulfate

Sodium thiosulfate, $Na_2S_2O_3.5H_2O$ (E. Merck, 99.5%) was used. A stock solution was prepared by dissolving the weighed amount in freshly boiled double distilled water. The dilute solution of desired strength was prepared by the dilution of the stock solution. The solution was standardized against iodine solution of known strength following the standard procedure (Jeffery *et al.*, 1989)[2]. A few drops of chloroform were added to the stock solution to prevent its slow decomposition.

Acetic acid

For preparing 1.0 mol L^{-1} stock solution, 58 ml acetic acid (Merck 100%) was diluted with doubly distilled water. It was standardized by titrating against standard sodium hydroxide solution, using phenolphthalein as an indicator.

Potassium Iodide

Iodate free potassium iodide (E. Merck, 99%) was used

Starch

For preparing indicator solution, starch (soluble) used was of Qualigens make.

Aniline

Aniline, which was of s.d. fine chem. Ltd. (99%) make, was used.

Iso propyl alcohol

Iso propyl alcohol, which was of BDH (99%) make, was used.

Benzamide

Benzamide, which was of ottokemi (98%) make, was used.

Sodium Benzoate

Sodium Benzoate, (E. Merck, 99%) was used.

Cobalt (III) Oxide

Cobalt (III) Oxide, Co_2O_3, (Sisco, 98%) was used.

Other chemicals

Sodium hydroxide (s.d. FINE CHEM. 97%); $CuSO_4.5H_2O$ (s.d FINE CHEM. 99%)

STANDARDISATION METHOD

Sodium thio sulphate (Hypo) solution

The hypo solution was standardised as follows.To a known volume of standard copper sulphate solution, potassium iodide was added and the liberated iodine was back titrated againsed hypo using starch as an indicator.

Iodine Solution

Iodine solution was standardised by taking its known volume in a conical flask, making it slightly acidic and titrating it against standard hypo solution using starch as an indicator.

Sodium Sulphite Solution

It was standardised iodometrically. In a volumetric flask, predetermined quantity of iodine, which was in excess over sulphite to be estimated, was taken. To this, Na_2SO_3 solution was added. The titration was performed in slightly acidic medium. The unreacted iodine was titrated against standard hypo using starch as an indicator.

Acetic Acid Solution

The acetic acid solution was standardised by titrating it against standard sodium hydroxide solution using phenolphthalein as an indicator.

EQUIPMENT

Reaction Vessel

The reactions were conducted in 0.15 L Erlenmeyer flasks open to air and room light. The reaction vessel was placed in 0.5 L beaker provided with an outlet at the top and an inlet at the bottom for circulating thermostated water for maintaining the desired temperature of the reaction mixture (± 1° C). The assembly was mounted on a magnetic stirrer.

pH meter

The digital pH meter (Systronics - μ - pH system 361) was used for measuring the pH of the reaction mixture.

Magnetic stirrer

The reaction vessel was mounted on a magnetic stirrer and the reaction mixture was continuously stirred magnetically at a speed of 1600±100 rpm for ensuring the rapid diffusion of oxygen into the reaction mixture and to keep the solid catalyst afloat. The magnetic stirrer was calibrated with the help of a Tachometer.

KINETICS PROCEDURE

The experimental procedure, which was exactly the same as described earlier by Brodzinsky *et al.* (1980)[3], Mudgal *et al.* (2008)[4];and Gupta *et al.*,

(2008)[5], is given here.All chemicals used were of reagent grade and their solution were prepared in double distilled water. The reactions were conducted in 0.15 L Erlenmeyer flasks, open to air, to allow the passage of atmospheric oxygen. The flask was placed in a beaker, which had an inlet at the lower part and an outlet at the upper part for circulating thermostated water for maintaining desired temperature, 30.0 ± 0.1° C.

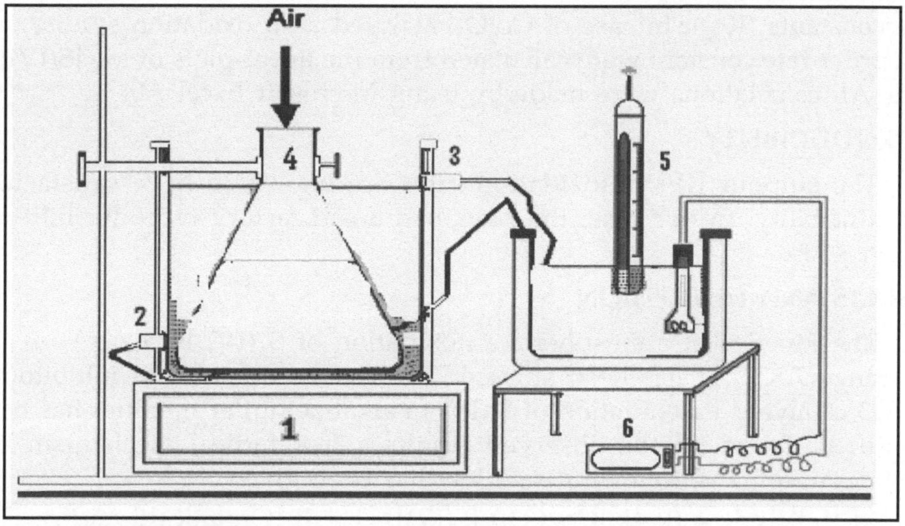

Fig. 1.1: Schematic diagram of the experimental setup for the kinetics study of S(IV) – O_2 oxidation reaction: ***1. Magnetic stirrer; 2.b Water inlet; 3. Water outlet; 4. Erlenmeyer flask (Reaction mixture); 5. Thermometer; 6. Thermostat.***

The reactions were initiated by adding the desired volume of freshly prepared standard Na_2SO_3 solution to the reaction mixture containing other additives such as buffer, catalyst, etc. The selection of a suitable stirring speed is necessary to save the reaction from becoming oxygen mass-transfer controlled. For this reason, the rate of the reaction was studied at different stirring speeds measured with the help of a tachometer(Mudgal *et al.*, 2008). The rate was found to become independent of stirring speed above 1200 rpm. This led us to select a stirring speed of 1600 ± 100 rpm for stirring the reaction mixture continuously and magnetically to allow the passage of atmospheric oxygen.

The kinetics was studied in buffered medium in which the pH remained fixed throughout the entire course of reaction for this purpose 10cm^3 of buffer made from Na, HPO_4 (1.0 mol L^{-1}) and KH_2PO_4(1.0 mol L^{-1}) for alkaline medium was used (total volume 100 cm^3) for obtaining the desired pH.The kinetics was followed by determining the unreacted S(IV) iodometrically in a slightly acidic medium (Mudgal *et al.*, 2008[4]; Gupta *et al.*, 2008 [5]; Prasad *et al.*, 1992[6]; Brodzinsky *et al.*, 1980[3]). For this purpose,

5.0 ml aliquot samples were withdrawn periodically and added to a titration flask containing known quantity of iodine and sufficient acetic acid to make the medium acidic. The unreacted iodine was titrated with standard sodium thiosulfate solution using starch as an indicator

TREATMENT OF KINETIC DATA

In this study, the treatment of kinetics results is based on first order rate constants (K_{obs}). In case of Co_2O_3 catalysed auto oxidation studies, the first order rate constant were calculated from the linear plots of log [S(IV)]vs time. All calculations were made by using Microsoft Excel 7.0.

REPRODUCIBLITY

The sulphur (IV) autoxidation rates are known to have satisfactory reproducibility. In our case, the rates had a satisfactory reproducibility to within ±10%.

RESULTS AND DISCUSSION

The kinetics of atmospheric autoxidation of S (IV) by Co2O3 in the pH range 7.82-9.42 has been studied. The role of organics as inhibitor of Co2O3 catalysed autoxidation of S (IV) in alkaline buffer medium has been identified. Based on the observed results a free radical mechanism has been proposed and following rate law has been given.

$$-d\ [S(IV)/dt = (k_1+k_2[Co2O3])\ [S(IV)]/\ 1 + B\ [Organics]$$

Experiment were carried out at 30d≤t°C≤45,4.02≤pH≤5.25, 1×10^{-3}mol/dm^3≤[S(IV)≤10×10^{-3} mol/dm^3, 5×10^{-6}mol/dm^3≤[Co2O3]≤2.5×10^{-5} mol/dm^3, 5×10^{-6}mol/dm^3≤[organics]≤8×10^{-4} mol/dm^3, Based on the experimental results, rate constants and order of the reactions were determined. Depending on the reaction conditions, the observed results for the Co2O3 catalysed S(IV) oxidation reaction in presence of organics has been tabulated and graphs have been plotted. The reaction order in S(IV) was first order for both reactions. The effect of Co2O3ion and inhibitor concentrations as well as initial pH of the solution on S (IV) oxidation rate was discussed. It was found that the rate of the S(IV) oxidation depends on the initial pH of the solution but independent on pH change during reaction. The effect of temperature of solution on S (IV) oxidation catalysed by Co2O3 in presence of organics was discussed. The values of k_{obs} were determined at three different temperatures in the range of 30°C to 40°C By plotting a graph between log k v/s 1/T yield us an apparent empirical energy of activation for the reaction. In contrast our results conclusively showed that organics studied here act as an inhibitor not catalyst for S (IV) autoxidation. The value of inhibition factor (B) of both uncatalysed and Co2O3 catalysed autoxidation of S(IV) in the present study are in the range of 10^3-10^4 as reported by Gupta *et al* (2008) and Prasad *et al* (2013).

MECHANISM

In aqueous solution SO_2 is present in four forms, $SO_2.H_2O$, HSO_3^-, SO_3^{2-} and $S_2O_5^{2-}$, governed by the following equations.

$$SO_2(g) + H_2O \overset{K_H}{\rightleftharpoons} SO_2.H_2O(aq.) \quad (1)$$

$$SO_2.H_2O(aq.) \overset{K_1}{\rightleftharpoons} HSO_3^{-1} + H^+ \quad (2)$$

$$HSO_3^{-1} \overset{K_2}{\rightleftharpoons} H^+ + SO_3^{-2} \quad (3)$$

$$2HSO_3^{-1} \overset{K_3}{\rightleftharpoons} H_2O + S_2O_5^{-2} \quad (4)$$

K_H is Henry's constant and K_1, K_2 are acid dissociation constants. K_3 is the formation constant for $S_2O_5^{2-}$ at 25°C the values are K_H = 1.23 mol $L^{-1}atm^{-1}$, K_1=1.4×10^{-2}, K_2=6.24×10^{-8}, and K_3=7.6×10^{-2}. In this experimental study in pH range (7.9 - 9.4), S(IV) would be largely present as SO_3^{2-}. Since the rate of reaction is nearly independent of pH, we have considered only SO_3^{2-} species to be reactive in the subsequently. In the present study, the dependence of oxygen shows that the formation of surficial complex by adsorption of O_2 on the particle surface of Co_2O_3 through the fast step. In alkaline medium the rate of Co_2O_3 catalyzed reaction is highly decelerated by the addition of organics like that of ethanol reported by Gupta *et al* this indicates the operation of a radical mechanism involving oxysulphur free radicals, like SO_3^-, SO_4^- and SO_5^-. The inhibition is caused through the scavenging of SO_4^- by inhibitors such as ethanol and benzene, etc. As reported by Sharma *et al* a radical mechanism operates in those reactions in which the inhibition parameter lies the range 10^3-10^4. In this study the value of inhibitor parameter is found to be be 4.9×10^3, which lies in the same range. This strongly supports the radical mechanism for the Co_2O_3 – catalyzed reaction in presence of organocs. Based on the observed results including the inhibition by organics, the following radical mechanism is proposed which similar to that proposed by Manoj *et al* sameena *et al* in the ethanol inhibition of the CoO catalyzed reaction.

$$Co_2O_3 + SO_3^{2-} \overset{K_1}{\rightleftharpoons} Co_2O_3.\ SO_3^{2-} \quad (5)$$

$$Co_2O_3.SO_3^{2-} + O_2 \overset{K_2}{\rightleftharpoons} Co_2O_3.SO_3^{2-}\ .\ O_2 \quad (6)$$

$$Co_2O_3.\ SO_3^{2-}.O_2 \xrightarrow{K_1} Co_2O_3 + SO_3^- + O_2^- \quad (7)$$

$$SO_3^- + O_2 \xrightarrow{K_2} SO_5^- \quad (8)$$

$$SO_5^- + SO_3^{2-} \xrightarrow{K_3} SO_5^{2-} + SO_3^- \quad (9)$$

$$SO_5^- + SO_3^{2-} \qquad SO_4^- + SO_4^{2-} \quad (10)$$

$$SO_5^{2-} + SO_3^{2-} \xrightarrow{K_4} 2SO_4^{2-} \quad (11)$$

$$SO_4^{-} + SO_3^{2-} \xrightarrow{K_6} SO_4^{2-} + SO_3^{-} \quad (12)$$

$$SO_4^{-} + x \quad \text{Nonchain product} \quad (13)$$

$$SO_4^{-} + \text{organics} \xrightarrow{K_7} \text{Nonchain product} \quad (14)$$

CONCLUSION

The following conclusions are deduced from the results of the organics inhibited Co2O3 catalysed autoxidation of S(IV) was that inhibit the oxidation with the fast influence. The value of Inhibition factor of both uncatalysed and Co2O3 catalysed autoxidation of S(IV) in the present study are in the range of 10^3 - 10^4 which shows that free radical mechanism is operative.

BIBLIOGRAPHY

1. Altwicker E.R., (1980), In *Advances in Environmental Sciences and Engineering*, Vol. 3. J.R. Pfaffin and E. N. Zieglar (Eds.), Gordon and Breach Science Publishers, New York, pp. 80-91.
2. Alyea H.N. and Backstrom H.L.J., 1929, The Inhibitive Action of Alcohols on the Autoxidation of Sodium Sulfite, *Journal of American Chemical Society*, 51, 90-107.
3. Anast J.M. and Margerum D.W., 1981, Trivalent Copper Catalysis of the Autoxidation of Sulfite, Kinetics and Mechanism of the Copper (III/II) Tetraglycine Reactions with Sulfite, *Inorganic Chemistry*, 20, 2319.
4. Ashmore P.G., (1963),*Catalysis and Inhibition of Chemical Reactions*. Butterworths, London.
5. Backstrom H.L.J., 1934, The Chain Mechanism of the Autoxidation of Sodium Sulfite Solutions, *J. Phys. Chem.*(B), 25, 122-138.
6. Bhargava P. and Gupta K. S., 1993, Kinetics of Oxidation of Sulfur(IV) by Peroxodisulfate, Relative Reactivity of Bisulfite and Sulfite ions, *Indian Journal of Chemistry*, 32A, 201-204.
7. Bhargava R., Prasad D.S.N., Rani A., Bhargava P., Jain U. and Gupta K.S., 1992, Kinetics of Autoxidation of Aqueous Sulfur Dioxide in Suspensions of Nickel(III) Oxide, *Transition Metal Chemistry*, 17, 238-241.
8. Bhargava R.,Rani A. and Gupta, K. S., 1992, Surface-mediated Oxidation of Aqueous Sulfur Dioxide in Ceramic Powder Suspensions, *Indian Journal of Chemistry*, 31A, 683-687.
9. Bhargava R., Rani, A. and Gupta, K.S., 1993, Oxidation of Aqueous Sulfur Dioxide in Suspensions of Magnesium Dioxide, Removal of SO_2 from Flue Gases, *Indian Journal of Chemistry*, 32A, 713-716.
10. Bigelow S.L., 1988, Catalytic Effects in the Oxidation of Sodium Sulfite by Air Oxygen, *Zeitschriftfuer Physikalische Chemie*, 26, 493-532.
11. Brandt C. and Van Eldik, R., 1995, Transition Metal Catalyzed Oxidation of Aqueous Sulfur(IV) Oxides, Atmospheric Relevant Process and Mechanisms, *Chemical Reviews*, 95, 119-190.
12. Buxton G.V., Salmon G.A., 2003,On the Chemistry of Inorganic Free Radicals in Cloud Water. Progress in Reaction Kinetics and Mechanism 28, 257-297.

13. Buxton G.V., Wang J., Salmon G.A., 2001, Rate Constants for the Reactions of NO_3, SO_4 – and Cl Radicals with formate and Acetate esters in Aqueous Solution, *Physical Chemistry Chemical Physics*, 3, 2618-2621.
14. Calvert J.G. and Stockwell W.R., 1984, Mechanisms and Rates of Sulfur Dioxides in Atmosphere. In: *SO_2, NO and NO_2 Oxidation Mechanisms. Atmospheric Considerations*, J. G. Calvert (Ed.), Butterworths, Boston, pp. 1-62.
15. Chebbi A., Carlier P., 1996, Carboxylic Acids in the Troposphere, Occurrence, Sources, and Sinks: A Review. *Atmospheric Environment*, 30, 4233-4249.
16. Clemitshaw K.C., 2006, Coupling between the Trophospheric Photochemistry of Nitrous Acid (HONO) and Nitric Acid (HNO_3), *Environmental Chemistry*, 3, 31-34.
17. Clifton C.L. and Huie R.E., 1989, Rate Constants for Hydrogen Abstraction Reactions of the Sulfate Radical, $SO\text{-}_4^{\cdot}$, Alcohols, *International Journal of Chemical Kinetics*, 21, 677-687.
18. Dogliotti L. and Hayon E., 1967, Flash Photolysis of Persulfate ions in Aqueous Solution, Study of Sulfate and Ozonide Radical Anions, *Journal of Physical Chemistry*, 71, 2511-2516.
19. Exner M., Herrmann H., Zellner R., 1994, Rate Constants for the Reactions of the NO_3 Radical with HCOOH/HCOO- and CH_3COOH/CH_3COO^-in Aqueous Solution between 278 and 328 K, *Journal of Atmospheric Chemistry*, 18, 359-378.
20. Fuzzi S., 1978, Study of iron(III) Catalyzed Sulfur Dioxide Oxidation in Aqueous Solution over a Wide Range of pH, *Atmospheric Environment*, 12, 1439-1442.
21. Gilvert B.C., Stell J.K., Peet W.J. and Radford K.J., 1988, Generation and Reaction of the Chlorine Atom in Aqueous Solution, *Journal of Chemical Society, Faradey Transactions*,1, 84, 3319-3330.
22. Grgic I., Dovzan A., Bercic, G., and Hudnik, V., 1998, The Effect of Atmospheric Organic Compounds on the Fe-catalyzed S(IV) Autoxidation in Aqueous Solution, *J. Atmos. Chem.* 29, 315-337.
23. Gupta K.S., 2002, Acid Rain Precursors, Sources Control and Damaging Effects, In *Proceedings Second SERC School on Mathematical Modelling of Atmospheric Pollution*, Sapna Book House, Bangalore, pp. 7-12.
24. Gupta K.S., 2002, Global Climate Change: Green House Effect, In, *Proceedings Second SERC School on Mathematical Modelling of Atmospheric Pollution*, Sapna Book House, Bangalore, pp. 13-24.
25. Gupta K.S., Jain U., Singh A., Mehta R.K., Manoj S.V., Prasad D.S.N., Sharma A., Parashar P., Bansal S.P., 2004, Kinetics and Mechanism of the Osmium(VIII)-catalysed Autoxidation of Aqueous Sulfur Dioxide in Acidic and Alkaline Media. *Journal of Indian Chemical Society*, 81, 1083-1092.
26. Gupta K.S., 2002, Air Pollution. In: Proceedings of Second SERC School on *'Mathematical Modelling of Atmospheric Pollution'* UGC-CAS in Fluid Mechanics, Sapna Book House, Banglore, pp. 7-11.
27. Gupta K.S., Bhargava P., Manoj S.V. and Bhargava R., 2000, Kinetics and Mechanism of Silver(I) Catalyzed Oxidation of Aqueous Sulfur(IV) in Acetate Buffered Medium. *Transition Metal Chemistry*, 25, 329-332.
28. Gupta K.S., Singh R., Saxena D., Manoj S.V. and M. Sharma., 1999, Role of Manganese Dioxide in the Autoxidation of Sulfur(IV) in Oxic and Anoxic Suspensions, *Indian Journal of Chemistry*, 38A, 1129-1138.

29. Gupta K.S., Bhargava P. and Manoj S.V., 1999, Kinetics of Silver(I) Catalysed Oxidation of Sulfur(IV) by Peroxodisulfate, *Indian Journal of Chemistry*, 38A, 692-697.

30. Gupta K.S., Bhargava P. and Manoj S.V., 2000, Kinetics of Tetraamminecopper(II) Catalysed Oxidation of Sulfur(IV) by Peroxydisulphate in Ammonia Buffer, *Transition Metal Chemistry*, 25, 274-278.

31. Gupta K.S., Bhargava P. and Manoj S.V. 2001, Kinetics of diamminesilver(I)-catalysed Oxidation of Sulfur(IV) by Dioxygen in Ammonia Buffers, *Transition Metal Chemistry*, 26, 71-75.

32. Gupta K.S., Mehta R.K., Sharma, A.K. Mudgal, P.K. Bansal S.P., 2008, Kinetics of the Uninhibited and Ethanol-inhibited CoO, Co_2O_3 and Ni_2O_3 Catalyzed Autoxidation of Sulfur(IV) in Alkaline Medium, *Transition Metal Chemistry*, 33, 809-817.

33. Hayon E., Treinin A. and Wilf J. 1972, Electronic Spectra, Photochemistry and Autoxidation Mechanism of the Sulfite-bisulfite Pyrosulfite Systems, The SO_2^-, SO_3^-, SO_4^- and SO_5^- Radicals, *Journal of American Chemical Society*, 94, 47-57.

34. Herrmann H., 2003, Kinetics of Aqueous phase Reactions Relevant to Atmospheric Chemistry, *Chemical Reviews*, 103, 4691-4716.

35. Herrmann H., Exner M., Jacobi H.W., Raabe G., Reese A., Zellner R., 1995, Laboratory Studies of Atmospheric Aqueous-phase Free-radical Chemistry: Kinetic and Spectroscopic Studies of Reactions of NO_3 and SO_4 Radicals with Aromatic Compounds,*Faraday Discussions*, 100, 129-153.

36. Hoffman M.R. and Jacob D.J., 1984, In *SO_2, NO and NO_2 Oxidation Mechanisms, Atmospheric Considerations*, Calvert, J.G.(Ed.), Butterworth, Boston, pp. 101-172.

37. Hoffmann M.R. and Boyce S.D., 1983, In *Trace Atmospheric Constituents: Properties, Transformations and Fates*; S.E. Schwartz, (Ed.), John Wiley and Sons, New York, pp. 147-189.

38. Hoffmann P., Karandashev V.K., Sinner T., and Ortner H.M., 1997, Chemical Analysis of Rain and Snow Samples from Chernogolovka/Russia by IC, TXRF and ICP-MS, *Fres. J. Anal. Chem.*, 357, 1142-1148.

39. Huie R.E. and Neta P., 1984, Chemical Behaviour of SO_3^- and SO_5^- Radicals in Aqueous Solutions, *Journal of Physical Chemistry*, 23, 5665-5669.

40. Huie R.E. and Peterson, N.C., 1983. In: *Trace Atmospheric Constituents; Properties, Transformations & Fates*; S.E. Schwartz, (Ed.), John Wiley and Sons, New York, pp. 118-143.

41. Huie R.E. and Wayne Sieck L., 1999, In*S-Centered Radicals*; Alfassi, Z.B. (Ed.), John Wiley & Sons: New York, pp. 63-99.

42. Huie R.E., 1995, In *Progress and Problems in Atmospheric Chemistry*, Barker, J.R (Ed.), World Scientific Publishing Co., Singapore, pp. 374-419.

43. Huie R.E., Clifton C.L., 1996, Kinetics of the Reaction of the Sulfate Radical with the Oxalate Anion. *International Journal of Chemical Kinetics*, 28, 195-199.

44. Humphrey R.E., Ward M.H. and Hinze W., 1970, Spectrophotometric Determination of Sulfite with 4,4'-dithiopyridine and 5,5'dithiobis-(2-nitrobenzoic acid), *Anal. Chem,*. 42, 698-702.

45. Huss A., Jr. Lim P.K. and Eckert C.A., 1978, On the 'Uncatalyzed' Oxidation of Sulfur(IV) in Aqueous Solutions, *Journal of American Chemistry* Society, 108, 6253.

46. Huss Jr. A., Lim P.K. and Eckert C.A., 1982, Oxidation of Aqueous Sulfur Dioxide. 1. Homogenous Manganese(II) and Iron (II) Catalysis at Low pH, *Journal of Physical Chemistry*, 86, 4224-4228.

47. J. Ziajka, W. Pasiuk-Bronikowska, 2003, Autoxidation of Sulphur Dioxide in the Presence of Alcohols under Conditions related to the Tropospheric Aqueous Phase. *Atmos. Environ.*, 37, 3913-3922.
48. Joos F. and Baltensperger U., 1991, A Field Study on Chemistry, S(IV) Oxidation Rates and Vertical Transport during Fog Conditions, *Atmos. Environ.* 25A, 217-230.
49. Kawamura K., Steiberg S., Ng L., Kaplan I.R., 2001, Wet Deposition of Low Molecular Weight mono- and di-carboxylic Acids, Aldehydes and Inorganic Species in Los Angeles. *Atmospheric Environment*, 35, 3917-3926.
50. Kerminen V.-M., Ojanen C., Pakkanen T., Hillamo R., Aurela, M., Merilainen J., 2000, Low-molecular-weight Dicarboxylic Acids in an Urban and Rural Atmosphere, *Journal of Aerosol Science*, 31, 349-362.
51. Kotronarou A. and Sigg L., 1993, SO_2 Oxidation in Atmospheric Water, Role of Fe(II) and Effect of Ligands, *Environ. Sci. Technol.* 27, 2725-2735.
52. Kraft J. and van Eldik R. 1989, Kinetics and Mechanism of the Iron(II1)-catalyzed Autoxidation of Sulfur(1V) Oxides in Aqueous Solution, Formation of Transient Iron(III)-sulfur(1V) Complexes, *Inorganic Chemistry*, 28, 2297-2305.
53. Kraft J. and van Eldik, R., 1989, The Possible Role of Iron (III)-sulfur (IV) Complexes in the Catalysed Autoxidation of Sulfur (IV)-oxides, A Mechanistic Investigation, *Atmos. Environ.* 23, 2709-2713.
54. Kuo D.T.F., Krik D.W. and Jia C.Q. 2006, The Chemistry of Aqueous S(IV)-Fe-O_2 System: State of the Art, *Journal of Sulfur Chemistry*, 27, 461-530.
55. Lee Y.J. and Rochelle, G.T. 1987, Oxidative Degradation of Organic Acid Conjugated with Sulfite Oxidation in Flue Gas Desulfurization, Products, Kinetics and Mechanism, *Environment Science and Technology*, 21, 266-271.
56. Leland J.K. and Bard, A.J., 1987, Photochemistry of Colloidal Semiconducting Iron Oxide Polymorphs, *J. Phys. Chem.* 91, 5076-5083.
57. Lente G. and Fabian I., 2002, Kinetics and Mechanism of the Oxidation of Sulfur (IV) by Iron (III) atmetal ion Excess, *J. Chem. Soc., Dalton Trans.* 778-784.
58. Lunak S. and Veprek-Siska J., 1976, Photochemical Autooxidation of Sulfite Catalyzed by Iron(III) ions, *Coll. Czech. Chem. Commun.*, 41, 3495-3503.
59. Manoj S.V., Mishra C.D., Sharma M., Rani A., Jain R., Bansal S.P. and Gupta K.S., 2000, Iron, Manganese and Copper Concentrations in Wet Precipitations and Kinetics of the Oxidation of SO_2 in Rain Water at Two Urban Sites, Jaipur and Kota, in Western India, *Atmospheric Environment*, 34, 4479-4486.
60. Manoj S.V., Singh R., Sharma M., Gupta K.S., 1999, Kinetics and Mechanism of Heterogeneous Cadmium Sulfide and Homogenous Manganese(II) Catalyzed Oxidation of Sulfur(IV) by Dioxygen in Acetate Buffered Medium, *Indian Journal of Chemistry*, 39A, 507-521.
61. Manoj S.V., Sharma M. and Gupta K.S., 1999, Role of Cuprous Oxide in Autoxidation of Aqueous Sulfur Dioxide and its Atmospheric Implications, *Atmospheric Environment*, 33, 1503-1512.
62. Martin L.R., 1984, In *SO_2, NO and NO_2 Oxidation Mechanisms, Atmospheric Considerations*, Calvert, J.G. (Ed.), Butterworth, Boston. pp 63-100.
63. Martin L.R. and Good T.W., 1991, Catalysed Oxidation of Sulfur Dioxide in Solution, The Iron–manganese Synergism, *Atmos. Environ.*, 25A, 2395-2399.
64. Munger J.M., Jacob D.J., Waldman J. M. and Hoffmann M.R., 1983, Fogwater Chemistry in an Urban Atmosphere, *J. Geophys. Res,.* 88, 5109-5121.

65. Neususs C., Pelzing M., Plewka A., Herrmann H., 2000, A New Analytical Approach for Size-resolved Speciation of Organic Compounds in Atmospheric Aerosol Particles, methods and First Results, *Journal of Geophysical Research,* 105, 4513-4528.

66. Novic M., Grgic I., Poje M. and Hudnik V., 1996, Iron-catalyzed Oxidation of S(IV) Species by Oxygen in Aqueous Solution, Influence of pH on the Redox Cycling of Iron, *Atmos. Environ,.* 30, 4191-4196.

67. Pasiuk-Bronikowska W., Bronikowski T., Ulejczyk M., 2003, Inhibition of the S(IV) Autoxidation in the Atmosphere by Secondary Terpenic Compounds, *Journal of Atmospheric Chemistry,* 44, 97-111.

68. Pasuik-Bronikowska W., Bronikowski T. and Ulejczyk M., 1997, Solubilization of Organics un Water Coupled with Sulfite Autoxidation, *Water Research,* 31, 1767-1775.

69. Pasuik-Bronikowska W., Bronikowski T., Ulejczyk M., 1998, Chemical Interactions of Aqueous Phase Pollutants, Sulfur Dioxide and Sobrerol, in U. Schurath and R. Roselieb (Eds.), Proc. 2nd Workshop of the EUROTRAC-2 Subproject Chemical Mechanism Development, Forschungszentrum Aachen, Aachen, pp. A12/1-4.

70. Pasuik-Bronikowska W., Bronikowski T., Ulejczyk M., 1999, Oscillations in the Rate of S(IV) Autoxidation Inhibited by Sobrerol, in R. Vogt and G. Axelsdottir (Eds.), Proc. Joint Workshop, Ford Forschungszentrum Aachen, Aachen, pp. 195-198.

References

1. Seinfeld, J.H., 1986, Atmospheric Chemistry and Physics of Air Pollution, John Wiley Inc, New York.

2. Cited in Huss, Jr. A, Lim, P.K. and Eckert, C. A., 1982, "Oxidation of Aqueous Sulfur Dioxide (i) Homogeneous Manganese (II) and Iron (II) Catalysis at Low pH" J. Phys. Chem. 86, 4224-4228.

3. Ali, M.; Saha, S. K. and Banerjee, P., 1991. Oxidation of Sulfite and Thiosulfate by the Cobalt(III) Complex of Dipicolinate in Aqueous Medium, *Bulletin Chemical Society of Japan*, 64, 2497.

4. Anast J.M. and Margerum D.W., 1981, Trivalent Copper Catalysis of the Autoxidation of Sulfite. Kinetics and Mechanism of the Copper(III/II) Tetraglycine Reactions with Sulfite, *Inorganic Chemistry*, 20, 2319.

5. Brandt, C., and van Eldik, R., 1998. Kinetics and Mechanism of Iron(III)-catalysed Autoxidation of Sulfur(IV) Oxides in Aqueous Solution: The Influence of pH, Medium and Aging, *Transition Metal Chemistry*, 23, 667.

6. Bhargava, R.; Rani, A. and Gupta, K. S., 1993. Oxidation of Aqueous Sulfur Dioxide in Suspensions of Magnesium Dioxide: Removal of SO_2 from Flue Gases, *Indian Journal of Chemistry*, 32A, 713-716.

7. Hoffmann, M.R. and Edwards J.O., 1975. Kinetics of the Oxidation of the Sulfite by Hydrogen Peroxide in Acidic Medium, *Journal of Physical Chemistry*, 79, 2096-2098.

8. Martin, L.R., 1984. In *SO_2, NO and NO_2 Oxidation Mechanisms: Atmospheric Considerations*; Calvert, J.G. (Ed.), Butterworth, Boston. pp. 63-100.

9. Scott, W.D. and Hobbs, P.V., 1967. The Formation of Sulfate in Water Drop, *Journal of Atmospheric Science*, 24, 54-57.

10. Junge, C.E. and Ryan, T.G., 1958. Study of the SO_2 Oxidation in Solution and its Role in Atmospheric Chemistry, Quart. J.Roy. Meteorological Society, 84, 46-55.

11. Miller, J.M. and de Pena, R.G., 1972. Contribution of Scavenged Sulfur Dioxide to the Sulfate Content of Rain Water, *Journal of Geophysical Research,* 77, 5905-5916.
12. Beilke, S. and Gravenhorst, G., 1978. Heterogeneous SO_2 -oxidation in the Droplet Phase, *Atmospheric Environment,* 12, 231-239.
13. Larson, T.V.; Horike, N.R.; Harrison, H., 1978. Oxidation of Sulfur Dioxide by Oxygen and Ozone in Aqueous Solution: A Kinetic Study with Significance to Atmospheric Rate Processes, *Atmospheric Environment,* 12, 1597-1611.
14. Brimblecombe, P. and Spedding D.J., 1974. The Catalytic Oxidation of Micromolar Aqueous Sulfur dioxide-I, *Atmospheric Environment,* 8, 937-945.
15. Tsunogai, S. "Oxidation Rate of Sulphite in Water and its bearing on the Origin of Sulphate in Meteoric Precipitation", Geochem. J. 5, 175-185 (1971).
16. Huss, A.; Jr. Lim, P.K. and Eckert, C.A., 1978. On the 'Uncatalyzed' Oxidation of Sulfur(IV) in Aqueous Solutions, *Journal of American Chemical Society,* 108, 6253-3253.
17. Calvert, J.G. and Stockwell, W.R., 1984. Mechanisms and Rates of Sulfur Dioxides in Atmosphere. In: *SO_2, NO and NO_2 Oxidation Mechanisms. Atmospheric Considerations,* J.G. Calvert (Ed.), Butterworths, Boston, pp. 1-62.
18. Brandt, C. and van Eldik, R., 1995. Transition Metal Catalyzed Oxidation of Aqueous Sulfur(IV) Oxides. Atmospheric Relevant Process and Mechanisms, *Chemical Reviews,* 95, 119-190.
19. Crutzen, P.J. and Lawrence, M.G. 2000. The Impact of Precipitation Scavenging on the Transport of Trace Gases: a 3-dimensional Model Sensitivity Study, *Journal of Atmospheric Chemistry,* 37(1), 81-112.
20. Halperin, J. and Taube, H., 1952. The Transfer of Oxygen Atoms in Oxidation Reduction Reactions, IV. The Reactions of Hydrogen Peroxide with Sulfite and Thiosulfate and of Oxygen, Manganese Dioxide and of Permanganate with Sulfite, *Journal of American Chemical Society,* 74, 380.
21. Penkett, S.A.; Jones, M.R. and Eggleton, A.E.G., 1979. A Study of SO_2 Oxidation in Stored Rain Water Samples, *Atmospheric Environment,* 13, 139-147.
22. Penkett, S.A., 1972. Oxidation of SO_2 and other Atmospheric Gasesby Ozone in Aqueous Solution, *Nature, Phys. Sci.,* 240, 105-106.
23. Hoffman, M.R. and Jacob, D.J., 1984. In: *SO_2, NO and NO_2 Oxidation Mechanisms. Atmospheric Considerations;* Calvert, J.G.(Ed.), Butterworth: Boston, pp 101-172.
24. Hoffmann, M.R. and Boyce, S.D., 1983. In *Trace Atmospheric Constituents: Properties, Transformations and Fates;* S.E. Schwartz, (Ed.), John Wiley and Sons: New York, pp. 147-189.
25. Kraft, J. and van Eldik, R. 1989. Kinetics and Mechanism of the iron(II1)-catalyzed Autoxidation of Sulfur(1V) Oxides in Aqueous Solution. 1. Formation of Transient iron(III)-sulfur(1V) Complexes, *Inorganic Chemistry,* 28, 2297-2305.
26. Kuo, D.T.F.; Krik, D.W. and Jia, C.Q. 2006. The Chemistry of Aqueous S(IV)-Fe-O_2 System: State of the Art, *Journal of Sulfur Chemistry,* 27, 461-530.
27. Grgic, I.; Hudnik, V., Bizjakats, M and Levec, J. 1991. Aqueous S(IV) Oxidation-catalytic Affects of some Metal ions, *Atmospheric Environment,* 25A, 1591-1597.
28. Manoj S.V., Mudgal, P.K. and Gupta, K.S., 2008. Kinetics of iron(III)-catalyzed Autoxidation of Sulfur(IV) in Acetate Buffered Medium, *Transition Metal Chemistry,* 33, 311-316.

29. Fuzzi, S., 1978, Study of iron(III) Catalyzed Sulfur dioxide Oxidation in Aqueous Solution over a Wide Range of pH, *Atmospheric Environment*, 12, 1439-1442.

30. Conklin, M.H. and Hoffmann, M.R., 1988. Metal Ion-Sulfur (IV) Chemistry. 3. Thermodynamics and Kinetics of Transient Iron(III)-Sulfur(IV) Complexes, *Environmental Science and Technology*, 22, 899-907.

31. Huss, Jr. A.; Lim, P.K. and Eckert, C.A., 1982. Oxidation of Aqueous Sulfur Dioxide. 1. Homogenous manganese(II) and Iron (II) Catalysis at Low pH, *Journal of Physical Chemistry*, 86, 4224-4228.

32. Wilkosz, I; Mainka, A; 2008. Mn (II)-catalysed S(IV) Oxidation and its Inhibition by Acitic Acid in Acidic Aqueous Solutions. *Journal of Atmospheric Chemistry*, 60, 1-17.

33. Grgic, I; Podkrajsec, B; Barzaghi, P; Harrmann, H; 2007. Scavenging of SO_4^- Radical Anions by Mono- and Dicarboxylic Acids in the Mn(II)-catalyzed S(IV) Oxidation in Aqueous Solution. *Atmospheric Environment*, 41, 9187-9194.

34. Manoj, S.V.; Mishra, C.D.; Sharma, M.; Rani, A.; Jain, R.; Bansal, S.P. and Gupta, K.S., 2000. Iron, Manganese and Copper Concentrations in Wet Precipitations and Kinetics of the Oxidation of SO_2 in Rain Water at Two Urban Sites, Jaipur and Kota, in Western India, *Atmospheric Environment*, 34, 4479-4486.

35. Connick, R.E. and Zhang, Y.X., 1996. Kinetics and Mechanism of Oxidation of HSO_3^- by O_2. 2. The Manganese(II) Catalyzed Reaction, *Inorganic Chemistry*, 35, 4613-4621.

36. Berglund, J.; Fronaeus, S.; Elding, L. I.,1993. Kinetics and Mechanism for Manganese-catalyzed Oxidation of Sulfur(IV) by Oxygen in Aqueous Solution, *Inorganic Chemistry*, 32, 4527-4538.

37. Podkrajsek, B.; Bercic, G.; Tursic, J. and Grgic, I. 2004. Aqueous Oxidation of S(IV) Catalyzed by Manganese(II): A Generalized Simple Kinetic Model, *Journal of Atmospheric Chemistry*, 47, 287-303.

38. Huss, Jr. A.; Lim, P.K. and Eckert, C.A., 1982. Oxidation of Sulfur Dioxide. 2. High Pressure Studies and Proposed Reaction Mechanisms, *Journal of Physical Chemistry*, 86, 4229-4233.

39. Lunak, S., El-Wakil, A. and Veprel-Siska, J. 1978. Autoxidation of Sulfite Catalyzed by 3d Transition Metals and Inhibited by 2-propanol: Mechanism of Inhibited and Induced Reactions,*Collections Czechoslovak Chemical Communications*, 43, 3306-3316.

40. Fuller E.C. and Crist, R.H. 1941. The Rate of Oxidation of Sulfite ions by Oxygen, *Journal of American Chemical Society*, 63, 1644-1650.

41. Hobson, D.B.; Richardson, P.J. and Robinson, P.J., 1986. Kinetics and Mechanism of Cobalt Catalyzed Reaction of Oxygen and Sulfite at very Low Concentrations, *Journal of Chemical Society Faraday Transactions*, 1, 82, 869-881.

42. Srivastava, R.D.; Macmillan, A.F. and Harris, I.J. 1968. The Kinetics of Oxidation of Sodium Sulfite, *Journal of Chemical Engineering*, 46, 181-184.

43. Gupta, K.S., Bhargava, P. and Manoj, S.V., 1999. Kinetics of Silver(I) Catalysed Oxidation of Sulfur(IV) by Peroxodisulfate, *Indian Journal of Chemistry*, 38A, 692-697.

44. Gupta, K.S.; Bhargava, P. and Manoj, S.V., 2001. Kinetics of Diamminesilver(I)-catalysed Oxidation of Sulfur(IV) by Dioxygen in Ammonia Buffers, *Transition Metal Chemistry*, 26, 71-75.

45. Gupta, K.S., Jain, U., Singh, A., Mehta, R.K., Manoj, S.V., Prasad, D.S.N., Sharma, A., Parashar, P., Bansal, S.P., 2004. Kinetics and Mechanism of the Osmium(VIII)-catalysed Autoxidation of Aqueous Sulfur Dioxide in Acidic and Alkaline Media. *Journal of Indian Chemical Society*, 81, 1083-1092.

46. Linn, Jr. D. E.; Dragon, M.J. and Miller, D.E., 1990. Catalysis of the Autoxidation of Aqueous Sulfur Dioxide using [Ni^{III}(cyclam)]: Evidence for a Novel Radical Chain Mechanism, *Inorganic Chemistry,* 29, 4256-4358.
47. Bronikowski, T; W. Pasiuk-Bronikowska, M. Ulejczyk, 2000. Inhibition of S(IV) Autoxidation, by Selenium, Works & Studies of the Institute of Environmental Engineering PAS, No. 54, 28-34.
48. Backstrom, H.L.J., 1934. The Chain Mechanism of the Autoxidation of Sodium Sulfite Solutions. *Z. Phys. Chem.*(B), 25, 122-138.
49. Rani, A.; Prasad, D.S.N.; Madnavat, P.V.S.; Gupta, K.S., 1992. The Role of Free Fall Atmospheric Dust in Catalysing Autoxidation of Aqueous Sulfur Dioxide, *Atmospheric Environment,* 26A, 667-673.
50. Prasad, D.S.N.; Rani, A.; Gupta, K.S., 1992. Surface-Catalyzed Oxidation of Sulfur(IV) in Aqueous Silica and Copper(II) Oxide Suspensions, *Environmental Science and Technology,* 26, 1361-1368
51. Bhargava, R.; Rani, A. and Gupta, K.S., 1993. Oxidation of Aqueous Sulfur Dioxide in Suspensions of Magnesium Dioxide: Removal of SO_2 from Flue Gases, *Indian Journal of Chemistry,* 32A, 713-716.
52. Rani, A.; Prasad, D.S.N.; Jain, U. and Gupta, K.S., 1991. Dynamics of Multiphase Glass Powder Catalysed Autoxidation Sulfur Dioxide in Bulk in Aqueous Phase, *Indian Journal of Chemistry,* 30A, 756-764.
53. Gupta, K.S.; Mehta, R.K.; Sharma, A.K.; Mudgal, P.K. and Bansal, S.P., 2008. Kinetics of Uninhibited and Ethanol–inhibited CoO, Co_2O_3 and Ni_2O_3 Catalyzed Autoxidation of Sulfur(IV) in Alkaline medium. *Transition. Metal Chemistry,* 33, 809-817.
54. Prasad, D.S.N.; Rani, A.; Madnavat, P.V.S.; Bhargava, R. and Gupta K.S., 1991. Kinetics of Surface Catalyzed Oxidation of Sulfur(IV) by Dioxygen in Aqueous Suspensions of Cobalt(II) Oxide, *Journal of Molecular Catalysis,* 69, 395-405.
55. Gupta, K.S., Singh,R.,. Saxena, D., Manoj S.V. and M. Sharma., 1999. Role of Manganese Dioxide in the Autoxidation of Sulfur(IV) in Oxic and Anoxic Suspensions, *Indian Journal of Chemistry,* 38A, 1129-1138.
56. Bhargava, R.; Prasad, D.S.N.; Rani, A.; Bhargava, P.; Jain, U. and Gupta K.S., 1992. Kinetics of Autoxidation of Aqueous Sulfur Dioxide in Suspensions of Nickel(III) Oxide, *Transition Metal Chemistry,* 17, 238-241.
57. Manoj, S.V., Sharma, M. and Gupta K.S. 1999. Role of Cuprous Oxide in Autoxidation of Aqueous Sulfur Dioxide and its Atmospheric Implications, *Atmospheric Environment,* 33, 1503-1512.
58. Prasad, D.S.N., Mehta R.K., Parashar P., Madnawat P.V.S., Rani A., Singh U., Manoj, S. V., Bansal S.P., Gupta K.S., 2003. Kinetics of Surface - Catalysed Autoxidation of Aqueous Sulfur Dioxide in Cobalt(III) Oxide Suspensions, *Journal of Indian Chemical Society,* 80, 391-394.
59. Cohen, S.; Chang, S. G.; Markovitz, S.S. and Novakov, T., 1981. Role of Flyash in Catalytic Oxidation of S(IV) Slurries, *Environmental Science and Technology,* 15, 1498-1502.
60. Madnavat, P.V.S.; Rani, A.; Sharma, M.; Prasad, D.S.N. and Gupta, K.S., 1993. Role of Surface and Leached Metal Ion Catalysis in Autoxidation of Sulfur(IV) in Power Plant Fly Ash Suspensions, *Atmospheric Environment,* 27A, 1985-1991.

61. Saxena, D.; Sharma, M.; Rani, A. and Gupta, K.S. 1995. Studies on Rates of Autoxidation of Aqueous Sulfur Dioxide in Several Fly Ash Suspensions. Implications for Acid Rain, *Journal of Environment Science and Health*, A-30, 1191-1210.
62. Brodzinsky, R.; Chang, S.G.; Mankovitz, S.S.; Novakov, T., 1980. Kinetics and Mechanisms of the Catalytic Oxidation of Sulfur Dioxide on Carbon in Aqueous Suspensions, *Journal of Physical Chemistry*, 84, 3353-3358.
63. Gupta, K.S.; Madnawat, P.V.S.; Bhargava, R.; Prasad, D.S.N.; Sharma, M. and Rani, A., 1992. Autoxidation of Aqueous Sulfur Dioxide in Suspensions of Minerals and Rocks. *Precip. Scavenging Atmos.-Surf. Exch., [Proc. Int. Conf.]*, 153-160.
64. Saxena, D.; Sharma, M.; Rani, A.; Singh, R. and Gupta, K.S., 1993. Kinetics of Oxidation of Aqueous Sulfur Dioxide by Lead Dioxide in Aqueous Suspensions, *Indian Journal of Environmental Protection*, 15, 575-579.
65. Prasad, D.S.N.; Rani A.; Sharma, M. and Gupta K.S., 1994. Rates of Autoxidation of Sulfur(IV) in Aqueous Suspensions of Limestone Powder, Implications for Scrubber Chemistry, *Indian Journal of Chemistry*, 1, 87-92.
66. Herrmann, H.; Ervens, H.; Jacibi, H.W.; Wokke, R.; Nowack, P. and Zellener, R., 2000. CAPRAM 2.3: A Chemical Aqueous Phase Radical Mechanism for Tropospheric Chemistry, *Journal of Atmospheric Chemistry*, 36, 231-284.
67. Bravo, H., 2002. Concentration of Benzene and Toluene in the Atmosphere of Southwestern Area at Mexico City Metropolitan Zone, *Atmospheric Environment*, 36, 3843-3849.
68. Bigelow, S.L., 1898. Catalytic Effects in the Oxidation of Sodium Sulfite by Air Oxygen, *Z Physik Chem.*, 26, 493-532.
69. Alyea, H.N. and Backstrom, H.L.J., 1929. The Inhibitive Action of Alcohols on the Autoxidation of Sodium Sulfite. *Journal of American Chemical Society*, 51, 90-107.
70. Altwicker, E.R., 1980. *In: Advances in Environmental Sciences and Engineering, Vol. 3. J.R. Pfaffin and E.N. Zieglar(Eds.)*, Gordon and Breach Science Publishers, New York, pp. 80-91.
71. Ziajka, P. and Pasiuk-Bronikowska, W., 2003. Autoxidation of Sulfur Dioxide in the Presence of Alcohols under Conditions related to Tropospheric Aqueous Phase, *Atmospheric Environment*, 37, 3913-3922.
72. Lee, Y.J. and Rochelle, G.T., 1987. Oxidative Degradation of Organic Acid Conjugated with Sulfite Oxidation in Flue Gas Desulfurization: Products, Kinetics and Mechanism, *Environment Science and Technology*, 21, 266-271.
73. Grgic, I.; Dovzan, A.; Bercic, G. and Hudnik, V., 1998. The Effects of Atmospheric Organic Compounds on the Fe-catalyzed S(IV) Autoxidation in Aqueous Solution, *Journal of Atmospheric Chemistry*, 29, 315-337.
74. Podkrajsek, B; Grgic, I; Tursic, J; Bercic, G, 2006. Influence of Atmospheric Carboxylic Acids on Catalytic Oxidation of Sulfur (IV). 54, 103-120.
75. Wolf, A.; Deutsch, F.; Hoffmann, P. and Ortner, H.M., 2000. The Influence of Oxalate on Fe-catalyzed S(IV) Oxidation by Oxygen in Aqueous Solution, *Journal of Atmospheric Chemistry*, 37, 125-135.
76. Ziajka, J; Beer, F. and Warneck, P., 1994. Iron-catalyzed Oxidation of Bisulfite Aqueous Solution: Evidence for a Free Radical Chain Mechanism, *Atmospheric Environment*, 28, 2549-2552.
77. Pasiuk-Bronikowska, W.; Bronikowski, T. and Ulejczyk, M., 1997. Solubilization of Organics in Water Coupled with Sulfite Autoxidation, *Water Research*, 31, 1767-1775.

78. Ziajka, J. and Pasiuk-Bronikowska, W., 1998 Effect of α-pinene and cis-verbenol on the rate of S(IV) oxidation catalyzed by Fe.*Proceedings of EUROTRAC Symposium '98:Transport and Chemical Transformation in the Troposphere,* Garmisch-Partenkirchen, Germany, 756-764.
79. Pasiuk-Bronikowska, W.; Bronikowski, T. and Ulejczyk, M., 1998. Chemical Intractions of Aqueous Phase Pollutants: Sulfur Dioxide and Sobrerol, in U. Schurath and R. Roselieb (Eds.), Proc. *2nd Workshop of the EUROTRAC-2 Subproject Chemical Mechanism Development,* Forschungszentrum Aachen, Aachen, pp. A12/1-4.
80. Pasiuk-Bronikowska, W.; Bronikowski, T. and Ulejczyk, M., 1999. Oscillations in the Rate of S(IV) Autoxidation Inhibited by Sobrerol, in R. Vogt and G. Axelsdottir (Eds.), Proc. *Joint Workshop,* Ford Forschungszentrum Aachen, Aachen, pp. 195-198.
81. Pasiuk-Bronikowska, W.; Bronikowski, T. and Ulejczyk, M., 2000. Transformation of Atmospheric Constituents and Pollutants Induced by S(IV) Autoxidation. *Chemistry and kinetics.* In: EUROTRAC-2 Annual Report, CMD Chemical Mechanism Development. ISS, Munich, pp. 123-126.
82. Rudzinski, K.A. and Pasiuk-Bronokowska., 2001. Isoprene Inhibition of S(IV) Autoxidation Initiated by Peroxydisulfate. In: *Transport and Chemical Transformation in the Troposphere,* Proc. EUROTRAC-2 Symp. 2000, P.M. Midgley; M.J. Reuther and M. Williams (Eds.), Springer, Berlin, pp 1-4.
83. Pasiuk-Bronikowska, W., Bronikowski, T., and Ulejczyk, M., 2003; Inhibition of the S(IV) Autoxidation in the Atmosphere by Secondary Terpenic Compounds, *J. Atmos. Chem.* 44, 97-111.
84. Mudgal, P.K.; Bansal, S.P. and Gupta, K.S. 2007. Kinetics of Atmospheric Oxidation of Nitrous Acid by Oxygen in Aqueous Medium, *Atmospheric Environment,* 41, 4097-4105.
85. Hayon, E.; Treinin, A. and Wilf, J., 1972. Electronic spectra, Photochemistry and Autoxidation Mechanism of the Sulfite-bisulfite Pyrosulfite Systems. The SO_2^-, SO_3^-, SO_4^- and SO_5^- radicals. *Journal of American Chemical Society,* 94, 47-57.
86. Ashmore, P.G., 1963. Catalysis and Inhibition of Chemical Reactions. *Butterworths,* London, pp. 375.
87. Gilbert, B.C.; Stell, J.K.; Peet, W.J. and Radford, K.J., 1988. Generation and Reaction of the Chlorine Atom in Aqueous Solution, *Journal of Chemical Society Faradey Transactions,* 84, 3319-3330.
88. Dogliotti, L. and Hayon, E., 1967. Flash Photolysis of Persulfate ions in Aqueous Solution. Study of Sulfate and Ozonide Radical Anions, *Journal of Physical Chemistry,* 71, 2511-2516.
89. Clifton, C.L. and Huie, R.E., 1989. Rate Constants for Hydrogen Abstraction Reactions of the Sulfate Radical, SO_4^-, Alcohols, *International Journal of Chemical Kinetics,* 21, 677-687.
90. Wine, P.H.; Tang, Y.; Thorn, R.P. and Wells, J.R., 1989. Kinetics of Aqueous Phase Reactions of the SO_4^- Radical with Potential Importance in Cloud Chemistry, *Journal of Geophysical Research,* 94, 1085-1094.
91. Ziajka, J.; Pasiuk-Bronikowska, W. and Warneck, P., 1996. The Role of Sulphate Radical Anions in S(IV) Oxidation by Chain Mechanism. In: *Proceedings of EUROTRAC Symposium 96,* P.M. Borrel, P. Borrel, T. Cvitas, K. Kelley, W. Sailar (Eds.), Computational Mechanics Publications, Southampton, pp. 401-405.

92. Ziajka, J.; Krejewska, M. and Pasiuk-Bronikowska, W., 2001. The Role of Myrtenal in the Autoxidation of S(IV) under Acidic Conditions. In: *Proceedings of Eight European Symposium of on the Physico-chemical Behaviour of Atmospheric Pollutants.* J. Hjorth, F. Reas, G. Angeletti (Eds.), CEC, JRC, Ispra, pp. CMD/APP 1-4.

93. Ziajka, J. and Pasiuk-Bronikowska, W., 2000. Myrtenol as an Inhibitor of S(IV) Autoxidation. In: *Proceedings of the EC/EUROTRAC-2 Joint Workshop, EC Cluster 4: "Chemical Processes and Mechanism" EUROTRAC-2: "Chemical Mechanism Development: M.J. Rossi, E.M. Rossi (Eds.),* EPFL, Lousanne, pp. 152-155.

94. Connick, R.E.; Zhang, Y.X.; Lee, S.; Adamic, R. and Chieng, P., 1995. Kinetics and Mechanism of Oxidation of HSO_3^- by O_2. 1. The Uncatalyzed Reaction. *Inorgnaic Chemistry,* 34, 4543-4553.

95. Vogel, A.I. A Text Book of Quantitative Inorganic Analysis, Longman Green, London, pp. 357-370 (1962).

96. Jeffery, G.H.; Basset, J.; Mendham, J. and Denney, R.C., 1989. Vogels's Textbook of Quantitative Chemical Analysis. Addison Wesley Longman Limited, Essex, pp. 383-385.

97. Brodzinsky, R.; Chang, S.G.; Mankovitz, S.S.; Novakov, T., 1980. Kinetics and Mechanisms of the Catalytic Oxidation of Sulfur Dioxide on Carbon in Aqueous Suspensions, *Journal of Physical Chemistry,* 84, 3353-3358.

98. Mudgal, P.K.; Sharma, A.K.; Mishra, C.D.; Bansal, S.P. and Gupta, K.S., 2008. Kinetics of Ammonia and Ammonium Ion Inhibition of the Atmospheric Oxidation of Aqueous Sulfur Dioxide by Oxygen. *Journal of Atmospheric Chemistry,* 61, 31-55.

99. Gupta, K.S.; Mehta, R.K.; Sharma, A.K.; Mudgal, P.K. and Bansal, S.P., 2008. Kinetics of Uninhibited and Ethanol–inhibited CoO, Co_2O_3 and Ni_2O_3 Catalyzed Autoxidation of Sulfur(IV) in Alkaline Medium. *Transition Metal Chemistry,* 33, 809-817.

100. Prasad DSN, Rani A, Gupta KS (1992) Environ Sci Technol 26:1361. doi:10.1021/es00031a013.

Pages: 27-49

Research in Chemistry and Chemical Sciences
Edited by: **Dr. Vijender Singh and Dr. Pawan Kumar 'Bharti'**
ISBN: 978-93-88854-40-5
Edition: **2020**
Published by: **Discovery Publishing House Pvt. Ltd., New Delhi (India)**

2

Recent Advances in the Synthesis and Application of Transition Metal Hydrotalcite based Catalysts for the Conversion of Two High GWP Gases N_2O and CH_4

Pinky Saikia[1,2], R.L.Goswamee[*1,2]

ABSTRACT

N_2O and CH_4 both are green house gases and due to increase of the concentration in the earth crust they cause air pollution hence, they have high global warming potential. Different sources including both industrial and human activities are responsible for the increase of N_2O and CH_4 in the environment. In comparison to preindustrial period the concentration of N_2O increases up to 122% whereas; that of CH_4 increases up to 267%. Thus, different methods were also developed such as N_2O decomposition, CH_4 oxidation which was carried out in presence of different types of catalysts. Generally, noble metal based and non-noble metal based catalysts are more useful for N_2O decomposition and CH_4 oxidation reaction. This chapter summarizes the use of different transition metal based Hydrotalcites type catalysts for N_2O decomposition and CH_4 oxidation reaction.

Keywords: *Hydrotalcites; mixed-metal oxides; catalytic decomposition; partial oxidation; GHSV*

INTRODUCTION

Nitrous oxide (N_2O) is the powerful greenhouse gas and the largest stratospheric-ozone-depleting substance [1-5]. In particular, N_2O has a global warming potential (GWP) of approximately 310 times higher than CO_2,

[1] **Advanced Materials Group, Materials Science and Technology Division, North-East Institute of Science and Technology (CSIR-NEIST), Jorhat - 785 006, Assam, (India)**

[2] **Academy of Scientific and Innovative Research (AcSIR), CSIR-NEIST Campus, (India)**

depleting concurrently ozone layer in a way similar to chlorofluorocarbons (CFCs) due to its long lifetime (114 years) in atmosphere [6,7]. Now-a-days, N_2O emissions have significantly increased compared to the pre-industrial period due to both industrial and different human activities [8]. This includes uses of chemical fertilizers, the combustion of fossil fuels and the large scale production of chemicals like nitric and adipic acid [9-11]. On the other hand, natural gas which is composed primarily of methane is one of the most abundant, low-cost C-containing feedstock available. Large amounts of NG are flared in refineries, chemical plants, oil wells and landfills which cause pollution since it releases both CO_2 and unburned CH_4 green house gases into the atmosphere [12]. Table 2.1 shows the current concentration of green house gases in the atmosphere collected from World Meteorological Organization's Greenhouse Gas Bulletin.

Table 2.1: Current concentration (2019) of green house gases in relation to preindustrial period (1750)

Greenhouse gases	1750 concentration	2019 concentration	Percentage increase relative to 1750	Ref.
Nitrous Oxide (N_2O)	275 ppb	333 ppb	122	[13]
Methane (CH_4)	700 ppb	1867 ppb	267	[13]

Mainly, from the global environment maintenance point of view the control of N_2O emissions from combustion and chemical processes have significant importance. A number of methods can potentially be employed to remove N_2O emissions, including thermal decomposition [14] selective adsorption [14,15], decomposition by the use of plasma technology [14] and catalytic decomposition [14]. Catalytic decomposition of N_2O to N_2 and O_2 offers a number of advantages over these alternative technologies for controlling N_2O emissions, including lower energy requirements and lower cost. The plasma technologies and selective adsorption need further development before they can be commercially viable. On the other hand, the conversion of CH_4 to valuable chemicals is another challengeable work. Methane can be converted either directly *via* a one step process or indirectly *via* several steps into many downstream fuels and chemicals [16]. In recent years, catalytic partial oxidation of methane (CPO) has received intensive attention because of its high methane conversion, and high selectivity for synthesis gas (CO and H_2). CPO [Eq.(1)] gives the H_2/CO ratio of 2, favourable for subsequent synthesis [17] and is weakly exothermic, therefore, the process needs less energy and capital cost than the conventional endothermic steam reforming.

$$CH_4 + 1/2O_2 \longrightarrow 2H_2 + CO \quad (1)$$

Therefore, reactions such as N_2O decomposition and CH_4 oxidation have significant environmental as well as commercial importance to control green gas emission. Catalysts used for the catalytic decomposition of N_2O and CH_4 oxidation can be classified into the following types – noble-metal (Ru, Rh, Pd, Pt, Ir) based supported catalyst, and non noble metal (Ni, Co and Fe) based catalysts and mesoporous oxide based catalyst [15,18,19]. Among these Hydrotalcites or Layered double hydroxides (LDHs) based mixed metal oxides attract so much attention.

Hydrotalcites or Layered double hydroxides (LDHs) can be represented by the general formula $[M_{1-x}{}^{2+}M_x{}^{3+}(OH)_2]^{x+}[A_{x/n}]^{n-3}$ .m H_2O, where M^{2+} (representing divalent metal ion e.g. Mg^{2+}, Ni^{2+}, Fe^{2+}, Co^{2+}, Cu^{2+}, Ni^{2+} or Zn^{2+}) and M^{3+}(representing trivalent metal ion e.g. Al^{3+}, Cr^{3+}, Ga^{3+},In^{3+}, Mn^{3+} or Fe^{3+}) metal cations are uniformly distributed, orderly prearranged in the $Mg(OH)_2$ type brucite like sheets and various charge-compensating anions (A^{n-}) (e.g. $CO_3{}^{2-}$, $NO_3{}^{2-}$,Cl^-, $SO_4{}^{2-}$ etc.) and water are present in their interlayer spaces [20-23]. The value of x is generally in the range of 0.2-0.33. The –OH groups in the LDH layers is oriented towards the interlayer region [24]. Due to the ability to exchange anions LDHs are also known as the anionic clays. In the brucite like layers the divalent metal cations coordinated octahedrally by –OH groups which have been replaced by the trivalent metal cations giving the positively charged layers. Figure 2.1 shows the schematic representation of Layered double hydroxides.

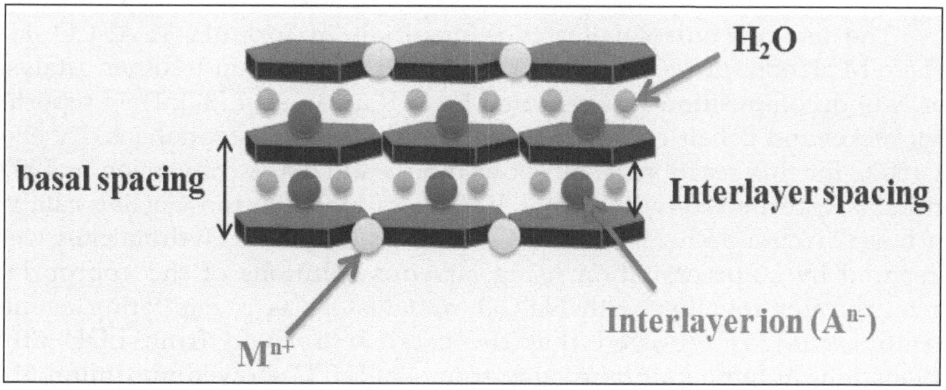

Fig. 2.1: Schematic representation of Layered double hydroxide

LDHs can be synthesized by different methods such as co-precipitation, hydrothermal method, oxide hydrolysis and sol-gel hydrolysis method [25-30]. LDHs have lots of applications such as organic/pharmaceutical synthesis, clean energy generation, degradation of pollutants to control environmental pollution and photochemical reactions [31,32]. Mixed-metal oxides obtained from the calcinations of LDHs possesses different catalytically important properties such as high surface area, uniform atomic level distribution of metal ion centres, acid-base bifunctionality and can be used as a catalyst for various environmentally important reactions e.g. the control of N_2O emission and CH_4 partial oxidation [33-36]. In this chapter we have focussed only the recent use of different transition metal based Hydrotalcites type catalysts for N_2O decomposition and CH_4 partial oxidation reaction.

CATALYTIC PROPERTIES OF HYDROTALCITES

LDHs or Hydrotalcites type materials after thermal decomposition or calcinations at intermediate temperatures (450-600°C) gives mixed metal oxide (MMO) which shows better catalytic activity due to larger surface area and numerous Lewis base sites [33-36]. Figure 2.2 shows the schematic representation of formation of mixed-metal oxides and its application for N_2O decomposition and CH_4 partial oxidation.

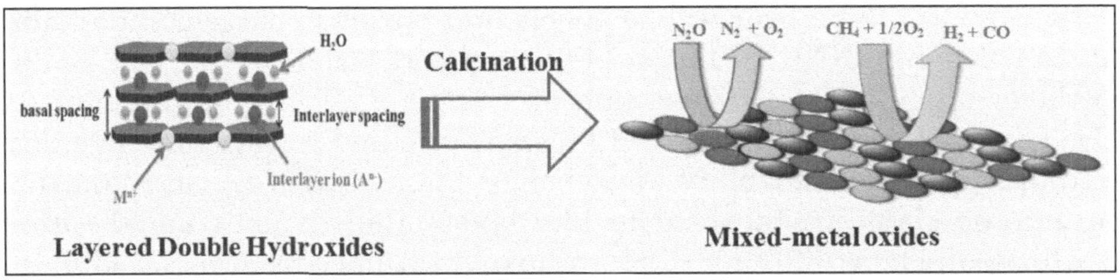

Fig. 2.2: Schematic representation of mixed-metal oxide and its application

Catalytic decomposition of N_2O

The use of Hydrotalcites type materials of formula M-Al-CO_3-HT, where M stands for Ni, Cu and Co and their comparison to other catalysts for N_2O decomposition was reported by S. Kannan *et al* [37]. They reported that nickel and cobalt containing catalysts showed substantial activity even at 150°C for this reaction. They showed 50% and 100% conversion at 190°C and 250°C, respectively, which is 100°C less than the most active catalyst such as Cu-ZSM-5,Rh-ZSM-5 and Co-ZSM-5 [38]. These Hydrotalcites were prepared by co-precipitation using aqueous solutions of the appropriate metal nitrates together with Na_2CO_3 and NaOH as precipitating agents. Armor *et al.*[39] reported that the catalyst derived from LDH after calcinations at temperature ranging from 450-500°C showed maximum N_2O decomposition. Since after calcinations mixed metal oxides are formed. They reported on catalytic decomposition of N_2O over calcined Co-Al-LDH which gave Co_3O_4 and $CoAl_2O_4$ phases after calcinations. The N_2O decomposition over calcined $[Co_{1-x}Al_x(OH)_2[CO_3]_{x/2}.H_2O$, where x= 0.25-0.33 at different Co:Al ratios (from 2:1 to 3:1) was also reported by S. Kannan *et al.*[40] in the temperature ranging from 150-280°C. The Co-Al LDH was synthesized by low super saturation and sequential precipitation methods. The obtained results indicated increasing activity with increasing Co^{2+}concentration on the catalyst surface as determined by X-ray photoelectron spectroscopy.

Co-Al 3: l-HT obtained by low super saturation method exhibited 84% conversion of N_2O while CoO-Al_2O_3 showed only 15% conversion at 450°C under similar reaction conditions.

Perez-Ramirez *et al.*[41] proved a positive influence on the activity for N_2O decomposition over materials with higher Co:Al molar ratios around 1.0-3.0 : 1.0. On the other hand, according to Chang *et al.* [42] the catalytic activity decreases with increasing cobalt concentration based on the ratio of Co:Al =1.0-3.0:1.0. The catalyst with Co:Al =1.0:1.0 showed up to 92% N_2O conversion at 450°C. S. Kannan [43] reported that Mg-Co-Al-O_x with Mg:Co:Al ratio 0.94 : 2.0 : 1.0 showed about 100% N_2O conversion with and without O_2 in the feed (2.5% O_2 and 2.0% H_2O) at 450°C. On the other hand, Obalova *et al.*[44] reported about 80% N_2O conversion over Mg-Co-Al-O_x with Mg:Co:Al ratio 2.0:2.0:2.0 at 450°C. On the other hand, the catalysts containing Mg in the structure were found to be less active catalysts compared to analogous Mg-Co(Cu)-Al-O_x [45] which was also confirmed by Obalova *et al.*[46,47]. The substitution of Ni with Mg resulted in significantly decreased catalytic activity as - Ni:Al (4.0:2.0) > Ni :Mg:Al (3.0 : 1.0 : 2.0 > 2.0 : 2.0 : 2.0) > Mg:Al (4.0:2.0). A maximum N_2O conversion of 79% was observed at 450 °C over Ni–Al–O_x (Ni: Al = 4.0:2.0). Upon calcinations at 450-500°C, a Ni-Al precursor formed crystalline NiO. Additionally, the ternary mixed metal oxides included MgO, which was inactive in N_2O decomposition. However, according to Perez-Ramirez *et al.*[47] the presence of magnesium in Ni–Al-O and Co-Al-O catalysts prevented deactivation of the catalysts due to preferential adsorption of SO_x on MgO. Consequently, the active sites remained available for N_2O reduction. According to Obalova *et al.*[46] the presence of both Ni and Mn in the systems Ni-Mn–O_x and Mg–Ni–Mn–O_x lower the decomposition of N_2O at 450°C (about 20%). The partial substitution of Mn with Al in the series Co-Mn resulted in higher activity [48] with Co:Mn:Al molar ratio 4.0:1.0:1.0. The N_2O conversion reached upto 82-97% conversion.

About 100% N_2O conversion was achieved over Co-Rh-Al-O_x catalyst at temperature of 300-350° C as reported by S. Kannan *et al.*[43] and K.S. Chang *et al.* [49] The material precursors were prepared by co-precipitation followed by calcinations at 450-500°C. Due to the low Rh concentration only spinels Co_3O_4 and $CoAl_2O_4$ were detected [41,43]. Kannan *et al.*[43] also studied the effect of rhodium loading (0.3-1.0 wt%) on the catalytic activity and reported an optimal amount of 0.7 wt% Rh for Co–Rh–Al–O_x (Co:Al = 3.0 : 1.0). As reported in many literatures the dispersion of Rh influenced the catalytic acivity [48-52]. According to P. Esclapez *et al.*[53] besides Rh dispersion particle size also effects on the high catalytic performance which was further studied by Alini *et al.*[54]. They studied H_2- reduced (5.0% H_2, 750 °C) Co–Rh–Al–O_x (Co : Rh : Al = 75.0 :0.5: 24.5) and Mg–Rh–Al–O_x (Mg : Rh : Al = 71.0 : 0.5 : 28.5, 71.0 : 1.0 : 28.0 or 80.0

: 1.0 : 19.0) at 450 °C, and reported that homogeneously dispersed Rh (0) with an average particle size in the range of 1.0–3.0 nm was the active species for N_2O decomposition. They reported with 2.6% water vapour in the feed, the activity of the Co-based catalysts decreased from 55 to 38%, while the samples containing magnesium enabled for complete conversion. On the other hand, varying in the Mg:Al molar ratios in the absence of H_2O did not cause significant changes in the catalytic activity. Catalysts with a higher Mg:Al ratio (Mg:Rh: Al = 80.0:1.0:19.0) deactivated faster in long-term stability tests (after 400 h) compared to Mg: Rh:Al with a molar ratio of 71.0:1.0:28.0. This effect was explained by re-oxidation of metallic rhodium. However, this deactivation in the presence of water vapour proved to be completely reversible, gaining full catalytic activity back by further heating the catalysts in reducing atmosphere. Other reduced materials such as Mg–Rh–Pd–Al–O_x (Mg :Rh : Pd : Al = 70.0 : 0.5 : 1.0 : 28.5 or 70.5 : 0.5 : 0.5 : 28.5) as well as Mg–Rh–La–Al (71.0 : 1.0 : 5.0 : 23.0) showed lower activity in the presence of water vapour compared to Mg–Rh–Al–O_x. These lower N_2O conversions, which were still higher than that for Co–Rh–Al–O_x, and due to the possible segregation of PdO during calcinations for the samples containing palladium. Segregated PdO was suggested to inhibit the synergistic interaction between both metallic rhodium and palladium. For La-containing materials, the formation of inactive La_2CO_5, this could also hinder the interaction of metallic rhodium and Mg–Al–O_x, and results in low catalytic activity. Perez-Ramirez *et al.*[41] also confirmed a promoting effect of magnesium on the structure of Co–Rh–Al–O_x. They investigated the effect of 0.125 bar SO_2 and 30.0 bar O_2 in the feed for Co–Al–O_x (Co:Al = 3.0 : 1.0, 0.7 wt% Rh) and Mg–Co–Rh–Al–O_x (Mg : Co : Al = 1.0 : 3.0 : 1.0, 0.7 wt% Rh). For Co–Al–O_x at 450 °C, the conversion did not change after introducing SO_2 and O_2 into the feed. However, at temperatures around 325°C, the catalyst was completely deactivated. After removal of SO_2 and O_2 from the feed, the activity did not return to its previous level. On the other hand, the catalyst showed a highest decrease of conversion from 80 to 60% during the first 10 h of the stability test at 300 °C. The presence of magnesium in Co–Rh–Al–O improved its stability in the presence of sulphur dioxide and oxygen and reduced deactivation as observed from the 100 h long-term stability tests. Although changes in the Mg:Al molar ratio and therefore the basicity of the oxide matrix did not cause significant differences in the activity for N_2O decomposition of the mixed metal oxides,[54] doping with some alkaline metals, such as Na, Li, K and Cs, was found to significantly increase the catalytic activity [55,56]. Various K-doped metal oxide catalysts for N_2O conversion were widely reported [56-58] in many literatures. However, in most cases, the presence of H_2O, O_2, and/or NO_x (NO and NO_2) inhibited N_2O conversion [46, 59, 60] and such effects depended on the catalyst used as well as the feed composition. Alkaline metals was deposited by using an impregnation method followed by calcinations did not change the structure of the support used. Wu *et al.*[59] reported Ni–Al–O_x (Ni:Al = 4.1:1.0) impregnated with potassium with K:Ni molar ratio of 0.05-0.2:1.0. The catalysts with a K:Ni molar ratio of 0.1:1.0 and calcined at 300-400 °C were the most active among the tested series. Complete conversion of N_2O over these catalysts was observed at 450°C. Materials with the same composition but calcined at 500°C revealed lower N_2O conversion by about 8%. It was observed that with increasing K loading of the samples catalytic activity decreased. Catalytic tests in the presence of 8.8% H_2O and/or 4.0% O_2 revealed that the presence of oxygen induced moderate inhibition on N_2O decomposition over Ni–Al–O_x and K/Ni–Al–O_x (Ni:Al = 4.1:1.0, K:Ni = 0.1 : 1.0). Although the mixture of H_2O and O_2 significantly inhibited N_2O decomposition, complete conversion of N_2O was still reached at 500°C over the catalysts containing potassium, whereas N_2O conversion over undoped Ni–Al–O_x was observed only 38%. The lower catalytic activity in the presence of H_2O and/or O_2 was most likely due to the competitive adsorption of both components on the same active sites responsible for N_2O decomposition. The same effect was observed over other Hydrotalcites-derived mixed metal oxides for N_2O decomposition such as over K-promoted Co–Al–O_x (Co:Al = 3.0:1.0, K/Co = 0.02-0.12 : 1.0) studied by Cheng *et al.*[58] The relationship between catalytic performance and content of potassium was further studied by Obalova *et al.*[55,61] Potassium (0.0–3.0 wt%) deposition on Co–Mn–Al–O_x (Co:Mn:Al = 4.0:1.0:1.0) was carried out by re-suspension of Hydrotalcites-like precursors in aqueous solutions of potassium nitrate. After calcinations at 500°C, the samples with 2.7-3.0 wt% K containing spinels as well as K_xMnO_2. Modification of the Co–Mn–Al–O system with different amounts of potassium significantly changed the catalytic activity. Maximum activity in N_2O decomposition was observed for samples doped with both 0.9 and 1.6 wt% K. All modified samples were tested for N_2O decomposition under various feed compositions, including 4.0% H_2O, 5.0% O_2, 0.17% NO and 0.1% NO_2. The presence of H_2O and O_2 in the feed decreased substantially the catalyst activity. However, the activity could be completely recovered when both components were eliminated from the feed whereas, the presence of NO_x influenced N_2O decomposition. The catalysts with 0.9 wt% potassium were the most active for feeds containing not only N_2O but also O_2 and NO [55]. Another series of Co–Mn–Al–O_x doped with potassium was obtained by impregnation of calcined Hydrotalcites-like compounds and washed precipitates with an aqueous solution of KNO_3 [56]. It was observed that among the tested samples, K (1.8 wt%)/Co-Mn-Al-O_x (Co:Mn:Al = 4.0:1.0:1.0) prepared by doping with potassium salt solution after co-precipitation exhibited highest activity. In the presence of 0.9% H_2O, 5.0% O_2 and 0.005% NO catalyst reached 90% conversion at 450°C. Catalytic tests of this material in the presence of 4.0% H_2O and 5.0% O_2 revealed only a 25% decrease in N_2O conversion during the stability test for 6 h. In comparison to this, no loss in N_2O conversion was observed for a N_2O-He feed and a time-on-stream of 360h. The excellent performance of this system confirms its great potential as an industrially relevant catalyst for N_2O abatement. Besides studies over deposited potassium, Xue *et al.*[62] investigated the effect of residual potassium remaining after synthesis. Ce–Co–O_x (Ce:Co = 0.21:1.0) was prepared from appropriate metal nitrates with KOH as the precipitating agent, followed by calcinations at 400 °C. Co_3O_4 and CeO_2 were also present in the material and the cooperative effect caused by their interaction was also reported. Decrease in catalytic activity was observed for catalyst with 0.7 mol% potassium at 50°C compared to that of the catalyst without residual K occurred. Potassium-doped catalysts showed about 96% conversion at 350°C. However, no catalytic or stability tests in the presence of other components (e.g. H_2O, O_2 and/or NO_x) were reported. The positive effect of K was compared to those of similar contents of Na (Fig. 2.3) and this effect decreased in the sequence as- Cs > Rb > K > Na > undoped > Li [63]. The study on residual amounts or additionally added Na was also carried out. The influence of residual Na, which remained in trace amounts after washing step was reported by Farris *et al* [64].

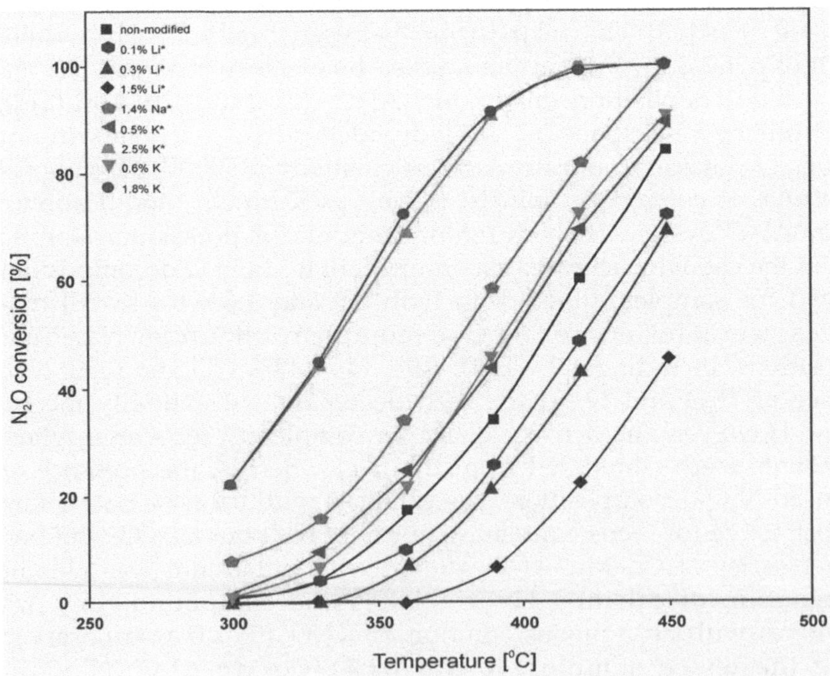

Fig. 2.3: Results of catalytic tests performed for Co–Mn–Al–O_x modified with Li, Na or K; (alkali metals added were labelled as *). Reaction conditions: 0.1% N_2O, He balance; total flow rate = 100 ml min^{-1}; mass of catalyst = 100 mg (adapted from ref. 56 Copyright @2010 with the permission of Elsevier)

They reported that both very low (below 0.16 wt%) and very high (above 15.0 wt%) residual Na contents caused low N_2O conversions upto 50%. An optimum Na content in the range of 3.0-6.0 wt% in Co–Al–O_x promoted the decomposition of N_2O, facilitating over 80% conversion at 475°C. Similar results were also observed by doping of 1.0-2.0 wt% Na. On the other hand, deposition of residual Na using impregnation followed by calcinations appears to be more efficient to promote the decomposition of N_2O. The optimum Na loading is dependent on the mixed metal oxides used which was reported by Xu *et al.*[65] They found that 1.5 wt% sodium as the optimum loading ensuring higher activity compared to that over undoped Co–Al–O_x. A similar value (1.4 wt%) was reported for Na/Co–Mn–Al–O_x as one of the most active catalysts [56]. Perez-Ramirez *et al.*[66] utilized Co–Rh–Al–O_x with different sodium contents ranging from 0.01 to 5.0 wt%. Catalyst with an optimum Na loading of 0.75 wt% led to higher conversion compared to the undoped support.

A broad range of studies covering different mixed metal oxides modified with several alkali promoters was reported by Obalova *et al.*[55,63] which revealed that the promoting effect of alkali metals was associated with their ionization potential, the charge transfer to the catalyst and a decrease in the binding energies of all catalyst components. The sequence of the promoting effect of alkali metals was explained in terms of charge donation from the alkali metal cations to surface oxygen and further to cobalt and manganese in Co–Mg–Al–O_x[63]. Only for the system modified with Li, the N_2O conversion of Co–Mg–Al–O decreased, as reported by Obalova *et al.*[56,67] On the other hand, according to A. Klyushina *et al.*[68] the synthesis methods also effect on the catalytic properties of Co-Mn-Al mixed oxides for N_2O decomposition. Three samples of mixed oxides of Co-Mn-Al with molar ratios of Co:Mn:Al= 4:1:1 were prepared by three different methods such as- calcinations of Hydrotalcites-like precursors (Co-Mn-Al-HT-ex), calcinations of corresponding nitrates (Co-Mn-Al-nitr) and calcinations of the product of mechanochemical reaction of Co, Mn, Al nitrates with NH_4HCO_3 (Co-Mn-Al-carb). Different conditions of synthesis led to the formation of spinel-like phase with different structural properties leading to different catalytic activity. N_2O conversions decreased with decreasing specific surface area in order Co-Mn-Al-carb > Co-Mn-Al-HT-ex > Co-Mn-Al-nitr. The synthesis from carbonate precursor led to the less ordered structure with smaller crystallite size causing higher surface area, better reducibility and increase of mean (Co + Mn) valence. However, its highest catalyst activity was determined by the lowest bond strength of active site-oxygen whereas specific surface area and amount of active sites per unit surface did not increase activity order. N_2O decomposition by using clay-supported LDH as vital component was also reported by Goswamee *et al.*[69] In this patent they used the honey comb monolith coated by clay supported LDH for the treatment of toxic N_2O. The catalytic reactions were carried out at temperatures from 400 to 600°C. The coated honey comb monolith was calcined at 450°C to get mixed-metal oxide. N_2O was decomposed to N_2 and O_2 and about 90-98% N_2O conversion was observed. Goswamee *et al.*[70] also reported the N_2O decomposition over SiO_2 supported Mg-Al LDH synthesized by sol-gel method using metal acetylacetonate as precursors. The catalytic reactions was carried out at 200-450°C. It was observed that N_2O was decomposed to N_2 and O_2 at very low temperature.

In conclusion mixed-metal oxides obtained from Layered double hydroxides or Hydrotalcites appear to be efficient catalyst for N_2O decomposition and thus this type of materials can be considered as a serious candidate for the removal of N_2O.

Catalytic Partial Oxidation of CH_4

Hydrotalcites are also used in the catalytic partial oxidation of CH_4. The use of Rh or Ni supported catalysts obtained from Mg-Al Hydrotalcites for catalytic partial oxidation of CH_4 was reported by F. Basile *et al* [71,72]. Catalytic partial oxidation of CH_4 over Ni supported Mg-Al oxide catalyst was reported by T. Shishido *et al.*[73] The catalyst was prepared by the solid phase crystallization (*spc*) method starting from Mg-Al Hydrotalcites (HT) anionic clay as the precursor. The precursor $[Mg_6Al_2(OH)_{16}CO_3^{2-}]\cdot 4H_2O$ was prepared by co-precipitation method from nitrates of the metal components. The *spc*-Ni/Mg-Al prepared showed high activity and selectivity to synthesis gas even at high space velocity of 6.72×10^5 ml $h^{-1}g^{-1}cat^{-1}$. Ni was supported by impregnating Mg-Al mixed oxide prepared from Mg-Al HT and it was observed that the catalytic activity of imp-Ni/Mg-Al was higher than those of Ni/á-Al_2O_3 and Ni/MgO catalyst, while it was close to that of *spc*-Ni/Mg-Al. The relatively high activity of the imp-Ni/Mg-Al was due to the regeneration of Mg-Al HT phase from the mixed oxide during the preparation. The partial oxidation of CH_4 over M/Mg/Al mixed oxides (where, M is Ru, Rh or Ir) was reported by F. Basile *et al.*[74] They prepared Ru and Rh containing Mg-Al mixed oxide with different compositions such as Rh/Mg/Al= 5:80:15, 5:71:24 and 5:65:30 as well as Ru/Mg/Al = 1:80:19 to 1:71:28. All of these catalysts showed total oxygen conversion, high methane conversion, and synthesis gas selectivity close to 90% (Fig. 2.4). It was observed that the sample in which only the MgO-type phase was present (Rh/Mg/Al 5:80:15) showed higher methane conversion and synthesis gas selectivity in comparison with the samples in which the MgO and spinel phases were present such as Rh/Mg/Al 5:71:24 and 5:65:30.

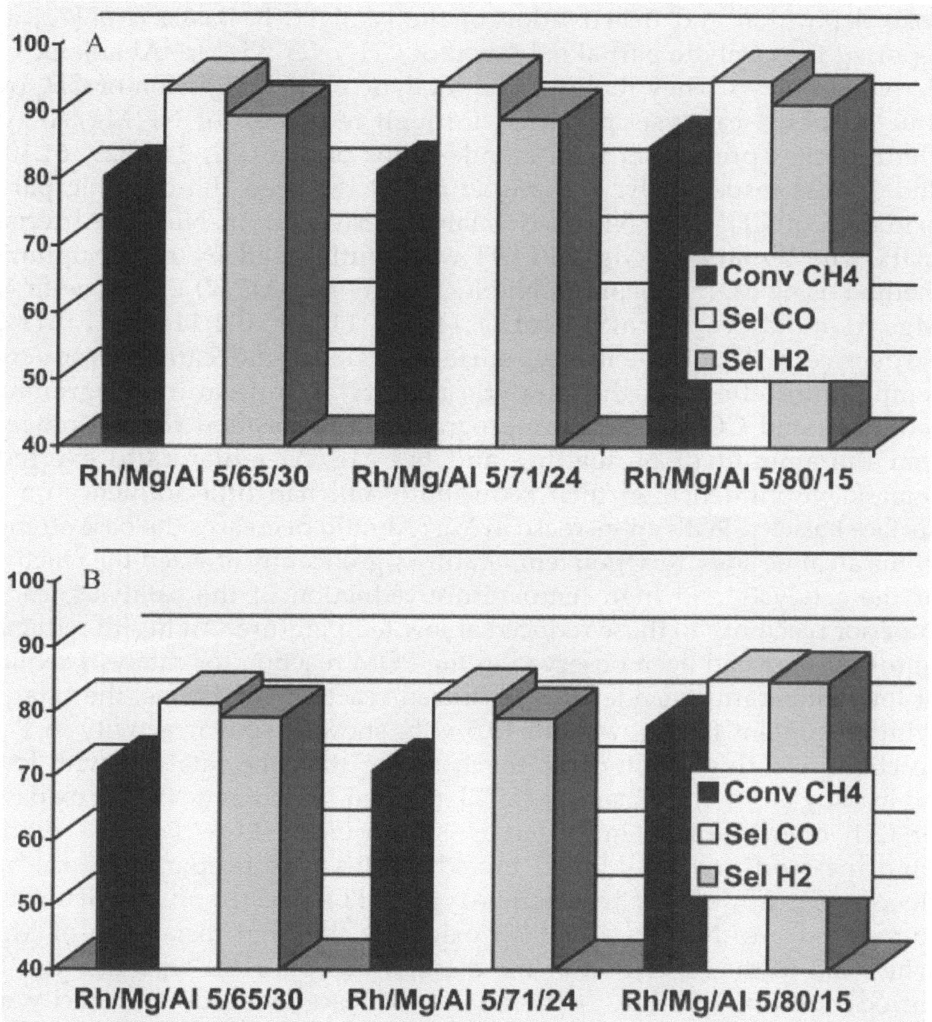

Fig. 2.4: Comparison of the activity of the Rh/Mg/Al catalysts containing 5% Rh (a.r.) in the partial oxidation of methane carried out at a residence time of 7 ms with an oven temperature of 773 K: (A) CH_4:O_2:He 2 : 1 : 4 v/v; (B) CH_4:O_2 :He 2 : 1 : 20 v/v. (adapted from ref.74 Copyright@2002 with the permission of RSC)

On the other hand, K.M. Lee *et al.*[75] reported the catalytic partial oxidation of CH_4 over calcined Ni-Mg/Al layered double hydroxides. It was observed that the catalyst composition and the calcinations temperature effect on the catalytic properties of Ni-Mg/Al LDHs. The catalyst performance was strongly related to the Ni particle size. Ni-Mg/Al mixed oxide catalyst obtained after calcinations at 1073 K with only Ni content and zero Mg/Al atomic ratio showed better catalytic activity about 90% CH_4 conversion due to the formation of $NiAl_2O_4$ spinels which reduced the coke deposition and deactivation of the catalyst. F. Basile *et al.*[74] also reported the catalytic partial oxidation of CH_4 over Ni/Mg/Al anionic clay derived catalysts. They reported the catalytic partial oxidation of CH_4 over four Ni based catalysts prepared through reduction of Ni/Mg/Al type Hydrotalcites precursors with atomic ratios of 10:61:29, 34:37:29, 61:10:29 and 71:0:29 respectively. Z. Jiang *et al.*[76] reported the catalytic partial oxidation of CH_4 over Ni-based catalyst derived from Ni-Mg/Al ternary LDH. The ternary Ni-Mg-Al LDH was synthesized by co-precipitation method using $Mg(NO_3)_2{\cdot}6H_2O$, $Ni(NO_3)_2{\cdot}6H_2O$ and $Al(NO_3)_2{\cdot}9H_2O$ with Ni/Mg/Al molar ratios at 1:11:4, 1:11:3, 1:11:2.4, 0.4:11:2.4, 1.9:11:2.4 respectively. The reducibility, surface basicity and catalyst reduction temperature effect on the catalytic activity. Temperature-programmed reduction and CO_2-temperature-programmed desorption results indicated that the amount of Ni-loading and the Mg/Al molar ratio exerted a remarkable influence on their reducibility but had little influence on the surface basicity. With an increase in Mg/Al ratio decreases the base strength of the alkaline sites. Reaction temperature significantly affected the reactivity of the catalysts and high temperature reduction of the catalysts lead to superior reactivity to those reduced at low temperature. An in situ reduction of the catalyst had been observed in the POM reaction for catalysts reduced at low temperature. Under the optimized reaction conditions, the catalysts with Ni content from 8 wt% to 15.5 wt% showed similar activity in POM reactions and this activity was much higher than the catalysts with lower Ni-loading (~ 4 wt). J. Zhang *et al.*[77] reported the catalytic partial oxidation of CH_4 over fluorine modified mesoporous Ni-Mg-Al mixed oxides. Fluorine-modified Ni–Mg–Al mixed oxides was prepared by thermal decomposition of Hydrotalcites-type (HT) precursor. Fluorine was introduced into Ni–Mg–Al mixed oxide *via* the high dispersion of MgF_2, which led to the formation of the mesoporous periclase-type catalyst. The introduction of fluorine to the mixed oxides enhanced the basicity and nickel homogeneous distribution. Fluorine acted as both electron and structure promoter and also improved the performance of Ni/Mg/AlO-F towards partial oxidation of CH_4 and deactivation was only observed even after 120 h run at 1053 K. F. Basile *et al.*[78] reported the effect of Mg/Al ratio of the Hydrotalcites type precursors on the dispersion and catalytic activity of Rh and Ru catalysts. The active and stable catalyst based on Rh and Ru nanoparticles strongly interacting with MgO or spinel matrix was prepared by calcinations and reduction of M/Mg/Al Hydrotalcites-type precursors. The $MgAl_2O_4$ spinel-type and MgO-type phases obtained by calcinations of the Rh/Mg/Al 5/71/24 (a.r.) sample were studied. Rh was more concentrated in the spinel phase but the larger amount of MgO phase led to a similar amount of Rh in the two phases. The reduction of the sample led to Rh disperse particles with a maximum of the particle-size distribution between 2 and 3 nm in particular the Rh(0) particle size supported on the spinel was larger than that supported on the MgO phase. The change of the M^{2+}/M^{3+} ratio changes the amount of the phases and the Rh distribution. In the catalysts with the M^{2+}/M^{3+} = 80/20 the amount of spinel phase was low or absent (depending on the Al/Rh concentration) and the Rh was completely soluted in the MgO phase. These phenomena lead to a narrow distribution of the Rh particle size and to a high methane conversion and *syn-gas* selectivity. The catalyst and the particle size distribution were stable for 100 h in hard reaction conditions. The increase of the M^{2+}/M^{3+} ratio applied to the Ru catalysts increases the amount of Ru in the MgO structure decreasing the segregation of RuO_2 and as a consequence, the catalytic activity increases. Therefore, the properties and the dispersion of the active metal depend on the type of oxide in which the metal is inserted and this parameter can be tailored by the M^{2+}/M^{3+} ratio. J. Zhang *et al.*[79] reported the partial oxidation of CH_4 over Ni/Mg/Al/La mixed oxides derived from LDH. A series of Ni/Mg/Al/La mixed oxides prepared by thermal decomposition of layered double hydroxides. It was observed that due to larger ionic radius of La^{3+} ion only small partial La^{3+} was imported into the HT structure. It was probably that most of lanthanum were dispersed on the surface or formed amorphous phases which existed between the crystal grains of the periclase-type solid solution. The content of La^{3+} was crucial for the catalysts performance toward POM. The addition of La^{3+} with less than 6.5% content gave rise to the strong basicity and better nickel dispersion with small particle sizes in the catalysts matrices, thus the corresponding mesoporous Ni/Mg/Al/La mixed oxides showed a high performance about 99% CH_4 conversion. Due to presence of La^{3+} improved the resistivity on carbon deposition and nickel sintering. As a result catalyst deactivation was hardly observed even after 86 h of reaction at 1053 K.

K. Takehira [80] reported the preparation of Ni catalysts loaded in egg-shell type by applying "Memory effect" in which Mg (Ni)-Al Hydrotalcites structure was reconstituted on the catalyst surface during the preparation. Mg-Al (3/1) Hydrotalcites was prepared by the co-precipitation from the nitrates of Mg(II) and Al(III) dried in air at 378 K, and calcined at 1123K for 1 h to form Mg–Al(3/1) mixed oxide. This catalyst was then used for CH_4 oxidation. It showed high and stable activity. J. Ashok [81] reported the CPO of CH_4 over Ni-Cu-Al catalyst. The precursors of Hydrotalcites-like structures of Ni–Cu–Al catalysts derived with different Cu/Al ratios were synthesized by co-precipitation method. The CH_4 decomposition activities were evaluated at 600-700°C and ambient pressure over calcined Ni–Cu–Al catalysts until the catalysts were deactivated completely. It was observed that addition of Cu to Ni enhanced methane decomposition activity when added in an appropriate amount. It was also observed that the Ni-Cu-Al with 60:25:15 ratio possessed higher hydrogen yield over the other compositions (60:05:35, 60:30:10, 65:00:35, 60:10:30, 60:15:25 and 60:20:20). Figure 2.5 and figure 2.6 shows the methane conversion rates (mol/min g-cat) and carbon accumulation (gC/g-cat) with time over Ni–Cu–Al catalysts at a temperature of 650°C and atmospheric pressure as well as the overall hydrogen yields over Ni–Cu–Al catalysts at 650°C with Cu loading. It was observed that among all the tested samples the Ni–Cu–Al (60:25:15) displayed higher activity with initial conversion of 53% and total carbon accumulation of 310 gC/g-cat over a total run time of 900min under the reaction conditions maintained in this study. The H_2 yields were increased with increase in the Cu content up to a molar composition of Ni–Cu–Al which was 60:25:15 and at above this Cu loading a rapid fall in H_2 yields was observed. Thus, it can be observed that a certain amount of copper can enhance methane decomposition activity of Ni.

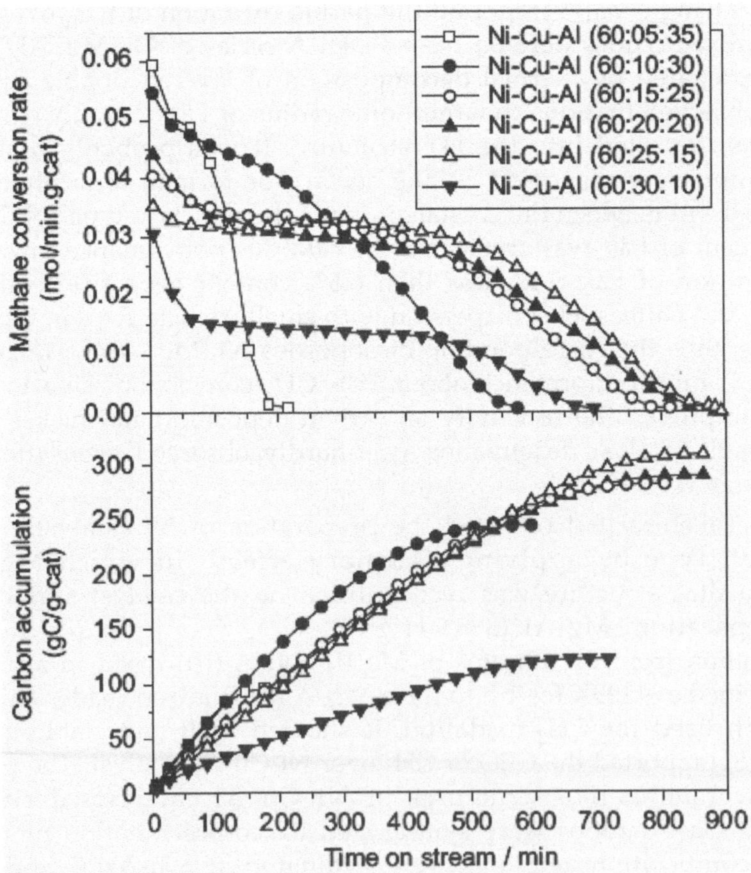

Fig. 2.5: The time on stream analysis over Ni–Cu–Al samples at 650°C: (a) Methane conversion rates and (b) carbon accumulation capacity (adapted from Ref. 81 Cpoyright@2008 with the permission of Elsevier)

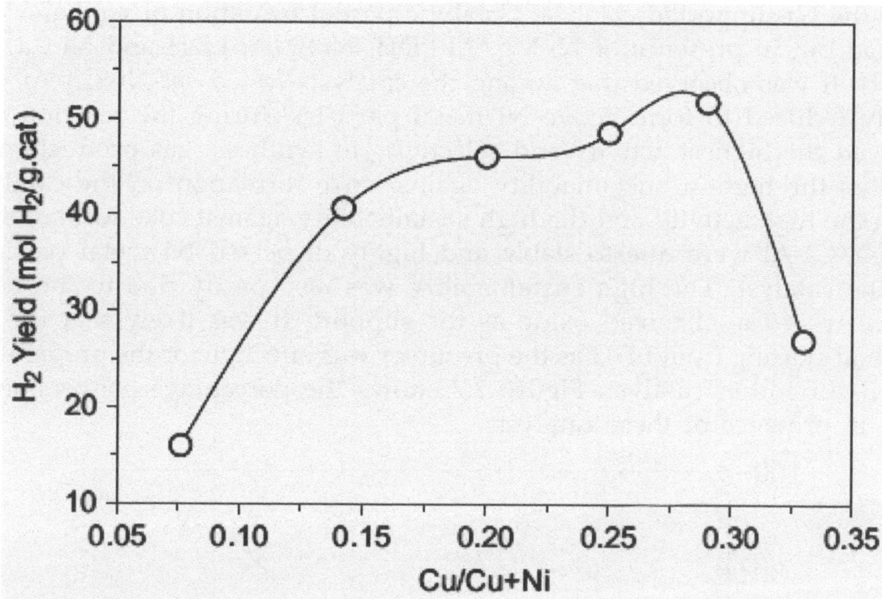

Fig. 2.6: Hydrogen yields against Cu content in Ni–Cu–Al catalysts studied at 650 °C (adapted from Ref. 81 Cpoyright@2008 with the permission of Elsevier)

F. Basile *et al.*[82] reported the CPO of CH_4 over Ni catalyst obtained from silicate intercalated HTlcs. Ni-containing catalysts obtained from Hydrotalcites-like compounds (HTlcs) intercalated with silicate anions were prepared to develop active and stable catalysts for the catalytic partial oxidation (CPO) of methane as an alternative to the conventional catalysts obtained intercalating carbonates. The results showed that Ni catalysts obtained by decomposition of HTlcs intercalated by silicate were a good alternative to the conventional carbonate intercalated compounds. Modifying the amount of silicates allowed the tailoring of the structural and textural properties of the catalysts, and then of their catalytic performances. Catalytic results have shown that Ni8exHT-x catalysts were stable with increasing the time-on-stream. Reducing the amount of active phase, the best results were achieved using the sample with a lower amount of silicates (stoichiometric). For this catalyst, the amount of magnesium available to form the MgO phase increased, thus a larger amount of Ni^{2+} species could be involved in the solid solution improving the catalyst stability.

H. Morioka *et al.* [83] reported the catalytic partial oxidation of CH_4 supported Ni catalysts prepared from Ni-Ca/Al-layered double hydroxide. They reported the synthesis of different types of Ni-M/Al-LDHs where, M=Mg, Sr and Ca respectively. The Ni-M/Al-LDHs were first synthesized by co-precipitation method and decomposed by calcinations to form the precursors. The precursors were in situ reduced during the reaction to give the Ni-supported catalyst. Catalytic partial oxidation of methane was carried out in presence of Ni-Mg/Al-LDH, Ni-Sr/Al-LDH and Ni-Ca/Al-LDHs. It was observed that among the catalysts tested *spc*-Ni/Ca–Al was easily reduced to form active Ni metal particles during the reaction and showed the highest activity and selectivity to synthesis gas production as well as the highest sustainability against coke formation on the catalyst. Both the high activity and the high sustainability against coke formation of *spc*-Ni/Ca-Al were due to stable and highly dispersed Ni metal particles on the catalyst. The high sustainability was also partly due to the basic property of Ca-Al mixed oxide as the support. It was likely that the *spc* method starting from LDH as the precursor was effective for the preparation of Ni supported catalyst. Figure 2.7 shows the percentage conversion of CH_4 in presence of these catalysts.

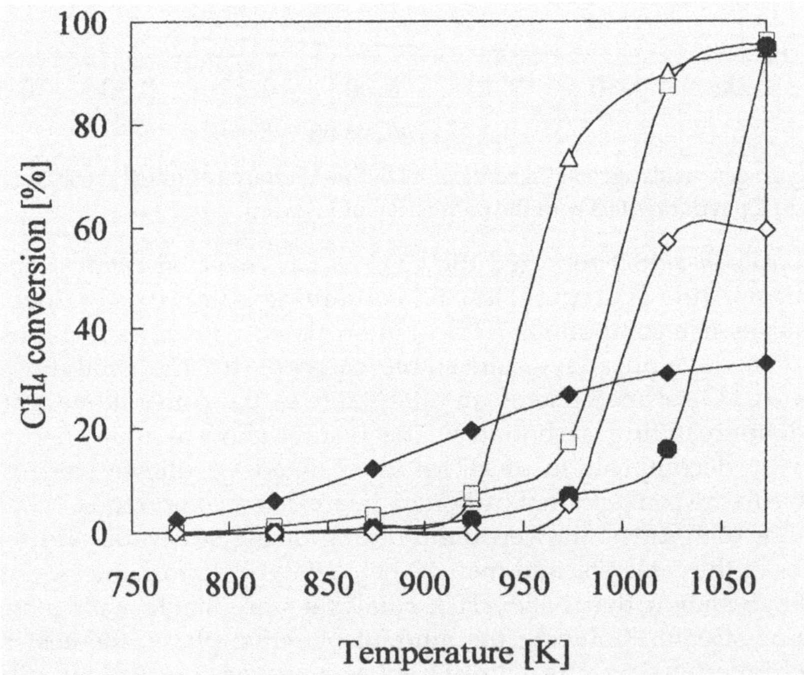

Fig. 2.7: The CH_4 conversion during the TPR over the Ni catalysts: (◆) *spc*-Ni/Mg–Al; (•) *spc*-Ni/Ca–Al; (◇) *spc*-Ni/Sr–Al; (Δ) *imp*-Ni/CaO; and (□) *imp*-Ni/Al_2O_3. (adapted from Ref. 83 Copyright@2001 with the permission of Elsevier)

D.V. Cesar *et al.*[84] reported the catalytic partial oxidation of CH_4 over Rh-Ni catalyst derived from Hydrotalcites like precursors. Ni-Mg-Al and Rh-Ni-Mg-Al LDHs were first synthesized by co-precipitation methods. These were then calcined at 500°C to obtain mixed metal oxide. The CPO reaction was carried out at 550 and 750°C. It was observed that $NiHT_x$ catalysts with high Ni content (x =1 and 5) showed high stability and high methane conversion for the partial oxidation of methane at 750°C. On the other hand those with lower Ni content (x = 15 and 25) exhibited low catalytic activity with low H_2/CO ratio (<2) and fast deactivation. At 550°C, the water gas shift reaction was favoured, increasing the hydrogen yield. However, the occurrence of the Boudouard reaction produced high carbon deposition with the formation of whisker-type carbon. In the bimetallic RhNiHT25, the Ni reducibility was improved due to the synergic effect between Rh and Ni, increasing the methane conversion and hydrogen selectivity. In addition to this, the noticeable increase in stability was related to the absence of carbon deposition after 30 h on stream (at 750 and 550°C). These results show that the bimetallic catalyst is promising for application in membrane reactors to produce high purity hydrogen. Thus, Hydrotalcites act as an active catalyst for CPO of CH_4.

We have also reported the catalytic partial oxidation of CH_4 in presence of N_2O over periclase type SiO_2@Ni(Mg,Al)O catalyst at the temperature range of 200-500 °C and Gas Hourly Space Velocity (GHSV) of 23,862 h^{-1} [85]. SiO_2@Ni-Mg-Al-LDH with SiO_2:LDH ratio 0:1 to 1:1 were prepared by 'soft chemical' sol-gel method by using metal acetylacetonate precursors.

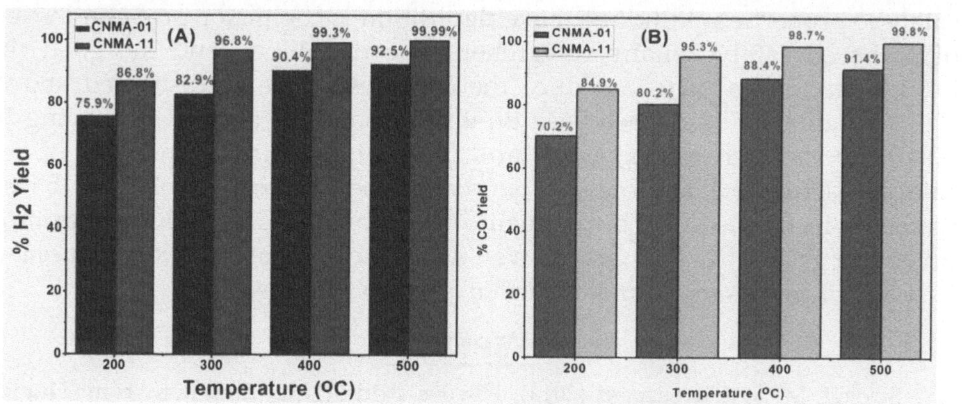

Fig. 2.8: Percentage yield of H_2 and CO in presence of calcined SiO_2@Ni-Mg-Al-LDH (A&B) (Ref 85)

After calcinations they formed MgO type solid solution. Mixed-metal oxide obtained from these LDHs possessed high surface area of 108.9 m^2/g and 403m^2/g respectively. The presence of SiO_2 increased the Ni dispersion as well as the Ni active surface area of the catalyst. Both H_2-TPR and XPS analysis showed that Ni^0 reduced from Ni^{2+}species of NiO-MgO solid solution acted as active species for catalytic partial oxidation (CPO) of CH_4 in presence of N_2O. These catalysts showed about 99.8% to 99.99% H_2 and 99.5% to 99.8% CO yield in the temperature range of 200-500°C. N_2O present on the feed act as oxygen source for CPO of CH_4 as it was first decomposed to N_2 and nascent oxygen. This nascent oxygen provide some less oxidizing oxygen species which does not re-oxidize Ni^0 like molecular oxygen and leads to partial oxidation of CH_4. Figure 2.8 shows the schematic representation of CH_4 partial oxidation in presence of these catalysts.

CONCLUSION

Now-a-days, LDHs attract so much attention towards catalytic activity due to their low cost, easy way of preparation and availability of large no. of composition/preparation variables. Due to the exchangeability of the intercalated anions in interlayer galleries LDHs layers can be tuned to get highly effective catalytic materials. In this review we summarize the different synthesis procedure and the use of LDH based catalytic materials for the treatment of different environmental harmful gases such as N_2O and CH_4 respectively. We also summarize the effect of synthesis procedure on the catalytic properties of LDHs. Mainly, the decomposition of N_2O, catalytic partial oxidation of CH_4 are discussed here. We have found that LDHs plays a vital role in these catalytic reactions. MMO (mixed-metal oxides) formed after calcinations and reduction of LDHs possesses different important properties such as high surface area, uniform atomic level distribution of metal centres, acid-base bi-functionality which helps in their catalytic properties. Although, coke deposition is the major problem in case of Ni-based catalyst many researchers also developed and designed the catalyst in such a way to reduce the coke resistance as discussed above. The formation of MgO periclase type solid solution as well as doping of alkali metals such as Na, Li, K and Cs leads to further increase of the catalytic activity. Therefore, the study on the application of LDH based materials in the use of the treatment of two highly GWP (global warming potential) gases N_2O and CH_4 as well as their other catalytic applications is very much necessary to make further progress in this field.

REFERENCES

1. Strokal, M. and Kroeze, C (2014). Nitrous oxide (N_2O) Emissions from Human Waste in 1970-2050. Curr. *Opin. Environ. Sustainability,* 9-10: 108-121.
2. Hungate, B.A., Dukes, J.S., Shaw, M.R., Luo, Y., Field, C.B (2003). Nitrogen and Climate Change. *Science,* 302: 1512-1513.
3. Erisman, J.W., Galloway, J., Seitzinger, S., Bleeker, A., Butterbach-Bahl, K (2011). How a Century of Ammonia Synthesis Changed the World. *Curr. Opin. Environ. Sustainability,* 3: 281-290.
4. Li, L., Xu, J., Han, J. H (2014). Reducing Nitrous Oxide Emissions to Mitigate Climate Change and Protect the Ozone Layer. *Environ. Sci. Technol.,* 48: 5290-5297.
5. Davidson, E.A., Kanter, D (2014). Inventories and Scenarios of Nitrous oxide Emissions. *Environ. Res. Lett.,* 9: 105012.
6. Rao, S., Riahi, K (2006). *The Role of Non-CO_2 Greenhouse Gases in Climate Change Mitigation: Long-term Scenarios for the 21st Century.* Energy J. 27: 177-200.

7. Ravishankara, R., Daniel, J.S., Portmann, R.W (2009). Nitrous oxide (N_2O): The Dominant Ozone-depleting Substance emitted in the 21st Century. *Science,* 326: 123-125.

8. Wayne, R.P (2000). Chemistry of the Atmosphere, 3rd ed; Oxford University Press: Oxford, U.K., 775.

9. Lee, S.J., Ryu, I.S., Kim, B.M.; Moon,S.H (2011). A Review of the Current Application of N_2O Emission Reduction in CDM Projects. *Int. J. Green House Gas Control,* 5: 167-176.

10. Wuebbles, D.J (2009). Nitrous Oxide: No Laughing Matter.*Sci.,* 326: 56-57.

11. Kapteijn, F., Rodriguez-Mirasol, J., Moulijn, J. A (1996). Heterogeneous Catalytic Decomposition of Nitrous Oxide. *Appl. Catal. B,* 9: 25.

12. Al-Sayari, S.A (2013). Recent Developments in the Partial Oxidation of Methane to Syngas. *The Open Catal. J.,* 6: 17-28.

13. WMO Greenhouse Gas Bulletin. The State of Greenhouse Gases in the Atmosphere Based on Global Observations through (2017). ISSN 2078-0796, 13.

14. Russo, N., Mescia, D., Fino, D., Saracco, G., Specchia, V. (2007). N_2O Decomposition over Perovskite Catalysts. *Ind. Eng. Chem. Res.,* 46: 4226-4231.

15. Konsolakis, M (2015). Recent Advances on Nitrous Oxide (N_2O) Decomposition over Non-Noble-Metal Oxide Catalysts: Catalytic Performance, Mechanistic Considerations, and Surface Chemistry Aspects. *ACS Catal.,* 5: 6397-6421.

16. Pena, M., Gomez, J., Fierro, J.L.G (1996). New Catalytic Routes for Syngas and Hydrogen Production. *Appl. Catal. A,* 144:7-57.

17. Yaremchenko, A.A., Kharton, V.V., Veniaminov, S.A., Belyaeb, V.D., Sobyanin, V.A. Marques, F.M.B (2007). Methane Oxidation by lattice Oxygen of $CeNbO_{4+\delta}$. *Catal.Commun.,* 8: 335.

18. Zhu, T., Flytzani-Stephanopoulos, M (2001). Catalytic Partial Oxidation of Methane to Synthesis Gas over Ni-CeO_2. *Appl. Catal.A,* 208: 403-417.

19. Zhang, R., Hua, C.,Wang, B., Jiang,Y(2016). N_2O Decomposition over Cu–Zn/γ–Al_2O_3 Catalysts. *Catalysts* 6:200; DOI:10.3390/catal6120200.

20. Cavani, F., Trifiro, F., Vaccari A (1991). Hydrotalcite-type Anlonlc Clays: Preparation, Properties and Applications. *Catal. Today,* 11:173-301.

21. Rives V (2001). Layered Double Hydroxides: Present and Future. *Nova Science Publishers, New York.*

22. Evans, D.G., Slade, R.C.T (2006). *Struct. Bonding,* 119: 1.

23. Duan, X., Evans, D.G. (2006). *Layered Double Hydroxides.* (Structure and Bonding Vol. 119, Series Editor D.M.P. Mingos). Springer-Verlag, Berlin, Heidelberg, pp. 234. ISBN-10 3-540-28279-3.

24. Fan, G., Li, F., Evans, D.G., Duan, X (2014). Catalytic Applications of Layered Double Hydroxides: Recent Advances and Perspectives. *Chem.Soc. Rev.,* 43: 7040.

25. Xue, B., Ting, F., Hui, Z (2014). Novel Morphology-Controlled Hierarchical Core@Shell Structural Organo-Layered Double Hydroxides Magnetic Nanovehicles for Drug Release. *ACS Appl. Mater. Interfaces* 6: 20498-20509.

26. Shao, M., Ning, F., Zhao, J., Wei, M., Evans, D.G., Duan, X (2012). Preparation of Fe_3O_4@SiO_2@ Layered Double Hydroxide Core-shell Microspheres for Magnetic Separation of Proteins. *J. Am. Chem. Soc.* 134: 1071-1077.

27. Aramendia, M.A., Borau, V., Jimenez, C., Marinas, J.M., Ruiz, J.R., Urbano, J.F (2002). Thermal Decomposition of Mg/Al and Mg/Ga Layered-double Hydroxides: A Spectroscopic Study. *J. Solid State Chem.* 168: 156-161.

28. Wang, Y., Li, F., Dong, S., Liu, X., Li, M (2016). A Facile Approach for Synthesizing Fe-based Layered Double Hydroxides with High Purity and its Exfoliation. *J. Colloid Interface Sci.* 467: 28-34.

29. Mishra, M., Das, M.R., Goswamee, R.L (2010). Synthesis and Coating of Silica Supported Nickel Oxide Particles over Ceramic Pre-forms through sol–gel Derived Layered Double Hydroxides. *J. Sol. Gel Tecnol.* 54: 57-61.

30. Prinetto, F., Ghiotti, G., Graffin, P., Tichit, D (2000). Synthesis and Characterization of sol–gel Mg/Al and Ni/Al Layered Double Hydroxides and Comparison with Co-precipitated Samples. *Micrporous Mesoporous Mater.* 39: 229-247.

31. Evans, D. G., Duan, X (2006). Preparation of Layered Double Hydroxides and their Applications as Additives in Polymers, as Precursors to Magnetic Materials and in Biology and Medicine. *Chem. Commun.*, 485.

32. Li F. and Duan X (2006). Applications of Layered Double Hydroxides. *Struct. Bonding,* 119: 193.

33. Tichit, D., Coq, B (2003). Catalysis by Hydrotalcites and Related Materials. *CATTECH,* 7:206.

34. Tichit, D., Lutic, D., Coq, B., Durand, R., Teissier, R (2003). The aldol Condensation of acetaldehyde and Heptanal on Hydrotalcite-type Catalysts. *J. Catal.,* 219: 167.

35. Tichit, D., Gerardin, C., Durand, R., Coq, B (2006). Layered Double Hydroxides: Precursors for Multifunctional Catalysts. *Topics in Catal.,* 39: 89.

36. Xu, Z. P., Zhang, J., Adebajo, M. O., Zhang, H., and Zhou, C.H. (2011). Catalytic Applications of Layered Double Hydroxides and Derivatives. *Appl. Clay Sci.,* 53:139.

37. Kannan, S., Swamy, C.S (1994). Catalytic Decomposition of Nitrous oxide on "in situ" Generated Thermally Calcined Hydrotalcites. *Appl. Catal. B Environ,* 3: 109-116.

38. LI, Y., and Armor, J N (1993). Simultaneous, Catalytic Removal of Nitric oxide and Nitrous oxide. *Appl. Catal. B,* 3: 55-60.

39. Armor, J.N., Braymer, T.A., Farris, T.S., Li, Y., Petrocelli, F.P., Weist, E.L., Kannan, S., and Swamy, C. S (1996). Calcined Hydrotalcites for the Catalytic Decomposition of N_2O in Simulated Process Streams. *Appl.Catal. B,* 7: 397-406.

40. Kannan, S., Swamy, C.S (1999). Catalytic Decomposition of Nitrous oxide over Calcined Cobalt Aluminum Hydrotalcites. *Catal. Today,* 53: 725-737.

41. Ramírez, J.P., Overeijnder, J., Kapteijn, F., and Moulijn, J.A (1999). Structural Promotion and Stabilizing Effect of Mg in the Catalytic Decomposition of Nitrous oxide over Calcined Hydrotalcite-like Compounds. *Appl. Catal. B,* 23:59.

42. Chang, K.S., Song, H., Park, Y.S., Woo, J.W (2004). Analysis of N2O Decomposition over Fixed Bed Mixed Metal oxide Catalysts made from Hydrotalcite-type Precursors. *Appl. Catal. A,* 273: 223.

43. Kannan, S (1998). Decomposition of Nitrous oxide over the Catalysts Derived from Hydrotalcite-like Compounds. *App. Clay Sci.,* 13: 347-362.

44. Obalova, L., Jiratova, K., Kovanda, F., Pacultova, K., Lacny, Z., Mikulova, Z (2005). Catalytic Decomposition of Nitrous oxide over Catalysts Prepared from Co/Mg-Mn/Al Hydrotalcite-like Compounds. *Appl. Catal., B,* 60: 289-297.

45. Chmielarz, L., Rutkowska, M., Kustrowski, P., Drozdek, M., Piwowarska, Z., Dudek, B., Dziembaj, R., Michalik, M (2011). An Influence of Thermal Treatment Conditions of Hydrotalcite-like Materials on their Catalytic Activity in the Process of N_2O Decomposition. *J. Therm. Anal. Calorim.*, 105:161-170.
46. Obalova, L., Jiratova, K., Kovanda, F., Valasakova, M., Balabanova, J., Pacultova, K (2006). Structure-activity Relationship in the N_2O Decomposition over Ni-(Mg)-Al and Ni-(Mg)-Mn mixed Oxides Prepared from Hydrotalcite-like Precursors. *J. Mol. Catal. A: Chem.*, 248: 210.
47. Obalova, L., Valasakova, M., Kovanda, F., Lacny, Z., Kolinova, K (2004). Study of the Catalytic Activity of Calcined Ni/Mg/Al (Mn) Hydrotalcites for N2O Decomposition* *Chem. Pap.*, 58:33.
48. Obalova, L., Pacultova, K., Balabanova, J., Jiratova, K., Bastl, Z., Valasakova, M., Lacny, Z., Kovanda, F (2007). Effect of Mn/Al ratio in Co–Mn–Al mixed Oxide Catalysts Prepared from Hydrotalcite-like Precursors on Catalytic Decomposition of N_2O *Catal. Today*, 119: 233.
49. Chang, K.S., Peng, X.J (2010). NO Presence Effects on the Reduction of N_2O by CO over Al–Pd–Co oxide Catalyst. *J. Ind. Eng. Chem.*, 16: 455-460.
50. Haber, J., Nattich, M., Machej, T (2008). Alkali-metal Promoted Rhodium-on-alumina Catalysts for Nitrous oxide Decomposition. *Appl. Catal. B*, 77: 278.
51. Haber, J., Machej, T., Janas, J., Nattich, M (2004). Catalytic Decomposition of N_2O *Catal. Today*, 90:15.
52. Yuzaki, K., Yarimizu, T., Aoyagi, K., Ito, S. I., Kunimori, K (1998). Catalytic Decomposition of N_2O over Supported Rh Catalysts: Effects of Supports and Rh Dispersion *Catal. Today*, 45:129.
53. Esclapez, S.P., Lopez-Suarez, F.E., Lopez, A.B., Illan-Gomez, M.J., Ura, B., Trawczynski, J (2009). Rh–Sr/Al_2O_3 Catalyst for N_2O Decomposition in the Presence of O_2.*Topics Catal.*, 52:1832.
54. Alini, S., Basile, F., Bologna, A., Montanari, T., Vaccari, A (2002). Preparation of Stable Catalysts for N_2O Decomposition under Industrial Conditions. *Stud. Surf. Sci. Catal.*, 143:131.
55. Obalova, L., Karaskova, K., Jiratova, K., Kovanda, F (2009). Effect of Potassium in Calcined Co–Mn–Al Layered Double Hydroxide on the Catalytic Decomposition of N_2O. *Appl. Catal., B*, 90: 132-140.
56. Karaskova, K., Obalova, L., Jiratova, K., Kovanda, F (2010). Effect of Promoters in Co–Mn–Al mixed oxide Catalyst on N_2O Decomposition. *Chem. Eng. J.*, 160: 480-487.
57. Chmielarz, L., Rutkowska, M., Kuœtrowski, P., Drozdek, M., Piwowarska, Z., Dudek, B., Dziembaj, R., Michalik, M (2011). An Influence of Thermal Treatment Conditions of Hydrotalcite-like Materials on their Catalytic Activity in the Process of N_2O Decomposition. *J. Therm. Anal. Calorim.*, 105: 161-170.
58. Cheng, H.,Huang, Y., Wang, A., Li, L., Wang, X., Zhang, T (2009). N_2O Decomposition over K-promoted Co-Al Catalysts Prepared from Hydrotalcite-like Precursors. *Appl. Catal., B*, 89: 391.
59. Wu, H., Qian, Z., Xu, X., Xu, X (2011). *Ranliao Huaxue Xuebao*, 39: 115.
60. Obalova, L., Kovanda, F., Jiratova, K., Pacultova, K., Lacny, Z (2008). Application of Calcined Layered Double Hydroxides as Catalysts for Abatement of N_2O Emissions. *Collect. Czech. Chem. Commun.*, 73: 1045-1060.

61. Obalova, L., Maniak, G., Karaskova, K., Kovanda, F., Kotarba, A (2011). Electronic Nature of Potassium Promotion Effect in Co–Mn–Al mixed oxide on the Catalytic Decomposition of N_2O. *Catal. Commun.,* 12, 1055-1058.

62. Xue, L., Zhang, C.B., He, H., Teraoka, Y (2007). Promotion Effect of Residual K on the Decomposition of N_2O over Cobalt–cerium mixed oxide Catalyst. *Catal. Today,* 126: 449-455.

63. Obalova, L., Karaskova, K., Wach, A., Kustrowski, P., Kutlakova, K. M., Michalik, S., Jiratova, K (2013). Alkali Metals as Promoters in Co–Mn–Al mixed oxide for N_2O Decomposition. *Appl.Catal. A,* 462-463: 227-235.

64. Farris, T.S., Li, Y., Armor, J.N., Braymer, T.A (1995). US Pat., 5472677 A.

65. Xu, X., Xu, X., Zhang, G., Niu, X (2009). *Ranliao Huaxue Xuebao,* 37: 595.

66. Ramirez, J.P., Garcia-Cortes, J.M., Kapteijn, F., Illan-Gomez, M.J., Ribera, A., Salinas Martinez de Lecea, C., Moulijn, J.A. (2000). Dual-bed Catalytic System for NO_x–N_2O Removal: A Practical Application for Lean-burn deNO_x HC-SCR. *Appl. Catal. B,* 25:191-203.

67. Karaskova, K., Obalova, L., Kovanda, F (2011). N_2O Catalytic Decomposition and Temperature Programmed Desorption Tests on Alkali Metals Promoted Co–Mn–Al mixed oxide. *Catal. Today,* 176: 208-211.

68. Klyushina,A., Pacultova, K., Karaskova, K., Jiratovae, K., Ritzb, M., Fridrichova, D., Volodarskajad, A., Obalova, L (2016). Effect of Preparation method on Catalytic Properties of Co-Mn-Al mixed Oxides for N_2O Decomposition. *J.Mol. Catal. A: Chem.* 425, 237-247.

69. Goswamee, R.L., Mishra, M., Sarma, A.K. Mixed Metal Oxidic Nanosheets Coated Monolithic Catalysts useful for the Decomposition of N_2O and a Process for the Preparation thereof. Patent No. WO/2014/080428.

70. Goswamee, R.L., Saikia, P., Borah, A., Allou, N.G.B. A Method for the Preparation of Silica@ Mg-Al LDH core shell Derived mixed Metal oxide Nano-sheet based Composite Catalyst for Decomposition of N_2O in Synthetic Automobile Exhaust Condition". File No. 201611022222.

71. Basile,F., Basini, L., Fornasari, G., Gazzano, M., Trifir, F., Vaccari, A (1996). New Hydrotalcite-type Anionic Clays Containing Noble Metals. *Chem. Commun.,* 2435-2436.

72. Basile, F., Basini, L., Amore, M.D., Fornasari, G., Guarinoni, A., Matteuzzi, D., Piero, G.D., Trifirò, F., Vaccari, A (1998). Ni/Mg/Al Anionic Clay Derived Catalysts for the Catalytic Partial Oxidation of Methane: Residence Time Dependence of the Reactivity Features. *J. Catal.*173: 247.

73. Shishido, T., Sukenobu, M., Morioka, H., Kondo, M., Wang, Y., Takaki, K., Takehira, K (2002). Partial Oxidation of Methane over Ni/Mg-Al oxide Catalysts Prepared by Solid Phase Crystallization method from Mg-Al Hydrotalcite-like Precursors. *Appl.Catal., A* 223: 35-42.

74. Basile, F., Fornasari, G., Gazzanob, M., Vaccari, A (2002). Rh, Ru and Ir Catalysts Obtained by HT Precursors: Effect of the Thermal Evolution and Composition on the Material Structure and use. *J. Mater. Chem.,* 12: 3296-3303.

75. Lee, K.M., Lee,W.Y (2002). Partial Oxidation of Methane to Syngas over Calcined Ni-Mg/Al Layered Double Hydroxides. *Catal. Lett.,* 83:1-2.

76. Jiang, Z., Su, J., Jones, M.O., Shi, H., Xiao, T., Edwards, P.P (2009). Catalytic Partial Oxidation of Methane over Ni-Based Catalysts Derived from Ni-Mg/Al Ternary Hydrotalcites. *Energy & Fuels,* 23:1634-1639.

77. Zhang, J., Wei, W., Sun, Y (2010). Fluorine-Modified Mesoporous Ni–Mg–Al Mixed Oxides for Partial Oxidation of Methane. *Catal. Lett.* 135:321-329; DOI:10.1007/s10562-010-0268-5.
78. Basile, F., Fornasari, G., Rosetti, V., Trifiro, F., Vaccari, A (2004). Effect of the Mg/Al Ratio of the Hydrotalcite-type Precursor on the Dispersion and Activity of Rh and Ru Catalysts for the Partial Oxidation of Methane. *Catal. Today,* 91-92: 293-297.
79. Zhang, J., Zhao, N., Wei, W., Sun, Y (2010). Partial Oxidation of Methane over Ni/Mg/Al/La mixed Oxides Prepared from Layered Double Hydrotalcites. *Int. J. Hydrogen Energy,* 35: 11776-11786.
80. Takehira, K., Shishido, T., Shoro, D., Murakami, K., Honda, M., Kawabata, T., Takaki, K (2004). Preparation of Egg-shell Type Ni-loaded Catalyst by Adopting "Memory Effect"of Mg–Al Hydrotalcite and its Application for CH_4 Reforming. *Catal. Commun.,* 5: 209-213.
81. Ashok, J., Subrahmanyam, M., Venugopa, A (2008). Hydrotalcite Structure Derived Ni–Cu–Al Catalysts for the Production of H_2 by CH_4 Decomposition. *Int. J. Hydrogen Energy,* 33: 2704-2713.
82. Basile,F., Benito, P., Fornasari, G., Gazzoli, D., Pettiti, I., Rosetti, V., Vaccari, A (2009). Ni-catalysts Obtained from Silicate Intercalated HTlcs Active in the Catalytic Partial Oxidation of Methane: Influence of the Silicate Content. *Catal.Today* 142: 78-84.
83. Morioka, H., Shimizu, Y., Sukenobu, M., Ito, K., Tanabe, E., Shishido, T., Takehira, K (2001). Partial Oxidation of Methane to Synthesis Gas over Supported Ni catalysts Prepared from Ni-Ca/Al-layered Double hydroxide. *Appl.Catal A,* 215: 11-19.
84. Cesar, D.V., Baldanza, M.A.S., Henriques, C.A., Pompeo, F., Santori, G., Munera, J., Lombardo, E., Schmal, M., Cornaglia, L., Nichio, N (2013). Stability of Ni and Rh–Ni Catalysts Derived from Hydrotalcite-like Precursors for the Partial Oxidation of Methane *Int. J. Hydrogen Energy,* 38, 5616-5626.
85. Saikia, P., Goswamee, R.L (2019). Catalytic Partial Oxidation of CH_4 to syn gas (H_2/CO) in Presence of N_2O over Periclase Type SiO_2@Ni(Mg,Al) O Catalyst Synthesized by non aqueous Route. *Catal.Commun.,* 119: 1-5.

Pages: 50-57

Research in Chemistry and Chemical Sciences
Edited by: Dr. Vijender Singh and Dr. Pawan Kumar 'Bharti'
ISBN: 978-93-88854-40-5
Edition: **2020**
Published by: **Discovery Publishing House Pvt. Ltd., New Delhi (India)**

3

DNA Binding and Cleavage Study of Copper Surfactant Complexes with Benzothiazole

Sonlata Bargotiya[1], Neha Mathur[1], Arun Kumar Sharma[2]

ABSTRACT

In this chapter we report the synthesis of coordination compounds using Cu(II) soap with nitrogen and sulphur donor ligands in a M:L (1:2) molar ratio of the type $Cu_2(C_{15}H_{31}COO)_4L_2$ *and* $Cu_2(C_7H_{15}COO)_4L_2$ *where L are 2-amino 6- bromo benzothiazole. These are characterized by elemental and spectral analysis namely 1H NMR, FT-IR, ESR. The interaction of complexes with Lactobacillus acidophilus DNA is investigated using agarose gel electrophoresis measurements and visualization of cleavage pattern has been done on UV transilluminator. The result suggests that copper(II) complexes bind to DNA via different modes. Gel electrophoresis study reveals the fact that copper complexes involving nitrogen and sulphur donor moieties cleaves super coiled DNA to nicked linear forms.*

Keyword: *DNA binding, DNA cleavage, Copper palmitate, Copper caprylate Substituted benzothiazole.*

INTRODUCTION

Deoxyribonucleic acid is a hereditary material that stores andtransfers the genetic information necessary for processes needed for the survival of an organism including growth, development, functioning and reproduction. Therefore designing, inventing,innovating and discovering of novel chemical nucleases that bind and modify the nucleic acids are important from chemical and biological point of view. Over the past few years, they have

[1] **Department of Chemistry, Pt. N.K.S. Govt. P.G. College, Dausa - 303 303, Rajasthan (India)**

[2] **Department of Chemistry, Govt. P.G. College, Jhalawar - 326 001, Rajasthan (India)**

significantly shown as promising diagnostic probes, reactive agents and therapeutics. Great efforts have been made to develop metallo-nuclease effective in cellular regulation with recognition of potential application in biotechnology and as chemotherapeutic agents. Naturally, a tremendous amount of attention has focused on the designing of DNA-binding agents[1]. Recently, the investigation centres on simple and efficient reagents, which can cleave nucleic acids under mild conditions[2]. This shows that nucleic acids provide exciting and difficult challenges for chemists and biochemist since their wide experimental discoveries forms a foundation for forensic science, biotechnology, pharmaceutical industries and upcoming researches. Simultaneously, with the recent advances in analytical techniques it is becoming more feasible, comfortable and accessible to study the mechanics of complex nucleic acids in a highly detailed perspective.

Before the detailed discussion of the binding and cleavage of DNA experiment a brief structural description of DNA is necessary. Nucleic acids were discovered by Friedrich Miescher in 1869[3]. It is composed of a deoxyribose sugar, a phosphate and heterocyclic bases (adenine, guanine, cytosine and thymine). Each base is complementary to another base on anti-parallel strand forming hydrogen bonds while backbones made of sugars and phosphate groups joined by ester bonds. It may be stated with remarks of Watson and crick[4] to the significant findings of some other scientists[5] that DNA is a double stranded, anti-parallel and a helix molecule which may be right handed (B-DNA) or left handed (Z-DNA). Hence, the poly anionic sugar phosphate backbone forms two distinct grooves, a wide major groove and a narrow minor groove attached to each sugar is one of four types of nucleo-bases. The sequence of four nucleo-bases along the backbone encodes the hereditary information[6].

The history of pioneering studies of Dimroth, Eichhorn, Lippard, Sigman, Dervan and Barton possibly forms an interface between biochemistry and nucleic acid research. With respect to the areas that we are focussing is the interaction of metal complexes with DNA. Such works are evidently cited in 1950s, most notably in F.P. Dwyer's work on the biological activity of metal polypyridyl complexes[7].

Now days, Melting temperature measurements for DNA in the presence of each of the first row transition metal ions are obtained to assess which metal ions stabilize or destabilize the duplex and the use of uranyl-bound nucleosides was investigated as a possible tool for electron microscopy-based DNA sequence determination[8]. Consequently, the studies on DNA hydrolysis cleavage by transition metal complex have been attracting great interest in the filled of artificial metallonuclease because such ions has been found at the catalytic sites of many natural nucleases[9]. Complexes composed of metals like zinc, copper, cobalt, nickel, ruthenium *etc.*, and bidentate polypyridyl ligands like 1,10-phenanthroline have been studied extensively for numerous applications including their biological activity as artificial nucleases[10].

EXPERIMENT

DNA Cleavage analysis of given compounds on bacterial DNA

1. Isolation of genomic DNA.
2. Bacterial DNA sample is supplemented with of 5mg/ml of complex A and B respectively.
3. Agarose Gel Electrophoresis and visualization of cleavage pattern on UV trans illuminator.

Protocol for isolation of genomic DNA and its suspension with synthesized complexes

24 hours old culture (primary culture) of *Lactobacillusacidophilus* is taken growing on nutrient broth (Peptone- 5g,Beef extract -3 g, Sodium chloride- 5 g, distilled water- 1000ml, pH- 7.0 autoclaved at 1210°C, 15 psi pressure and 15 min.). The media was inoculated with the ATCC 25922 culture of *Lactobacillus acidophillus.*

The primary culture was transferred to the fresh nutrient broth (25ml primary culture and 25 ml fresh medium) to obtain secondary culture. Take the culture in three test tubes (one untreated and other to treated with complex $CP(BTA)_{Br}$ and $CC(BTA)_{Br}$ respectively.

Incubate it for 24 hrs and collect 1000 1 bacterial culture.

- Centrifuge 6000 rpm for 10 min and collected pellet. Now, to this pellet add 250 1 cell lysis buffer. Incubate it for 60°C for 1 hr. Again centrifugate at 7000 rpm for 10 mins.

  Collect the pellet again and add 250 1 phenol : chloroform : iso amyl alcohol (25 : 24 : 1). Do again centrifuge at 1000 rpm for 10 min, collect the upper aqueous layer.
- Add double amount of chilled ethanol + 50 1 of sodium acetate and finally centrifuge again. Collected the desired bacterial DNA solution for proceeding analysis.

Three flasks were taken (secondary culture) loaded with two different concentrations of sample $CP(BTA)_{Br}$ and $CC(BTA)_{Br}$.

- Flask one served as untreated control,
- Flask 1 with 5 mg/ml i.e. $CP(BTA)_{Br}$,
- Flask 2 with 5 mg/ml i.e. $CC(BTA)_{Br}$.

- The secondary cultures were incubated for 48 hrs for the DNA cleavage.

- After the incubation, DNA was isolated and the bands were visualized on UV transilluminator.

Protocol for Agarose gel electrophoresis:

Prepare 0.5 X TBE by diluting appropriate amount of 10X TBE buffer.

Weigh 0.6 g of agarose and add to 50 ml of IX TAE. This gives 1.2% agarose gel.

Boil till agarose dissolves completely and a clear solution results. Meanwhile place the combs of electrophoresis set such that it is approximately 2 cm away from the cathode.

- Pour the agarose solution in the central part of tank when the temperature reaches approximately 60°C. Do not generate air bubbles. The thickness of the gel should be around 0.5 to 0.9 cm. Keep the gel undisturbed at room temperature for the agarose to solidify.

  Pour 0.5 X TBE buffer into the gel tank till the buffer level stands at 0.5 to 0.8 cm above the gel surface. Gently lift the combs, ensuring that wells remain intact. Connect the power cord to the electrophoresis power supply according to the convention red: anode, black: cathode.
- Load the samples in the wells in the desired order. Set the voltage to 50 V and switch on the power supply. Allow the gel to run for more than half the length of gel.Switch off the power supply and visualized Gel under UV-Transilluminator for interpretation of the results

DNA Cleavage Analysis on UV trans-illuminator

After the cleavage of the DNA with the chemical treatment at 5 mg/ml concentration the banding pattern was analyzed by agarose gel electrophoresis using 1.2% agrose gel.

The cleavage pattern was detected after 48 hrs and 96 hrs of incubation; the bands were visualized on UV- transilluminator.

DNA ladder was used 100-1000bp (100 bp step up ladder, Merck).

Loading of the samples (after 24 hrs of incubation).

Lane M- DNA Ladder

Lane 1- uncleaved control *Lactobacillus acidophilus* Genomic DNA Lane 2- cleaved DNA with sample $CP(BTA)_{Br}$ 5 mg/ml

Lane 3-cleaved DNA with sample $CC(BTA)_{Br}$ 5 mg/ml

RESULT AND DISCUSSION

From a detail historical background and valuable articles on metal depended cleavage of nucleic acids, one can probably come onto the pathway of this biological event[11]. Interactions of transition-metal complexes with nucleic acids have been studied two categories:

(i) Those involving a redox reaction of the metal complex with oxidation of the nucleic acid.

(ii) Those involving coordination of the metal centre to the sugar-phosphate backbone so as to mediate the cleavage of the nucleic polymers. Both redox and cleavage reactions of metal complexes with nucleic acids have been explored with much success in the development of tools for molecular biology, biochemistry and genetics.

The ability of the synthesized complexes to affect DNA cleavage was investigated by gel electrophoresis using *Lactobacillusacidophilus* DNA. The complexes were found to exhibit significantnuclease activity. The cleavage efficiency of the complexes was compared with that of the control (untreated DNA).

In the present study, the DNA gel electrophoresis experiment was conducted at 35°C using our synthesized complexes as oxidants. Control experiment using DNA alone does not show any significant cleavage of DNA even on longer exposure time. But on treatment of DNA with synthesised complexes, redox property of the metalcomplexes mediates oxidation of nucleic acids and the metal complexes were able to degrade DNA effectively. On comparing the DNA cleavage by both complexes we see that more effective cleavage is obtain by $CC(BTA)_{Br}$ than $CP(BTA)_{Br}$. This can easily be visualised by cleavage patterns of bacterial DNA (Fig. 3.1). In the figure we see that lane I represents the untreated DNA. This DNA is not degraded throughout the lane. Lane II consists of DNA treated with $CP(BTA)_{Br}$. Visualizations predict a bit of smearing in DNA. Lane III shows DNA cleavage pattern treated by $CC(BTA)_{Br}$. We see that here the cleavage is much more effective than that of lane II.

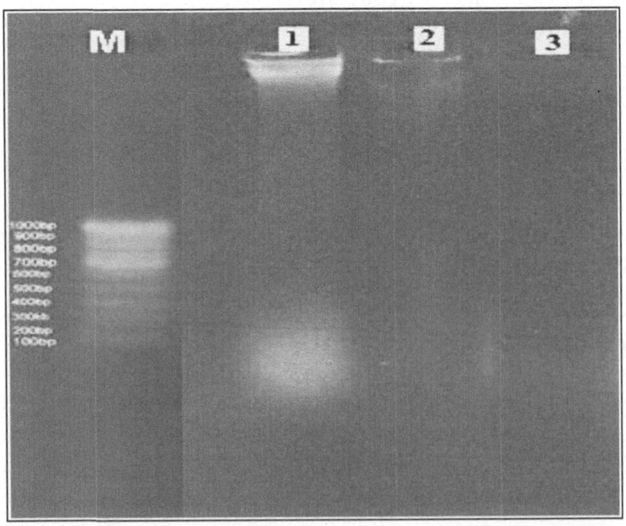

Fig. 3.1. Image Depicting the Cleavage Patterns of *Lactobacillus acidophilus* DNA

The gel electrophoresis images clearly reveal that the intensity of all the treated DNA samples has vanishes, possibly because of the disruption of the DNA. It shows that the control DNA alone does not show any apparent cleavage whereas the DNA treated with synthesised complexes show cleavage. A general oxidative mechanism has been suggested for DNA binding and cleavage by abstraction of a hydrogen atom from sugar units and predicts the release of specific residues arising from transformed sugars, depending on the position from which the hydrogen atom is removed.The possible proposed mechanism can take place at two levels[12]:

1. Carbohydrate level
2. Nucleic base level

At carbohydrate level abstraction of one of the hydrogen of deoxyribose can initiate the cleavage process. At nucleic base level it can occurs probably at guanine. Base metal ion in the complexes may also react and attacks at the C4′ position of the sugar moiety and finally cleaves the DNA (Fig. 3.2). Due to the cleavage, intensity of DNA band decreases led to extensive degradations, resulting in the disappearance of bands on agarose gel, which can be observed in lane II & III of Fig 3.1.

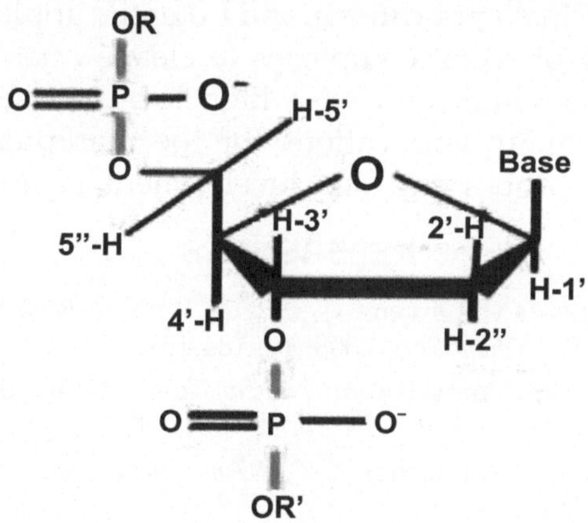

Fig. 3.2: Backbone of *Lactobacillus acidophilus* DNA Specifying the Site of Incision

However, the nature of reactive intermediates involved in the DNA cleavage by the complexes is not clear. The results indicate thatthe metal ions play an important role in the cleavage of isolated DNA. As the complex was observed to degrade the DNA, it can be concluded that the complexes inhibits the growth of the pathogenic organism by cleaving the genome.

Hence, we conclude that the synthesised complexes effectively cleave the *Lactobacillus acidophilus* DNA. Metal complexes showed higher activity than free ligands. Not only this, synthesised transition metal complexes possess a number of biological applications. Among transition metal complexes the activity of copper complexes is significantly high[13-14].

These compounds show bright path towards pharmaceutical as well as chemical sciences, showing a significant promise as therapeutic, diagnostic probes and foot printing agents.[15]. But still there is need to explore some of more biological properties for their wide applicability and significant usage in multiple fields because it is an untapped area with potentially tremendous value.

CONCLUSION

Both the synthesized complexes effectively cleave the *Lactobacillus acidophilus* DNA. Not only this, synthesized transition metal complexes possess a number of biological applications. Among transition metal complexes the activity of copper complexes is significantly high. These compounds show bright path towards pharmaceutical as well as chemical sciences, showing a significant promise as therapeutics, diagnostic probes and foot printing agents. But still there is need to explore some of more biological properties for their wide applicability and significant usage in multiple fields because it is an untapped area with potentially tremendous value. Such a new innovations and inventions may be useful to foot printing studies, studying specific DNA binding agents, as diagnostic researches in biotechnology, medicinal applications, and potential applications for genomic research. The ability of metal complexes to cleave nucleic acids efficiently, in a non-degrading manner and with high levels of selectivity for a site, sequence will offer many applications for the manipulation of genes, the design of structural probes and the development of novel therapeutics.

REFERENCES

1. Flores A F C, Flores D C, Oliveira G, Pizzuti L, Silva R M S, Martins M A P and Bonacorso H G, *J BrazChem Soc.*, 2008, 19, 184-193.
2. Yuan C X, Wei Y B and Yang P, *Chin J Chem.*, 2006, 24(8), 1006-1012; DOI:10.1002/cjoc.200690188
3. Pyle A M, Long E C and Barton J K, *J Am Chem Soc.*, 1989, 111(2), 4520-4522; DOI:10.1021/ja00194a070
4. Arounaguiri S, Easwaramoorthy D, AshokKumar A, Datta Gupta A and Maiya B G, *Proc Indian AcadSciChem Sci.*, 2000, 112, 1-17.
5. Liu H K and Sadler P J, *AccChem Res.*, 2011, 44(5), 349-359; DOI:10.1021/ar100140e
6. Erkkila K E, Odom D T and Barton J K, *Chem Rev.*, 1999, 99(9), 2777-2796; DOI:10.1021/cr9804341
7. Deepalatha S, Sambasiva P and Venkatesan R, *SpectrochimicaActa Part A*, 2005, 64(1), 178-187; DOI:10.1016/j.saa.2005.07.014
8. Dhara K, Ratha J, Manassero M, Wang X, Gao S and Banerjee P, *J InorgBiochem.*, 2007, 101(1), 95-103; DOI:10.1016/j.jinorgbio.2006.08.010
9. Alvarez G M, Alzuet G, Borras J, Maccias B and Castineiras A, *Inorg Chem.*, 2003, 42(9), 2992-2998; DOI:10.1021/ic020611n
10. Dimroth K, Witzel H, Huelsen W and Mirbach W, *Ann Chem.*, 1959, 620, 94-108.

11. Butzow J J and Eichhorn G L, *Biochemistry,* 1971, 10, 2019-2027.
12. Elmroth S K and Lippard S J, *J Am Chem Soc.,* 1994, 116(8), 3633-3634; DOI:10.1021/ja00087a073
13. Sigman D S, Mazumder A and Perrin D M, *Chem Rev.,* 1993, 93(6), 2295-2316; DOI:10.1021/cr00022a011
14. Dervan P B, *Nature,* 1992, 359, 87-88; DOI:10.1038/359087a0
15. Barton J K, *Science,* 1986, 233, 727-734.

Pages: 58-81

Research in Chemistry and Chemical Sciences
Edited by: Dr. Vijender Singh and Dr. Pawan Kumar 'Bharti'
ISBN: 978-93-88854-40-5
Edition: **2020**
Published by: **Discovery Publishing House Pvt. Ltd., New Delhi (India)**

4

Thermodynamics, Kinetics Study and Statistical Approach of Arsenic Removal in Waste Water utilizing Activated Carbon from Saw Dust in different Impregnation Ratio

Swapnila Roy[1*], Ashok Kumar Shaw[2]

ABSTRACT

The present study is highlighted on arsenic removal efficiency in synthetic water utilizing low-cost starting material converted to activated carbon(AC), activated by magnesium chloride($MgCl_2$) in different impregnation ratio(IR) (0.25, 0.5,1.0) upon thermal treatment. Comparative batch studies were conducted in different experimental conditions to investigate the influence of different process parameters on arsenic removal. The phenomenon of arsenic ion uptake was realized by Langmuir and Freundlich adsorption model. Langmuir isotherm showed satisfactory fit to the experimental data. The rate of adsorption implied that the pseudo-second-order rate well fitted the adsorption kinetics better than the pseudo-first-order rate equation. Significant process parameters including adsorbent dosage, pH and contact time were optimized using Response surface methodology (RSM). Results of RSM analysis indicated good correlation between experimentally recorded and theoretically predicted %arsenic removals. The mechanism of adsorption process was illustrated by calculating Gibbs free energy, enthalpy and entropy from thermodynamic studies. In this present investigation, it was represented that regeneration % of activated carbon(IR:1.0) prepared from saw dust in 5 adsorption-

[1] **Regent Institute of Science and Technology,Bara Kanthalia, Barrackpore, P.O: Sewli Telinipara, Kolkata - 700 121 (India)**

[2] **Regent Education and Research Foundation, Bara Kanthalia, Barrackpore, P.O: Sewli Telinipara, Kolkata - 700 121 (India)**

desorption cycles are 90.92%, 86.46%, 80.13%, 71.01%, and 62.53% respectively. The optimum contact time, dosage of adsorbent and pH for activated carbon with I.R(1.0) were found to be 70 min,1.5 g L^{-1} and pH 2.00 respectively. In that condition, it was performing high level of arsenic removal efficiency (92.4%). So it may be concluded that as saw dust is easily available material, so chemically synthesized activated carbon can be used for arsenic removal in waste water.

Keywords: *Arsenic removal, Activated Carbon, Isotherm model, Kinetics, Thermodynamics, Process Optimisation, Response surface methodology.*

INTRODUCTION

For many years, groundwater is assumed to be as the most safe for drinking without any treatment[1]. But now it is considered to be polluted as because of presence of arsenic ion. Dissolution of minerals depends on the water composition and the time of contact between the source minerals and the water. Fish, shellfish, meat, poultry, dairy products and cereals can also be dietary sources of arsenic, although exposure from these foods is generally much lower compared to exposure through contaminated groundwater. In seafood, arsenic is mainly found in its less toxic organic form.The maximum limit of arsenic in drinking water is 0.01mg/L according to the guidelines of water quality.The greatest threat to public health from arsenic originates from contaminated groundwater[2,3]. Inorganic arsenic is naturally present at high levels in the groundwater of a number of countries, including Argentina, Bangladesh, Chile, China, India, Mexico, and the United States of America. Drinking-water, crops irrigated with contaminated water[4] and food prepared with contaminated water are the sources of exposure. Due to natural effects, the arsenic dispersed into the nearest water courses or agricultural fields in the forms of arsenate ion [As (V)] and arsenite ion [As (III)], leading to a high arsenic concentration in thewater courses around the mines. Arsenic exists in the –3, 0, +3 and +5 oxidation states. Environmental forms include arsenious acids,arsenic acids, arsenites, arsenates, methyl arsenic acid, dimethyl arsinic acid, arsine, etc. Arsenic(III) is a hard acid and preferentially complexes with oxides and nitrogen.

Arsenic is used industrially as an alloying agent, as well as in the processing of glass, pigments, textiles, paper, metal adhesives, wood preservatives and ammunition. Arsenic is also used in the hide tanning process and, to a limited extent, in pesticides, feed additives and pharmaceuticals. The first symptoms of long-term exposure[5,6] to high levels of inorganic arsenic (for example, through drinking-water and food) are usually observed in the skin, and include pigmentation changes, skin lesions and hard patches on the palms and soles of the feet (hyperkeratosis). These occur after a minimum exposure of approximately five years and may be a precursor to skin cancer. In addition to skin cancer, long-term exposure to arsenic may also cause cancers of the bladder and lungs. The International Agency for Research on Cancer (IARC) has classified arsenic and arsenic compounds as carcinogenic to humans, and has also stated that arsenic in drinking-water is carcinogenic to humans. A great deal of research over recent decades has been done to lower the concentration of arsenic in drinking water and still there is a need to develop low cost viable techniques[7] Existing major arsenic removal[8,9,10] technologies include oxidation, adsorption, precipitation, coagulation and membrane separation[11,12].

The present study focused on arsenic uptake[13,14] where activated carbon was used, prepared from saw dust which was impregnated by magnesium chloride in different ratio and synthesized chemically.

OBJECTIVE OF THE STUDY

The present study on arsenic removal was investigated with the objective to prepare chemically activated carbon from saw dust[15] using magnesium chloride as an activating agent. The physical and chemical properties of the prepared activated carbon were determined and estimation of arsenic removal efficiency using different experimental procedure by adsorption as a function of contact time, adsorbent dose and pH.

MATERIALS AND METHODS

Materials

Magnesium chloride ($MgCl_2.6H_2O$) [Merck, Germany], Saw dust (available in local market) were collected for preparation of activated carbon. All chemicals of reagent grade and ultrapure distilled water were used in all the preparations.

Preparation of Adsorbents

In this present study activated carbon was prepared from saw dust using magnesium chloride ($MgCl_2$) as an activating agent. The particular quantity of washed and dried saw dust was mixed with required amount of activating agent ($MgCl_2$), according to different impregnation ratio (I.R= 0,25,0.50,1.0).

$$\text{Impregnation ratio (I.R)} = \frac{\textit{Weight of active agent added}}{\textit{Weight of carbonising material added}} \quad (1)$$

The required quantity of distilled water was added and boiled until slurry like mixture was obtained. Then the mixture was dried in a container for one day at 105±5°C. Then these three containers were placed in Muffle furnace at 800° C for 4 hours. After that when these containers were attained steady state temperature, these were kept in cool environment for about 10 hours. Finally these were taken out. The prepared activated carbon was washed by dilute HCl to remove excess HCl present in the activated carbon. Then these three activated carbon were oven dried and kept in desiccators for further experiment.

Physicochemical Properties of Adsorbents

The different physiochemical properties[16,17] (oil yield, bulk density, porosity, moisture content, ash content and pH) of the prepared activated carbons were estimated using standard procedures. All the experiments were performed thrice and results are given in table 4.1.

Table 4.1: Physicochemical Analysis

Sl. No.	Characteristics	Chemically Activated ($MgCl_2$)		
		0.25	0.5	1.0
1.	Moisture content (%)	6.21	5.32	3.87
2.	Ash content (%)	16.24	15.06	13.07
3.	Decolorizing power, (mg/g)	30.87	35.83	43.64
4.	pH	7.8	7.6	7.2
5.	Yield of carbon (%)	61	72	86
6.	Bulk Density	0.67	0.73	0.78
7.	Porosity	0.63	0.69	0.75

Yield of Carbon

After carbonization followed by cooling, the activated carbon was weighed. Then the percentage yield of carbonizing was achieved by applying this formula

$$\%\ \text{yield of carbon} = \frac{\textit{weight of char}}{\textit{weight of raw material}} \tag{2}$$

Determination of Bulk Density

The dry empty 10 mL centrifuge tube was cleaned and weighed ($W1$) and then the centrifuge tube was filled with the prepared activated carbon powder and then weighed ($W2$). The difference in the weights denotes the weight of the activated carbon powder in tube. The bulk density was estimated using the following equation:

$$\text{Bulk Density} = \frac{W2 - W1}{\textit{volume of centrifuge tube}} \tag{3}$$

Porosity Determination

The porosity of the activated carbon was estimated using the formula:

$$\text{Porosity} = \frac{\textit{pore volume}}{\textit{total volume}}$$

The pore volume of prepared activated carbon was achieved using the formula:

$$\text{Pore volume}=\frac{\textit{Bulk density of activated carbon}}{\textit{density of water}}$$

$$\text{Hence, porosity} =\frac{\textit{Bulk density of activated carbon}}{\textit{density of water X Total volume}} \tag{4}$$

Determination of Moisture Content

The empty crucible was dried at 110°C and then cooled in a desiccators and weighed (*W*1). Then the prepared known weight of activated carbon powder with crucible were weighed(*W*2) and dried in an oven at 110°C.This weight was taken constantly at 30 minutes interval until the weight became constant. Then activated carbon with crucible was cooled in a desiccator and reweighed (*W*3). The weight difference of the activated carbon was used to measure the moisture content (X_o) of the activated carbon from saw dust.

$$X_o = \frac{W2 - W3}{W2 - W1} \times 100 \tag{5}$$

Determination of Ash Content

The empty crucible was oven dried at 110°C and cooled in a desiccator and weighed (*W1*). The known weight of prepared dried activated carbon powder was put in the crucible and weighed (*W*2) and then kept in the muffle furnace at 800°C for 1 hour and then allowed to cool .Finally the crucible was reweighed (*W*3). The percentage ash content of activated carbon sample was obtained from the following equation:

$$\text{Ash\%} =\frac{W_{ash}}{W_0} \times 100 = \frac{W3 - W1}{W2 - W1} \times 100 \tag{6}$$

Where W_{ash}= weight of ash (g)

Determination of pH

1 g activated carbon from saw dust was weighed. Then it was dissolved in 3 ml distilled water. The mixture was heated and stirred for few minutes. Then it was filtered and pH was determined using a digital pH meter.

Preparation of Synthetic Arsenic Solution

Stock arsenic ion solution(1000 mg L^{-1}) was prepared by dissolving accurately weighed quantity in double-distilled water. Experimental arsenic solution of different concentrations were prepared by diluting the stock solution with suitable volume of distilled-water.

EXPERIMENTAL

Experimental set up

Experiments were conducted in temperature controlled incubator shaker (INNOVA 4430, New Brunswick Scientific, Canada). Temperature fluctuations in the reactor were negligible .The samples were collected for stirring for particular time interval. The dissolved arsenic in each conical flask was estimated by using ion AAS[18] (Perkin Elmer).

Percentage of arsenic removal efficiency was calculated with a standard RSM design (CCD) and 20 experiments were carried out. The percent removal (%) of arsenic is determined by using the following equation:

$$R(\%) = \frac{C_i - C_0}{C_i} \times 100 \qquad (7)$$

Where C_i is the initial fluoride concentration (mg L^{-1}) and C_0 is the final fluoride concentration in solution (mg L^{-1}).

Batch Experiment

In this present batch study, the required quantity of activated carbon was added to the arsenic solution, then it was stirred for different contact time with different dosage of adsorbent in different pH of solution. This powder like activated carbon is very suitable for arsenic removal in water.

Thermodynamic and Kinetics Studies

Adsorption Isotherm

The Langmuir and Freundlich isotherms study were carried out by using AC (different IR ratio) for arsenic removal in water. The interaction between arsenic ions and adsorbents can be better explained by these isotherm models.

Langmuir Isotherm

The linear form of Langmuir model is given by the following equation:

$$\frac{C_e}{Q_e} = \frac{1}{Q_0 b} + \frac{C_e}{Q_0} \qquad (8)$$

Where C_e is the residual fluoride concentration at equilibrium, Q_e is the fluoride concentration adsorbed on the sorbent at equilibrium, Q_o denotes maximum fluoride concentration and b is the Langmuir constant.

Freundlich Isotherm

From the following equation Freundlich constants were calculated as follows or batch sorption studies.

$$\text{Ln } Q_e = \ln K_F + \left(\frac{1}{n}\right) \ln C_e \qquad (9)$$

Where Q_e is the amount of arsenic adsorbed at equilibrium, and K_F and n are Freundlich

constants indicates adsorption capacity and adsorption intensity respectively.

Adsorption Kinetics

The adsorption process was carried out at various temperatures to determine the optimum temperature for maximum adsorption efficiency and for obtaining the reaction rate constant activation energy. 100 mL of arsenic solution of concentration 50 mg L^{-1} was taken in 250 mL conical flask and 1.5 g adsorbent was added to it. Then this mixture was agitated at 150 rpm for 1 hour. From this experiment kinetic rate constant at different temperatures were estimated.

Pseudo First order kinetics

The rate constant was estimated using the following equation:

$$\frac{dq_t}{dt} = k_1 (q_e - q_t) \quad (10)$$

where, q_e = arsenic adsorbed at equilibrium/unit weight of adsorbent (mg/g), q_t is the amount of arsenic adsorbed at any instant (mg/g) and k_1 is the rate constant (min^{-1}).

Integrating at these conditions as t=0 and q_t=0 to t=t and q_t=q_t, the final equation is written as given below:

$$\text{Log}(q_e - q_t) = \log q_e - \frac{k_1 t}{2.303} \quad (11)$$

Pseudo Second order kinetics

The model equation is described as follows:

$$\frac{t}{q_t} = \frac{1}{k_2 q_e 2} + 1/q_e(t) \quad (12)$$

Where k_2 denotes the pseudo-second-order rate constant of adsorption (g mg^{-1} min^{-1}) and q_e and q_t are the amount of arsenic adsorbed (mg/g) at equilibrium and at time t respectively.

Activation Energy

From the obtained the rate constant, activation energy of the adsorption of arsenic was calculated using Arrhenius Eq (6).given as follows:

$$\text{Ln}k_2 = \text{In}A_0 - \frac{Ea}{RT} \quad (13)$$

Where E_a=activation energy (kJmol^{-1}); R=gas constant(8.314 J mol^{-1} K^{-1}); and A_0=Arrhenius constant.

Adsorption Thermodynamics

The adsorption thermodynamic parameters of arsenic were estimated using the following formulas:

$$K_c = \frac{C_a}{C_e} \tag{14}$$

Where, K_c=coefficient of distribution for the adsorption; C_a=arsenic adsorbed per unit mass of the adsorbent (mg L^{-1}); C_e=equilibrium concentration of adsorbate in aqueous phase (mg L^{-1}).

$$\Delta G_0 = -RT\ln K_c \tag{15}$$

Where,G_0(kJ mol^{-1})=change of Gibb's free energy; R=universal gas constant; and T=absolute temperature (K); and

$$1nK_c = \frac{\Delta S_0}{R} - \frac{\Delta H_0}{RT} \tag{16}$$

WhereΔH_0 (kJ mol^{-1})=change of enthalpy; ΔS_0(J mol^{-1} K^{-1})=change of entropy.

RESULTS AND DISCUSSION

Characterisation of Activated Carbon (saw dust)

XRD (X-ray Diffraction) Analysis

X-ray diffraction analysis of activated carbon was conducted using X-ray diffractometer equipment (Bruker, D8 Advance) with a Cu Kα radiation. The diffraction pattern of activated carbon from saw dust (IR:1.0)as prepared, was represented in figure 4.1.

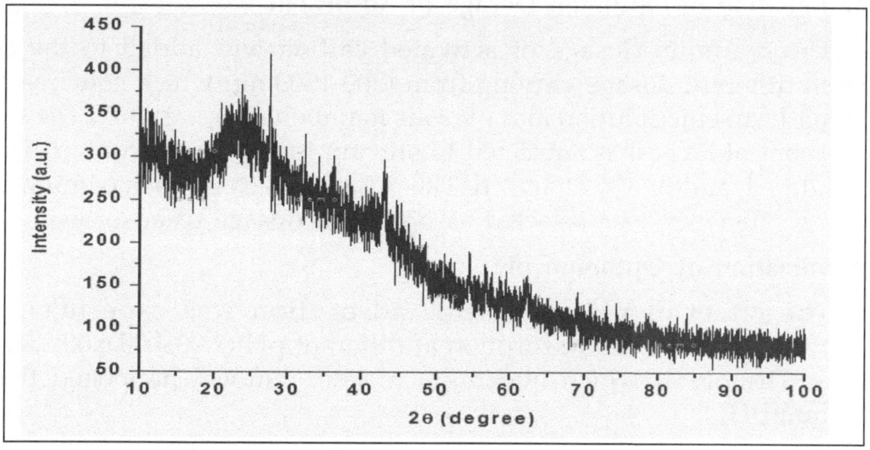

Fig. 4.1: XRD of activated carbon from saw dust

Boehm Titration

The acidic and basic properties of surface of the samples were estimated by the Boehm Titration method. In this method, 0.2 g AC(different impregnation ratio)sample was added to 25 ml of 0.1 M $NaHCO_3$ and similarly to 25 ml of 0.1 M Na_2CO_3.The mixtures were stirred for 24 hours and then it was filtered. After removal of carbon, the excess of base and acid was titrated with 0.1 M HCl solution and 0.1 M NaOH solution, respectively. Chemically number of acidic sites were estimated by chemical neutralization of carboxyl, phenolic and lactonic groups by NaOH; carboxyl and lactonic groups by Na_2CO_3; and carboxyl groups by $NaHCO_3$. Similarly, the number of basic sites was estimated from the amount of consumed hydrochloric acid by AC (Table 4.2).

Table 4.2: Acidic and basic surface characteristics of the activated carbons

Sample: (AC from saw dust)	Groups			Total acidity (meq g^{-1})	Total basicity (meq g^{-1})
	Carboxylic (meq g^{-1})	Phenolic (meq g^{-1})	Lactonic (meq g^{-1})		
IR:0.25	0.16	0.2	0.24	0.86	0.98
IR:0.5	0.17	0.23	0.22	0.87	0.99
IR:1.0	0.18	0.27	0.23	0.85	1.01

Determination of Optimum Contact Time

Contact time play a significant role in adsorption study. To study the effect of contact time, 100 mL of arsenic solution of 100 mg $L^{-1}$and pH 2.0±0.02, was mixed with 1.5 gL^{-1}activated carbon, stirred at different contact times (10-100 min) and then filtered. These filtrates were analyzed for residual arsenic concentration using AAS.

Determination of Optimum Dosage of Adsorbent

The optimum dosage of activated carbon was added to the conical flask in different dosage varying from (200-1500mg) which contains 100mL of 50mg L^{-1}arsenic solution and pH was maintained as 2.0±0.02. The solution in the conical flask was subjected to stirring for optimum contact time and then filtered, and finally analyzed. The dosage which gives maximum arsenic removal efficiency was selected as optimum dosage of adsorbent.

Determination of Optimum pH

The effect of pH on arsenic adsorption was experimented by performing equilibrium adsorption at different pH (2.00,4.00,6.00,8.00,10.00) values. The pH at which maximum arsenic removal happened that was optimum pH.

Interaction Effect

Effect of Adsorbent dose

Within the experimental range of adsorbent dose in between 0.2 g-1.5 gL^{-1}, percent removal of arsenic firstly increased (upto1.0 gL^{-1}), then decreased slowly. The adsorbent dose in the range of 0.2-1.0 gL^{-1}, arsenic removal efficiency increased due to the number of ions increases on the adsorbent surface as the attraction force between adsorbate ions and adsorbent. While increasing dosage of adsorbent higher than 1.5 gL^{-1}, number of arsenic ions decreased gradually on the adsorbent surface because surface of adsorbent was saturated by adsorbate ions, and in that case the repulsive force occurred between arsenic ions and adsorbent surface. Comparing three adsorbents(different IR ratio), weight of active agents were increasing according to the increased ratio. So the adsorption capacity of adsorbate was higher, with increasing ratio. From figure 4.2, it was observed that the removal efficiency of arsenic increased with increasing IR, so it can be inferred that activated carbon(IR=1.0) was the best adsorbent for arsenic removal among three adsorbents.

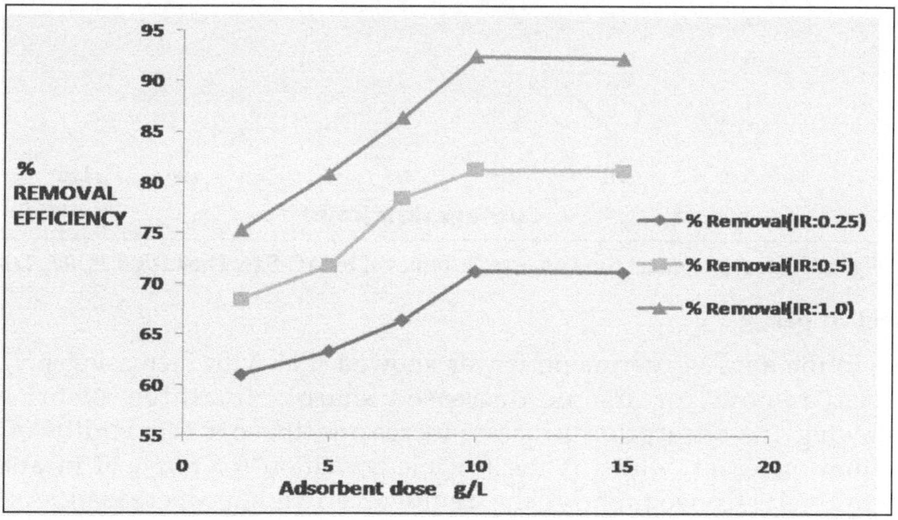

Fig. 4.2: Effect of adsorbent dose on arsenic removal by AC-Saw Dust (IR:0.25, 0.5, 1.0)

Effect of Contact time

It was observed from figure 4.3 the experimental results that on increasing the contact time at pH 2 and optimum dosage of adsorbent, arsenic removal efficiency increased. As the contact time increased, higher the number of arsenic ions attached on the adsorbent surface. Chemically the accumulation of arsenic ions on adsorbent surface increased due to attractive force which resulted in increasing the arsenic removal in solution. But after certain point (70 min), removal efficiency decreased. The reason behind this phenomena was that maximum number of the arsenic ions attached on adsorbent surface when reaction time was 70 minutes. Comparing three adsorbents (IR:0.25,0.5,1.0), the number of pores were higher (IR:1.0) than two other adsorbents due to presence of more activating agents for preparation of carbon, consequently the adsorption capacity was the highest for that activated carbon (IR:1.0). As a result in particular contact time, adsorption capacity was highest shown by AC(IR:1.0) than other two adsorbents. From figure 4.3, it was observed that the removal efficiency of arsenic increased in case of AC(IR:1) which was reflected in the plot.

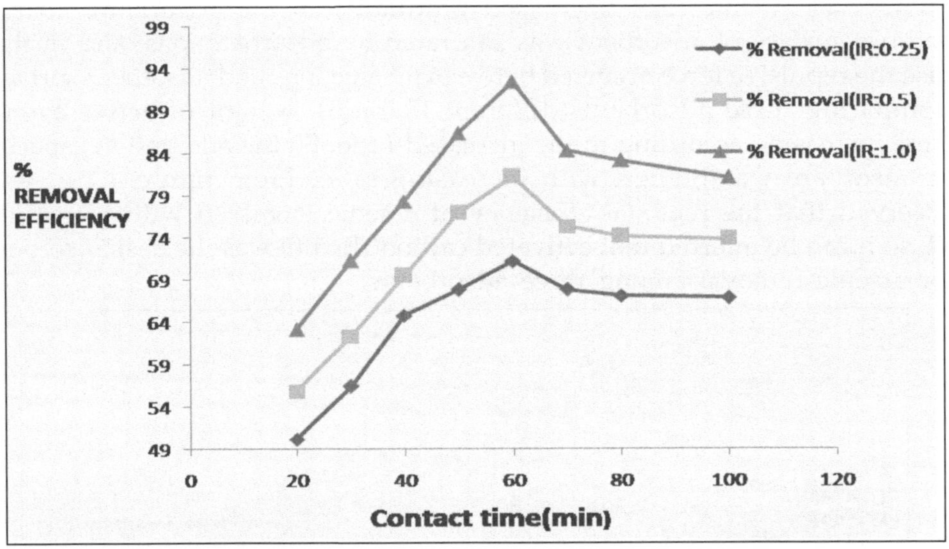

Fig. 4.3: Effect of contact time on arsenic removal by AC-Saw Dust (IR:0.25, 0.5, 1.0)

Effect of pH

In the above experiment, it was showed that with increasing pH, the percent removal of arsenic decreased sharply for three adsorbents. Following the adsorption process, increasing the pH the acidity of the medium increases, which is the feasible condition for removal of arsenic (Figure 4.4). Consequently, the removal efficiency decreased. As the adsorption capacity of activated carbon (IR:1) was the highest than other two adsorbents(explained before),so at particular pH(optimum dosage of adsorbent and optimum contact time) the number of adsorbate ions increased on AC(IR:1) than AC(IR:0.25) and (IR:0.5).Overall, AC(IR:1) was the best adsorbent among three for further experiment.

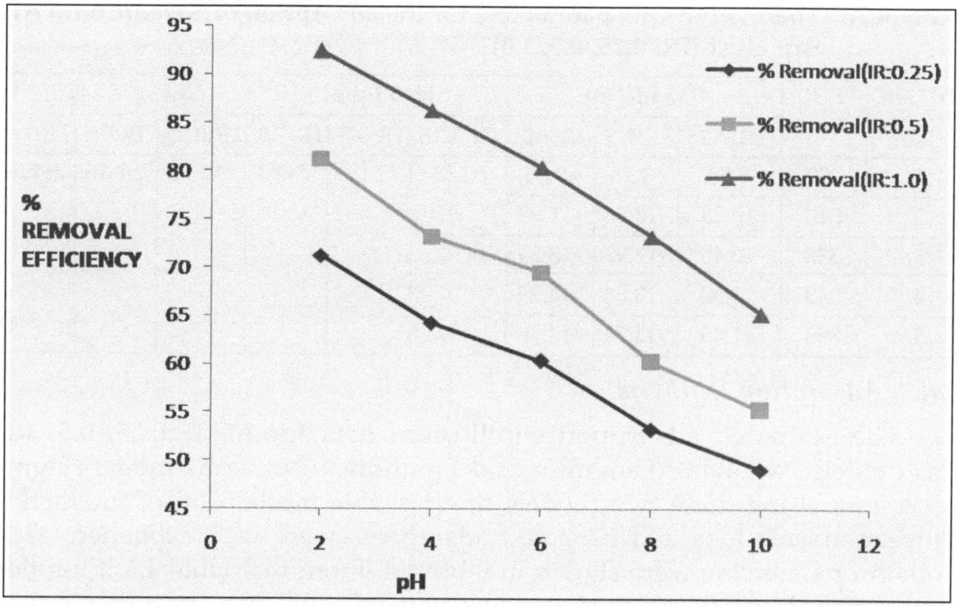

Fig. 4.4: Effect of pH on arsenic removal by AC-Saw Dust (IR: 0.25,0.5,1.0)

Thermodynamics and Kinetics Study

Estimation of thermodynamic parameters of three activated carbon for arsenic removal

From the experimental study following equation (8-10) it was depicted that the negative value of ΔG^0 increased with increasing in the temperature(up to 333 K). It implied that the adsorption was thermodynamically feasible in nature and the positive values of ΔH^0 indicated endothermic nature of the reaction due to consuming energy from the reaction system. The values of ΔH^0 and, ΔS^0 were estimated from the slopes and intercept of the plot ln K_c vs. (1/T) (Fig. not given) and the values were listed in table 4.3. It was observed that the negative value of ΔG^0 at all temperatures represented that the arsenic removal reaction was spontaneous in nature. In this case ΔG^0 decreased up to 333K and after that it increased which denoted that the adsorption reaction was feasible up to 333K. As a result the randomness in between arsenic ion and activated carbon surface was increased. Due to endothermic reaction, it was expected that the adsorption capacity of arsenic ions by activated carbon was increasing with temperature. But after 333K,the reverse reaction occurred. Mathematically entropy of the reaction was estimated from the experimentally obtained data that was positive for these adsorbents. So it can be inferred that as temperature was increased above 333K, the desorption took place on the adsorbent surface, consequently the concentration of arsenic in solution was increased in small amount in solution.

Table 4.3: Thermodynamic parameters for the adsorption of Arsenic onto AC-Saw dust (IR: 0.25, 0.5, 1.0)

Sl. No.	T, K	ΔG, kJ/mol			ΔH, kJ/mol			ΔS,J mol^{-1} K^{-1}		
		IR:0.25	IR:0.5	IR:1.0	IR:0.25	IR:0.5	IR:1.0	IR:0.25	IR:0.5	IR:1.0
1.	293	-8.93	-9.13	-9.83	62.33	72.19	79.43	252.11	257.13	267.39
2.	313	-10.23	-10.86	-11.93						
3.	333	-12.45	-12.97	-13.54						
4.	343	-13.32	-13.86	-14.29						
5.	353	-11.45	-11.74	-12.56						

Batch Adsorption Isotherm

The estimated adsorption equilibrium data for AC(IR:0.25, 0.5, 1.0) was modeled applying Langmuir and Freundlich isotherms model (Figure 4.5 & 4.6) .Using these two models the probable mechanism of interaction between arsenic ions and prepared adsorbents were well explained . The isotherm parameters were shown in table 4.4. From that table 4.4 it implied that Langmuir model showed good agreement with three adsorbents than Freundlich model in present study of arsenic sorption. According to the Langmuir model, the monolayer arsenic adsorption occurred in these three adsorbents which depends on the nature of surface.

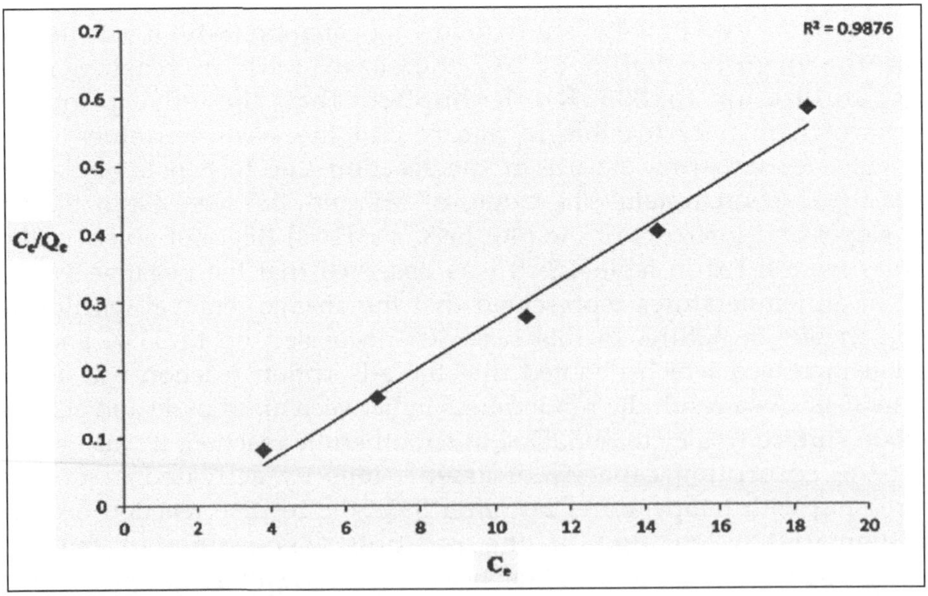

Fig. 4.5: Langmuir Isotherm plots of arsenic removal onto AC-Saw dust (IR:1.0)

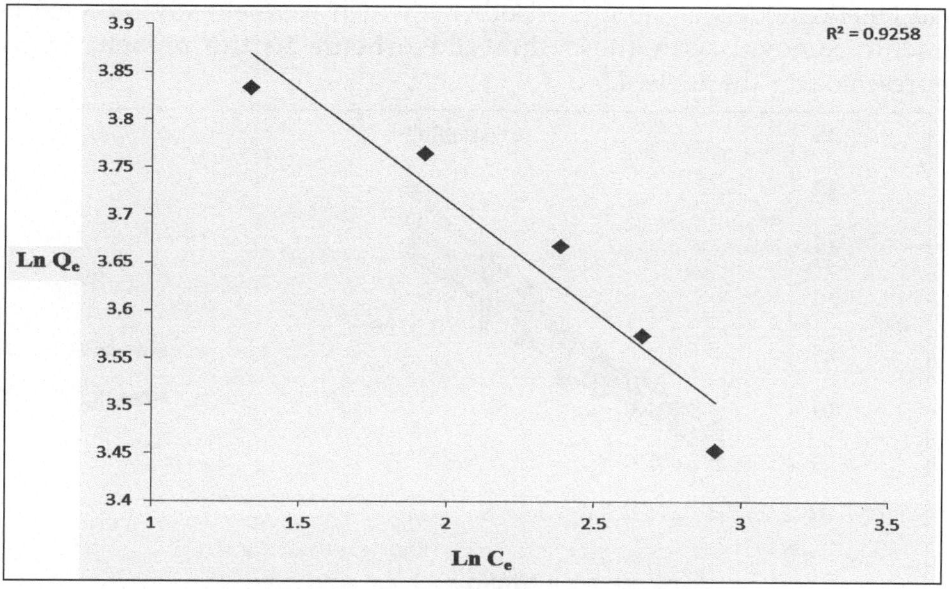

Fig. 4.6: Freundlich Adsorption Isotherm plots of arsenic removal onto AC-Saw dust(IR:1.0)

Table 4.4: Langmuir and Freundlich isotherm model constants and correlation coefficients for arsenic adsorption onto AC-Saw Dust (IR: 0.25, 0.5, 1.00) at optimized conditions

Adsorbents	Langmuir			Freundlich		
	Q_e(mg g^{-1})	b(L mg^{-1})	R^2	K_F(mg g^{-1})	n(L mg^{-1})	R^2
(1)AC(IR:0.25)	24.52	0.31	0.998	41.54	3.23	0.9968
(2)AC(IR:0.5)	31.23	0.41	0.998	43.13	3.03	0.9947
(3)AC(IR:1.00)	34.52	0.47	0.996	45.82	3.85	0.9678

Batch Adsorption kinetics

The present adsorption kinetics studies were carried out for arsenic removal using three adsorbents having different IR ratio of AC. The parameters of kinetic studies were shown in table 4.5. From this study, it was observed that pseudo second order kinetics study were well fitted than pseudo first order reaction. From the pseudo second order kinetic reaction it was indicated that adsorption capacity of both adsorbent were dependent on available binding site. The plot of t/q_tVs t (Figure 4.7) in pseudo second order kinetic modeling were represented. From the pseudo second order rate constant k_2 at different temperatures, the activation energy E_a(Activated carbon) was determined using the Arrhenius energy equation (Eq.16). The comparative study of adsorption capacities, isotherm and kinetic models of various adsorbents which were already reported for arsenic removal with these three adsorbents in the present study, represented in the table 4.5.

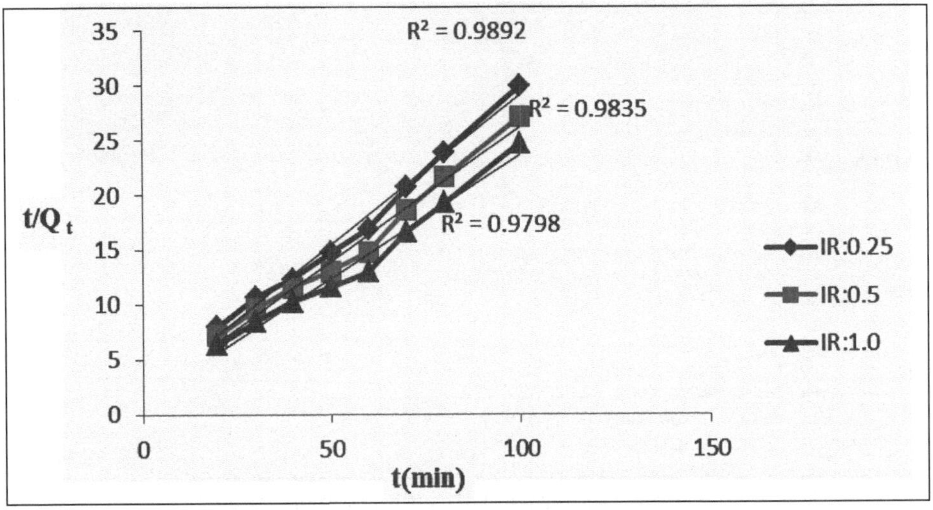

Fig. 4.7: Pseudo second order kinetic model for adsorption of arsenic by AC-Saw dust(IR:0.25,0.5,1.0)

Table 4.5: Comparison of pseudo first order and pseudo second order rate constants for AC-Saw dust (IR:0.25,0.5,1.00) at optimized conditions

Adsorbents	Pseudo first order kinetics			Pseudo second order kinetics		
	k_1(min)	q_e(mg g^{-1})	R^2	k_2(g mg^{-1})	q_e(mg g^{-1})	R^2
(1)AC(IR:0.25)	0.0033	19.21	0.9237	0.0821	36.72	0.9892
(2)AC(IR:0.5)	0.0011	22.11	0.9311	0.0782	29.79	0.9835
(2)AC(IR:1.00)	0.0009	25.54	0.9362	0.0652	23.49	0.9798

Response Surface Methodology for Optimization of Adsorption Parameters

The determination of optimum conditions for arsenic adsorption by AC dependent on the three process variables, which were adsorbent dose, pH and contact time of the solution. The experimental ranges along with the levels of variables were given in table 4.6. The percent removal of arsenic was the response of the system. Statistically the prediction of the optimum condition was obtained following the quadratic equation model given below (Eq. 17).

$$Y= \beta_0 + \Sigma^k_{i=1} \beta i\ xi + \Sigma^k_{i=1} \beta ii\ xi2 + \Sigma_{i=1} \Sigma_{j=i+1} \beta ij\ xixj + \varepsilon \quad (17)$$

Here,Y=response (i.e. dependent variable), β_0=constant coefficient, β_i=β_{ii}=β_{ij}=coefficients of linear, quadratic and interaction effect, x_i and x_j=factors (independent variables)

And ε=error.

Percentage of arsenic removal efficiency was calculated with a standard RSM design (CCD)[19] and 20 experiments were carried out. The percent removal (%) of arsenic was determined by using the following equation (Eq. 18):

$$R\ (\%) = \frac{C_i - C_0}{C_i} \times 100 \qquad (18)$$

Where C_i is the initial arsenic concentration (mg L^{-1}) and C_0 is the final arsenic concentration in solution (mg L^{-1}).

Design Expert Version 11.1.6 (Stat Ease, USA) was applied for graphical analysis of the experimentally obtained data. The optimum values of the independent variables were obtained by solving the regression equation and by analyzing the contour plots. The coefficient of correlation and the quadratic model equation was used to predict the interaction effect of different factors within the specified range, which can be described mathematically.

Estimation of Response Surface for Maximum Arsenic Removal

The results of the 20 experiments performed as per CCD analysis was shown in table 4.7. The maximum arsenic removal was obtained 92.41% at 70 min contact time, at pH 2.00 and 1.5 gL^{-1} of adsorbent. The response variable which was expressed as a function of independent variables defined in quadratic model, developed by Design Expert software is expressed in the form of different numerical factors in equation(19)given below:

Table 4.7: Central composite design (CCD) used for optimizing three independent variables along with the obtained response

Sl. No.	A: Contact time min	B: Adsorbent doseg/L	C: pH	R1%
(1)	(2)	(3)	(4)	(5)
1.	45	1	5	78.45
2.	45	1	5	78.45
3.	45	1	5	78.45
4.	45	1	5	78.45
5.	45	1	5	78.45
6.	45	1	5	78.45
7.	45	1	10.04	76.28
8.	45	1	0.04	88.78
9.	45	1.84	5	70.34
10.	45	0.16	5	66.78

(Table Contd...)

(1)	(2)	(3)	(4)	(5)
11.	87	1	5	79.43
12.	3	1	5	52.43
13.	70	1.5	8	80.31
14.	20	1.5	8	65.48
15.	70	0.5	8	67.37
16.	20	0.5	8	62.57
17.	70	1.5	2	92.4
18.	20	1.5	2	71.29
19.	70	0.5	2	89.45
20.	20	0.5	2	70.86

$$\text{Removal \% of Arsenic(R1)} = +78.33 + 7.67^*A + 1.85^*B - 5.12^* + 1.57^* AB - 2.51^*AC + 1.56^*BC - 3.81^*A^2 - 2.88^*B^2 + 2.15\ C^2 \quad (19)$$

It is observed that A, B, C, AB, B^2,$C^2$are significant model terms. The fitness of the model was verified by the correlation coefficient (R^2) between the experimental and model predicted values (Figure 4.8) of the response variable. Statistically, R^2 value of 0.9668 indicated that the model was statistically significant. Therefore, the model was applied to predict the percentage removal of arsenic in solution within the limits of the experimental factors.

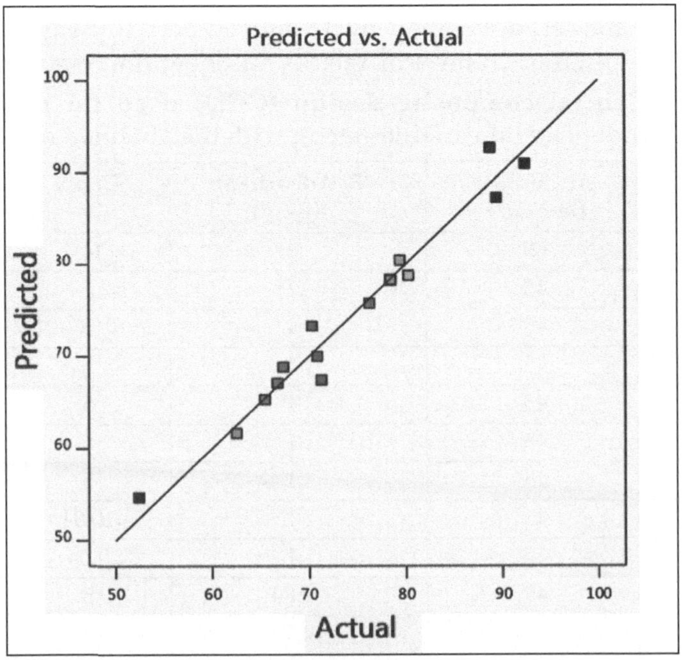

Fig. 4.8: Graphical Plot showing Predicted Response Vs Actual Response

Interaction Effect of Process Variables

Effect of Variation in Adsorbent Dose and pH

The combined effect of adsorbent dose and pH for adsorption on arsenic removal was illustrated in the RSM plot of figure 4.9. It was found that percentage of arsenic removal decreased on increasing pH the from 2.00 to 8.00 and also increased in the range of adsorbent dose from 0.33-1.5 gL^{-1}. The higher values of arsenic removal may be obtained by increase in adsorbent dose and also with decrease in pH. Due to increase in adsorbent dosage, the electrostatic force of attraction between the arsenic ions and adsorbent increased. From this given plot, maximum removal efficiency 92.41% was obtained at an 1.5 gL^{-1} adsorbent dose, at pH 2.00 and 70 min of contact time.

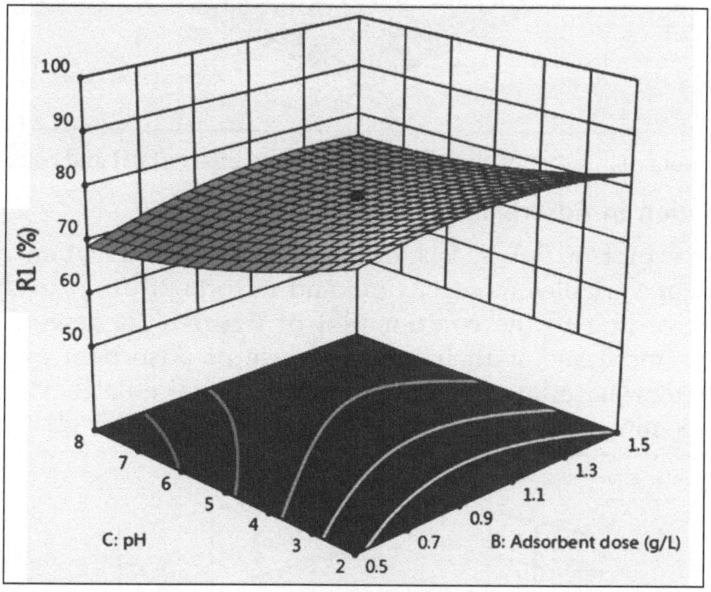

Fig. 4.9: Response surface plot showing the combined effect of absorbent dose and pH

Effect of Variation in pH and Contact Time

The effect of different pH and contact time were required to remediate arsenic in solution using activated carbon. It was proved from figure 4.10 that both the independent process variables play significant role on the % arsenic adsorption process. From this contour plot, maximal removal efficiency of 92.41 % was achieved at pH 2.00 and 70 min of contact time, while the other variable was set at the middle value. As the contact time increased from 10-80 min, the 70 min of contact time uptake capacity increased at particular adsorbent dose which implied that the percentage of adsorption increased (due to higher attractive force between ions and adsorbent), consequently percentage efficiency of removal of arsenic ions increased.

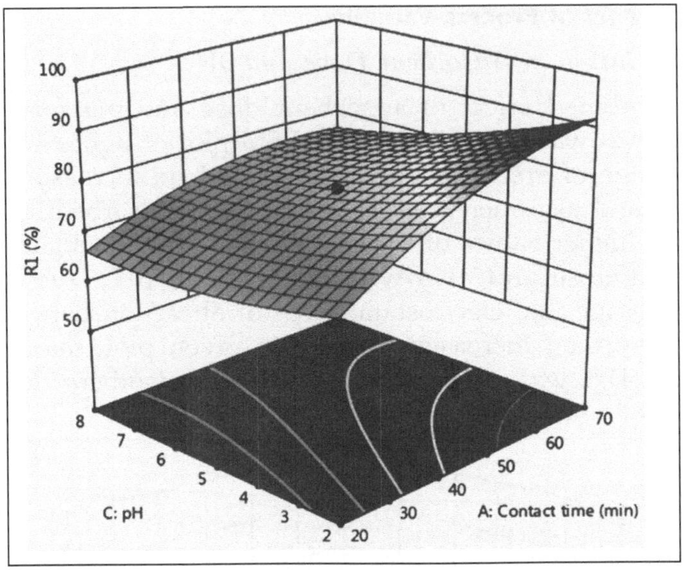

Fig. 4.10: Response surface plot showing the combined effect of pH and contact time

Effect of Variation in Adsorbent dose and Contact Time

The above plot of figure 4.11 depicted that the interaction effects of the independent variables (contact time and adsorbent dose) in the above response . According to the contour plot of figure 4.11, arsenic removal efficiency was increased with increasing dose of adsorbent and contact time. This trend was followed by maximum removal efficiency of 92.41%, obtained at 70 min contact time and adsorbent dose of 1.5 gL^{-1}.

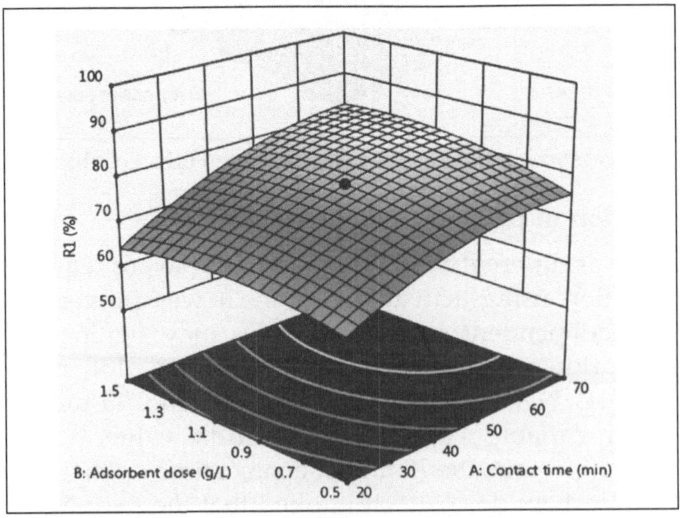

Fig. 4.11: Response surface plot showing the combined effect of absorbent dose and contact time

Conformational Study

The optimized data are supported by numerical modeling[20],which are verified by confirmatory experiments (Figure 4.12) as suggested by the model(adsorbent dose 1.5 gL^{-1}; pH 2.00; contact time 70 minutes).These are found to be optimum condition for maximum percent fluoride removal and in that condition the maximum fluoride removal obtained as 92.41% and experimentally it is 92.46%. The difference between the removal efficiency in the two conditions being 0.05%. Here error data obtained after repeating the experiment.

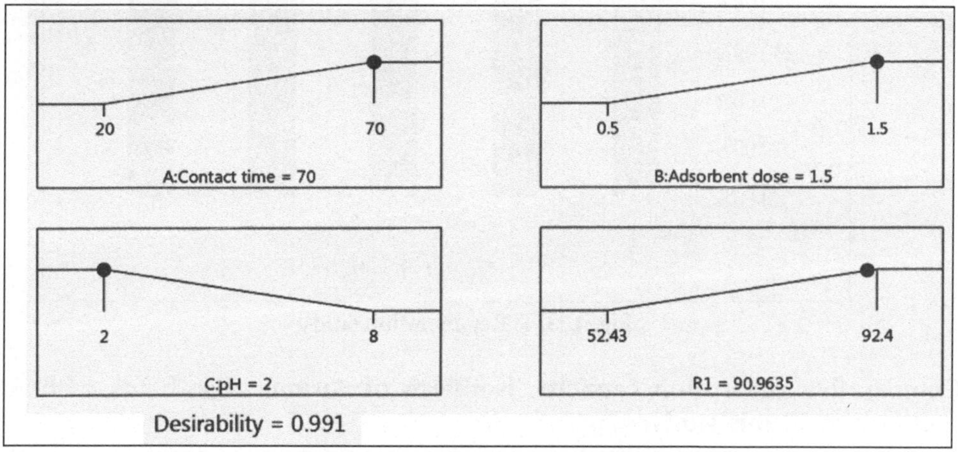

Fig. 4.12: Desirability Function

Regeneration Study

The regeneration study of adsorbent in water treatment method was very important. As the activated carbon (IR:1.0) prepared from saw dust showed higher arsenic removal efficiency (92.4%) compared to other activated carbon (IR:0.25,0.5), so its desorption study was determined by 5 adsorption–desorption cycles. The present adsorption-desorption study was carried out with 100 ml of 50 $mg{\cdot}L^{-1}$ of synthetic arsenic solution at the starting of each cycle. The study was investigated with 1% sodium hydroxide as desorbing agent. The adsorption capacities of each cycle were90.92%, 86.46%, 80.13%, 71.01%, and 62.53%.These experimental results (Figure 4.13) proved that activated carbon (IR:1.0) prepared from saw dust can be reused for arsenic removal in water.

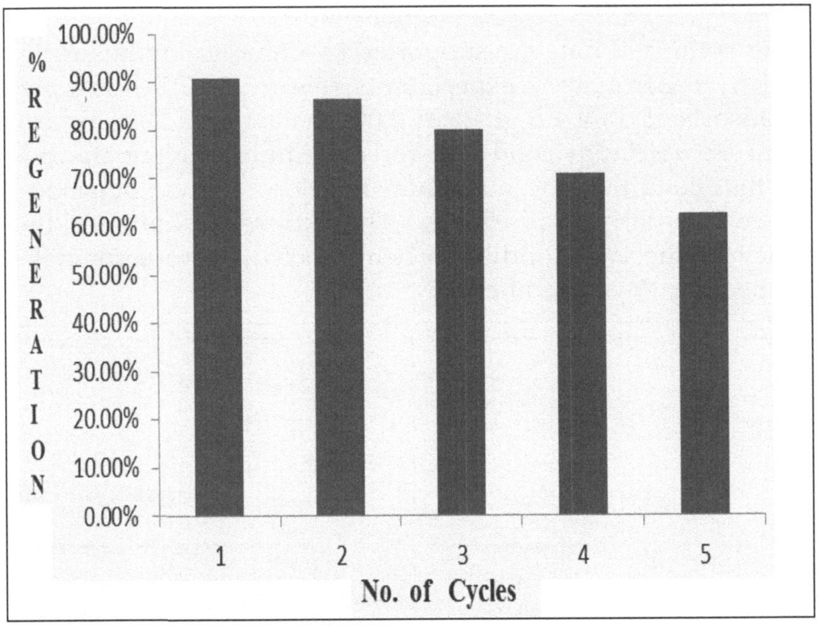

Fig. 4.13: % Regeneration study

Comparative adsorption capacity, isotherm of various adsorbents with AC synthesized in this study

Adsorbent	Maximum adsorbent capacity(mg·g^{-1})	Reference
Hydrous Titanium Dioxide	8.3	[21]
Iron and Cesium mixed oxide	2.42	[22]
ZrO_2	9.2	[23]
Monoclinic Fe_2O_3/Graphene	2.904	[24]
Al doped Phenolic bead	20	[25]
Silver containing Yeast cell	0.975	[26]
Polymer Nanocomposite(Fe_3O_4)	2.83	[27]
Activated Carbon (Saw dust, IR:1.0)	19.59 mg·g^{-1}	Present Study

CONCLUSION

The present work deals with the aim of studying arsenic adsorption process onto activated carbon prepared from saw dust in different impregnation ratio. The adsorption studies were carried out as a function of pH, contact time and dosage of adsorbent. The following conclusions may be inferred on the basis following experiment:

- It was proved that the adsorption equilibrium data were well fitted to the Langmuir adsorption model rather than Freundlich adsorption model at different pH for three adsorbents.
- The obtained experimental results showed good agreement with pseudo–second order kinetic modelin case of three adsorbents.
- Thermodynamic parameters such as change in Gibbs free energy (ΔG^0), enthalpy (ΔH^0), andentropy (ΔS^0) were determined from thermodynamic studies. Additionally, the nature of the adsorption process was spontaneous and endothermic.
- The desorption study was carried out using 1% NaOH as desorbing agent onto activated carbon (IR:1.0) in 5 cycles. The results showed that this adsorbent can be reused for further de-fluoridation.

As saw dust is very cheap and easily available and adsorbents were synthesized chemically from these materials which can be serve as effective adsorbent for removal of arsenic ion from solution. Additionally, from comparative study it was shown that this was better adsorbent for arsenic removal in water.

REFERENCES

1. Viraraghavan T; Subramanian K.S; Aruldoss J.A. Arsenic in Drinking Water Problems and Solutions. Water Science Technology. 1999, 40, 69-76.
2. Khan A.H; RasulS.B; Munir A; Habibuddowla M; Alauddin M; Newaz S.S; Hussan A. Appraisal of a Simple Arsenic Removal method for Groundwater of Bangladesh. J. Environ. Sci. Health. 2000, *35*, 1021-1041.
3. Kinniburgh D.G; Smedley P.L; Trafford J.M; Milne C.J; Hug S.M.I; Ahmed K.M; Burden S. The National Hydrochemical Survey. In: Kinniburgh D.G. and Smedley P.L. (Eds.), Arsenic Contamination of Groundwater in Bangladesh. Volume 2: Final Report. British Geological Survey Report, WC/00/19. British Geological Survey, UK (Chapter 6),. 2001, *7*, 77-103.
4. Smedley P.L; Nicolli H.B; Macdonald D.M.J; Barros A.J; Tullio J.O.Hydrogeochemistry of Arsenic and other Inorganic Constituents in Ground Waters from La Pampa, Argentina. Applied Geochemistry. 2002, 17, 259-284.
5. Jain C.K; Ali I.Arsenic: Occurrence, Toxicity and Speciation Techniques. Water Research. 2000, 34, 4304-4312.
6. Elizalde-Gonzalez M.P; Mattusch J; Wennrich R; Morgenstern P. Sorption on Natural Solids for Arsenic Removal. Chemical Engineering Journal. 2001, 81, 187-195.
7. Bajpai, S; Chaudhuri, M. Removal of Arsenic from Ground Water by Manganese Dioxide—coated Sand. î Journal of Environmental Engineering. 1999, 126, 782-787.
8. Ramaswami A; Tawachsupa S; Isleyen M. Batch-mixed Iron Treatment of High Arsenic Waters. Water Research. 2001 35, 4474-4479.
9. Berg M; Tran C.H; Nguyen C.T; Pham V.H; Schertenleib R; GigerW. Arsenic Contamination of Groundwater and Drinking Water in Vietnam: A Human Health Threat. Environmental Science and Technology. 2001, 35, 2621-2626.

10. Ongley K.L; Armienta A.M; Heggeman K; Lathorop A.S; Mango H; Miller W; Pickelner S. Arsenic Removal from Contaminated Water by the Soyatal Formation, Zimapan Mining District, Mexicoóa Potential Low-cost Low-tech Remediation System. Geochemistry: Exploration, Environment, Analysis. 2001, 2, 0-9.
11. Korngold E; Belayev N; Aronov L. Removal of Arsenic from Drinking Water by Anion Exchangers. Desalination. 2001, 141, 81-84.
12. Cheng R.C; Liang S. Enhanced Coagulation for Arsenic Removal, American Water Works Association. 1994, 86, 79-90.
13. Raji C; Anirudhan T.S. "Chromium (VI) Adsorption by Sawdust Carbon, Kinetics and Equilibrium," Indian Journal of Chemical Technology. 1997, 2, 228-236.
14. Su C.; Puls W.R. Arsenate and Arsenite Removal by Zerovalent Iron: Kinetics, Redox Transformation, and Implications for *in situ* Groundwater Remediation. Environ. Sci. Technol. 2001 35, 1487-1492.
15. ShirzadSiboni M; Samarghandi M.R; Azizian S; Kim W.G; Lee S.M. "The Removal of Hexavalent Chromium from Aqueous Solutions using Modified Holly Sawdust: Equilibrium and Kinetics Studies", Environ.Eng.Res. 2011 16, 55-60.
16. Evbuomwari B.O; Agbede A.M; Atuka M.M. A Comparative Study of the Physico-chemical Properties of Activated Carbon from Oil Palm Waste, *International Journal of Science and Engineering Investigations*. 2013, 2, 75-79.
17. Jun T.Y; Arumugam S.D; Latip N.H.A; Abdulla A.M; Latif P.A. Effect of Activation Temperature and Heating Duration on Physical Characteristics of Activated Carbon Prepared from Agriculture Waste. 2010, *Environment Asia 3 (Special issue)*, 143-148.
18. APHA, AWWA, WEF. Standard Methods for Examination of Water and Wastewater. 22nd ed. Washington: American Public Health Association. 2012, 1360 pp ISBN 978-087553-013-0.
19. Roy, S; Manna, S; Sengupta, S; Ganguli, A; Goswami, S; Das, P. Comparative Assessment on Defluoridation of Waste Water using Chemical and Bio-reduced Graphene Oxide Batch, Thermodynamic, Kinetics and Optimization using Response Surface Methodology and Artificial Neural Network. Process Saf. Environ. Protect. 2017, 111, 221-231.
20. Singh, K.P; Gupta, S; Singh, A.K; Sinha, S. Optimizing Adsorption of Crystal Violet Dye from Water by Magneticnanocomposite using Response Surface Modeling Approach. J. Hazard. Mater. 2011. 186, 1462-1473.
21. Xu Z; Li Q; Gao S; Shang JK ., As(III) Removal by Hydrous Titanium dioxide Prepared from One-step Hydrolysis of Aqueous $TiCl_4$ Solution. Water Res. 2010, 44, 5713-5721.
22. BasuT; Ghosh UC. Nano-structured iron (III) - cerium (IV) Mixed oxide: Synthesis, Characterization and Arsenic Sorption Kinetics in the Presence of Co-existing Ions Aiming to Apply for High Arsenic Groundwater Treatment. Appl Surf Sci. 2013, 283, 471-481.
23. Cui H; Su Y; Li Q,; Gao S; Shang JK. Exceptional Arsenic (III, V) Removal Performance of Highly Porous, Nanostructured ZrO_2 Spheres for Foxed Bed Reactors and the Full-scale System Modeling. Water Res. 2013, 47, 6258-6268.
24. Wang C; Luo H; Zhang Z; Wu; Zhang J; Chen S. Removal of As(III) and As(V) from Aqueous Solutions using Nanoscale Zero Valent Iron-reduced Graphite Oxide modified Composites. J Hazard Mater 2014, 268, 124-131.

25. Sharma A; Verma N; Sharma A; Deva D; Sankararamakrishnan N. Iron Doped Phenolic Resin based Activated Carbon Micro and Nanoparticles by Milling: Synthesis, Characterization and Application in Arsenic Removal. ChemEng Sci. 2010, 65, 3591-3601.
26. Selvakumar R; Arul Jothi N; Jayavignesh V; Karthikaiselvi K; Immanual Antony G; Sharmila PR; Kavitha S; Swaminathan K. As(V) Removal using Carbonized Yeast Cells Containing Silver Nanoparticles. Water Res. 2011 45, 583-592.
27. Vunain E; Mishra AK; Krause RW. Fabrication, Characterization and Application of Polymer Nanocomposites for Arsenic(III) Removal from Water. J Inorg Organomet Polym. 2013, 23, 293-305.

Pages: 82-103

Research in Chemistry and Chemical Sciences
Edited by: **Dr. Vijender Singh and Dr. Pawan Kumar 'Bharti'**
ISBN: 978-93-88854-40-5
Edition: **2020**
Published by: **Discovery Publishing House Pvt. Ltd., New Delhi (India)**

5

Fate and Transport of Per- and Poly-fluorinated Alkyl Substances (PFAS) in the Environment

Meena, L.,* V. Davamani, E. Parameswari, T. Anitha[1] and R.P. Premalatha[2]

INTRODUCTION

In the global context of anthropogenically-induced changes, the dissemination of persistentorganic pollutants (POPs) in natural environments, which may pose threats to human healthand wildlife, has emerged as a major issue in the last 60 years. While legacy POPs are stillunder close scrutiny of environmental monitoring programs, the past two decades have alsowitnessed the identification of POPs as emerging concern. Such is the case of perfluoroalkyl and polyfluoroalkyl substances (PFASs). PFASs comprise a large group of man-made chemicals which constitutes more than 3000 in number (Wang *et al.*, 2017) and it contain the common structural element of one or more fully fluorinated alkyl moieties (C_nF_{2n+1}), known as a perfluoroalkyl group (Buck *et al.*, 2011). These chemicals are used to make products that are stain and stick resistant,have been linked to health effects in adults and adverse birth outcomes They are C_2-C_{16} chemicals with unique properties, hydrophobic and lipophobic with no natural counterparts. PFASs are synthetic fluorosurfactants that have been produced and are catered to requirements of industrial processes, consumer goods, and specialty applications including firefighting foamformulations. Per- and

Dept. of Environmental Sciences, Tamil Nadu Agricultural University, Coimbatore, (India)

[1] Horticultural College & Research Institute, Tamil Nadu Agricultural University, Periyakulam, (India)

[2] Dept. of Soil Science & Agricultural Chemistry, Tamil Nadu Agricultural University, Coimbatore, (India)

polyfluoroalkyl substances (PFASs) are a group of anthropogenic fluorinatedchemicals that have been widely used for the past six decades (Buck *et al.,* 2011). Due to their uniquecharacteristics, such as water and oil repellency, high surface activity, and thermal stability,PFASs have been used in many different industrial and commercial applications, including surface repellent coatings (e.g., food contact paper, textiles, leather and cookware), surfactants (e.g., fire-fighting foams, mist suppressants, and cleaning products), photographic devices, and pesticides.

As a group, PFASs are defined by fluorocarbon chains (4-18 carbons) andcan be further classified based on compound structure and functional groups, and include perfluorosulfonates (PFSAs), perfluoro carboxylates (PFCAs), and fluorotelomer sulfonates (FTSs). Several PFSAs, such as perfluorooctanesulfonate (PFOS), and PFCAs, such as perfluorooctanoate (PFOA), have been detected in various biota and human blood samples from around the world, including the high Arctic (Butt *et al.,* 2010; Houde *et al* 2011). PFASs enter Arctic systems directly through runoff from local sources (e.g., airports) (Prevedouros *et al.,* 2006) or indirectly through longrange oceanographic or atmospheric transport (Armitage *et al.,* 2006). Although many PFASs are being phased out of use in North America, there is concern about the continued approval fortheir use by other governing bodies and the existing stock of highly stable PFASs in the environment, as these chemicals arenot likely to fully break down (Lindstrom *et al.,* 2011). Further, the use offluorotelomer substances is increasing; FTS are not as environmentally stable as the PFSAs they are replacing in industry, but they can degrade to the persistent PFCAs, rendering them of environmental concern. (Lindstrom *et al.,* 2011)

Studies on PFASs in the Arctic have focused mainly on the marine environment and, as such, less is known about the concentrations in various freshwater biota, especially lower trophic-level invertebrates (Muir *et al.,* 2013). The concentrations of 70 PFASs in 95 samples of leachate were measured in a survey of U.S landfills of varying climates and waste ages.

Many of the consumer products are disposed in landfills at the end of their useful life and the presence of PFASs in landfill leachate is well documented, though the range of concentrations that varies widely (Busch *et al.,* 2010). For example, the reported range of perfluorooctanoic acid (PFOA) concentrations in U.S. landfill leachate (n =13) was 0.15 to 9.2 μg/ L. (Huset *et al.,* 2011). For Chinese landfill leachate, concentrations of PFOA have been reported to be as high as 214 μg/L. (Yan *et al.,* 2015). This study also compared PFAS compound profiles and how their sources can affect PFAS accumulation in organisms and help explain the mobility of PFAS.

Table. 5.1: Discovery and Manufacturing History of Select PFAS

PFAS Compounds	Development Time Period							
	1930s	1940s	1950s	1960s	1970s	1980s	1990s	2000s
PTFE	Invented	Non-Stick Coatings			Waterproof Fabrics			
PFOS		Initial Production	Stain and Water Resistant Products	Firefighting foam				U.S. Reduction of PFOS, PFOA, PFNA (and other select PFAS2)
PFOA		Initial Production	Initial Production					
PFNA					Initial Production	Architectural Resins		
Fluorotelomers								Predominant form of firefighting foam

(ITRC- interstate technology regulatory council fact sheet)

HISTORY/STATUS

First created in the 1930s and 1940s, PFAS are among some 4,700 man-made chemicals that contain fluorine atoms bonded to a carbon chainpoly- and perfluoroalkyl substances (PFAS) have beenused since the 1940s as surfactants in products for stain-proof and grease-proof applications and are used globally since the 1960's for a wide range of industrial, commercial and domestic applications due to their unique surface-active properties.

International Status

Stockholm Convention

The objective of the Stockholm Convention is to protect human health and the environment from persistent organic pollutants. It differentiates three categories of POPs:

- Intentionally produced POPs that are slated for elimination
- Intentionally produced POPs are to be reduced and ultimately eliminated, except where there is a specified "acceptable purpose," such as disease vector control, or exempted usage, in which case the production and/or use of the substance is restricted;and POPs that are unintentionally produced as the result ofhumanactivity and which are slated for continued minimization and, where feasible, ultimate elimination of total releases derived from anthropogenic sources.

Table 5.2: 9 new POPs added to the Stockholm Convention in 2009

POPs	Pesticide	Industrial Chemical	By-product
Chlordecone	+		
HBB		+	
a-HCH	+		+
b-HCH	+		+
g-HCH	+	+	+
OBDE		+	+
PFOS		+	
PeCBz	+	+	+
Endosulfan	+		

ENVIRONMENTAL SIGNIFICANCE

PFAS are found in a wide range of consumer products that people use daily. They are useful in the way being manufactured. Some are listed below:

- PFOS as AFFF-foam, food packaging, textile, oil and gas industry. Metal and plastic coating comprising of coating of photographic films, papers, printing plates Carpets, furniture, outdoor clothing,leather polish chromium, zinc, gold,copper, nickel, tin,brass, etc.,Impregnation of dispersion media such asink, paint, varnish, manufacture ofvideo endoscopes, It is also used in insecticides, cleaning fluids, hydraulic fluids, detergents shampoos, carpet cleaner and handcreams.

- PFOA used for polymer-production, dyes, polishes, adhesives, lubricants
- N-alkylsubstitutedperfluorooctane-sulfonamide in photographic paper, Insecticides, teflon production in non sticks, herbicides.

PFAS can accumulate and stay in the human body for long periods of time. There is evidence that exposure to PFAS can lead to adverse health outcomes in humans. PFOA and PFOS can cause reproductive and developmental, liver and kidney, and immunological effects in laboratory animals.

It is the most commonly encountered perfluorinated compound in the environment and tissues of wildlife (Giesy, 2010). PFOA has been widely used as an emulsion polymerization aid in the production of Teflon (Lindstrom, 2011). C8 science panel studies has given that many water utilities & well owners may be subjected to:

- Diagnosed hypertension
- Coronary artery disease
- Chronic kidney disease
- Liver disease
- Osteoarthritis
- Rheumatoid arthritis,
- Neuro-developmental disorders in children (e.g., ADD)
- Asthma and chronic obstructive pulmonary disease (COPD)
- Stroke
- Nineteen types of cancer (other than kidney and testicular)
- Type II diabetes
- Birth defects
- Miscarriages and still births
- Preterm birth and low birth weight
- Diagnosed high cholesterol
- Ulcerative colitis (autoimmune disease)
- Thyroid disease
- Testicular and kidney cancers

PROPERTIES

PFOA and PFOS are made up of "chains" of eight carbon atoms that are attached to fluorine and other atoms. Replacement chemicals, like GenX, tend to have fewer carbon atoms in the chain, but have many similar physical and chemical properties as their predecessors (e.g. they both repel oil and water). The perfluoroalkyl moiety within a PFAS molecule is highly resistant to abiotic degradation, which has led to the accumulation of PFAS breakdown products (perfluoroalkyl sulphonic and carboxylic acids) in the environment.

The family of PFAS comprises 42 families and its subfamilies, several hundredcompounds with carbon chain lengths generally from C_2 to C_{16} (Buck *et al.*, 2011). Inspite of being very diverse class of compounds, they are unified by the presence of a perfluoroalkyl group, but comprising anionic, cationic, and zwitterionic species, which will interact differently with soil and aquifer matrices (Hanson *et al.*, 2017; Wang *et al.*, 2017).The surfactant properties of PFOA and PFOS complicate their physiochemical properties such as partitioning coefficients.

Adsorption to soil or sediment occurs via two mechanisms: interaction of hydrophobic fluorinated carbon tail with the organic carbon fraction of the soil, and to a lesser extent through electrostatic interactions of the polar head group with the charged clay fraction (Higgins and Luthy, 2006). Longer-chained PFASs sorbs to soils more readily, and PFASs with sulfonate groups sorbs more carboxylates (Kucharzyk *et al.*, 2017). Organic rich soils retard movement of PFAS, when f_{oc}increases, K_d also increases. Oil and other organics may also increasesorption. Electrostatic effects includes that positively charged PFAS (i.e. someprecursors) sorbs to negatively chargedminerals and negatively charged PFAS sorbs to positivelycharged minerals, here electrostatic repulsion can decrease PFASsorption.

Some of these substances (principally perfluorooctane sulfonic acid (PFOS) and perfluorooctanoic acid (PFOA) have been identified as PBT, being persistent in the environment and having bioaccumulative and toxic properties in humans and wildlife. Perfluorooctane sulfonate (PFOS) is a perfluoroalkyl sulfonic acid (PFSA), and is themost prominent PFSA (DEPA, 2013).

SOURCES

Per- and polyfluoroalkyl substances (PFASs) are used in many consumer product. Commercial and consumer products containing PFAS:

- Paper and packaging
- Clothing and carpets
- Outdoor textiles and sporting equipment
- Ski and snowboard waxes
- Non-stick cookware
- Cleaning agents and fabric softeners
- Polishes and waxes, and latex paints

- Pesticides and herbicides
- Hydraulic fluids
- Windshield wipers
- Paints, varnishes, dyes, and inks
- Adhesives
- Medical products
- Personal care products (for example, shampoo, hair conditioners, sunscreen, cosmetics, toothpaste, dental floss) (Kotthoff *et al.*, 2015)

Potential Manufacturing Sources that releases PEAS to the Environment

- Textiles & leather (Kotthoff *et al.*,2015; ATSDR, 2015): applications include protective clothing and outerwear, umbrellas, tents, sails, architectural materials, carpets, and upholstery.
- Paper products (Schaider *et al.*, 2017): uses include non-food paper packaging (for example, cardboard, carbonless forms, masking papers) and food-contact materials (for example, pizza boxes, fast food wrappers, microwave popcorn bags, baking papers, pet food bags).
- Metal plating & etching (OSHA, 2013; KEMI, 2015 and EPA, 2015): corrosion prevention, mechanical wear reduction, aesthetic enhancement, surfactant
- Wire manufacturing (Schaider *et al.*, 2017): coating and insulation.
- Industrial surfactants, resins, molds, plastics (Kotthoff *et al.*, 2015; Miteni, 2016 and Chemours, 2017): manufacture of plastics and fluoropolymers, rubber, and compression mold release coatings; plumbing fluxing agents; fluoroplastic coatings, composite resins, and flame retardant for polycarbonate
- Photolithography, semiconductor industry (Putte *et al.*, 2010): photoresists, top anti-reflective coatings, bottom anti-reflective coatings, and etchants, with other uses including surfactants, wetting agents, and photo-acid generation

Other ources include

- Aqueous film-forming foams (AFFFs) (Anderson *et al.*, 2016; Hale 2016)
- Flame retardants (Gou *et al.*, 2009)
- Waste Disposal (Ahrens *et al.*, 2015)
- Wastewater Treatment (Ahrens *et al.*, 2009)
- WWTP Operations
- Biosolids (Sepulvado *et al.*, 2011).

PFAS TRANSPORT SOURCES

PFASs comprise >3,000 individual compounds that are increasingly reported as bioaccumulate, with understanding of their toxicology evolving.

Some PFASs can travel miles from their point of release, as they are mobile and persistent, potentially creating large plumes.

PFASs—perfluorooctane sulfonate (PFOS) and perfluorooctanoic acid (PFOA)—are highly mobile, once introduced to the aquatic environment (Fujii *et al.*, 2007), and are not removed by conventional wastewater treatment (Filipovic and Berger, 2015). The sources of PFASs to surface- and groundwater can be divided into:

(*i*) Point sources

(ii) Diffuse sources.

Table 5.3: The sources of PFASs to surface- and groundwater

Sources	Contamination sources	References
Point source	Municipal WWTPs into rivers	Becker *et al.*, 2008
	Surface water of PFAS production sites	Steenland *et al.*, 2013
	Surface water of military airfields.	Ahrens *et al.*, 2015
	Groundwater through landfill sites	Yan *et al.*, 2015
Diffuse sources	Contamination of groundwater was suggested to originate from rain and snow	Filipovic *et al.*, 2015

TRANSPORT MECHANISM

Mobility of PFAS in water will in part be influenced by the degree to which the PFASsorb to sediments or soils during transport. There are two sorption mechanisms which control the degree of PFASsorption to sediments and soils during transport in water:

1. Hydrophobic sorption to naturally-occurring solid organic particles; and
2. Surface sorption to charged mineral surfaces.

SORPTION MECHANISM

Hydrophobic Sorption of PFAS to Naturally-Occurring Solid Organic Carbon

PFAS can sorb to naturally-occurring solid organic carbon particles present insediment or soil during transport in water, The degree to which a PFASsorbs to naturally-occurring solid organic carbon particles in sediment or soil duringtransport in water can be estimated by the PFAS-specific organic-carbon partitioncoefficient (Koc), the PFAS-specific octanol-water partition coefficient (Kow), or thePFAS- and soil-specific distribution coefficient (Kd). Sorption of PFCAs and PFSAs will increase with increasing chainlength and with increasing solid phase fraction of organic carbon (foc).

In addition, sorption increases with decreasing pH and increasing concentration of Ca2+. This finding suggests that the degree of PFAS hydrophobic sorption to soils and sedimentsis a site-specific phenomenon and depends on the specific PFAS present at a site as well as the specific soil type.

Surface Sorption of PFAS to Charged Mineral Surfaces

All of the PFCAs, PFSAs, PFPAs, and some of the precursors are strong or weak acids that exist as anions in natural waters at almost all pH, surface sorption tocharged mineral surfaces naturally present in soils or sediments may be a significantmechanism controlling the mobility of these PFAS in water during transport

Study 1: Tang *et al.* (2010) investigated PFOS adsorption onto goethite and silica by batchadsorption experiments under various solution compositions. They found that PFOS adsorption onto silica surfaces was marginally affected by solution pH, ionic strength,and calcium concentration. However, in contrast, they found that PFOS uptake by goethite increased significantly at lower pH and higher calcium concentrations, whichwas likely due to enhanced electrostatic attraction between the negatively charged PFOS molecules and positively charged goethite surface.

Study 2: Ferrey *et al.* (2012) investigated PFOS and PFOA sorption onto mineral surfaces by constructing laboratory microcosms with sediment from beneath a landfill and amending the microcosms with PFOS and PFOA. They found that sorption of PFOAand PFOS at near neutral pH was controlled by electrostatic sorption on ferric oxide minerals, and not by sorption to organic carbon.

Study 3: Lipson *et al.* (2013) investigated PFOS transport in bedrock groundwater at a well characterized site where AFFF was released to the ground as part of fire-fighting activities during a catastrophic fire at a petroleum storage facility in the United Kingdom. The PFOS diffusion coefficient estimated through model calibration was significantly lower than the standard estimation method and it was hypothesized that PFOS transport was influenced by an anion exclusion effect associated with surface charge on the aquifer mineral surfaces.

Study 4: Apart from the two sorption mechanisms as discussed above, mobility of PFAS mayalso be influenced by the presence of co-contaminants (Lipson *et al.*, 2013).

Guelfo *et al.* (2013) studied the sorption of PFAS to multiple soils.

1. In the presence of non-aqueous phase liquid (NAPL), which may be relevant at AFFF-impacted sites; and
2. In the presence of non-fluorinated AFFF surfactants i.e PFAS with more than 6 - CF_2 groups demonstrated variable sorption properties affected by the presence of NAPL and nonfluorinated AFFF. Shorter chain PFAS generally showed an increase in the sorption due to the presence of co-contaminants. The authors concluded that "PFAS groundwater transport at AFFF-impacted sites will depend on the solid phasecharacteristics as well as the PFAS concentration and chain length".

PFAS TRANSFORMATIONS

Biotic Transformations

PFCAs and PFSAs are generally considered to be recalcitrant to biodegradation vianaturally-occurring microorganisms in water or soil. Biodegradation studies in which PFOS or PFOA were monitored for loss of parent compound have been conductedusing a variety of microbial sources and exposure regimes (Parsons, 2008). Underaerobic conditions with activated sludge, no loss or biotransformation of PFOS orPFOA was observed. Under anaerobic circumstances, some removal of PFOS and PFOA has been observed, but no metabolites or increase of fluoride was measured.To date, no laboratory data exist that demonstrates that PFCAs or PFSAs undergo significant and complete biodegradation under environmental conditions.

Precursors are known to be transformed into PFCAs and PFSAs under natural circumstances. Biotransformation of the 8:2 Telomer Alcohol (FTOH 8:2) is relatively well studied (Parsons *et al.*, 2008). The aerobic degradation of FTOH 8:2 begins with oxidation of the alcohol to an acid moiety, and then a subsequent oxidation to the complete degradation of the non-fluorinated aliphatic portion of the molecule. As aresult, a PFCA is created as a by-product, in this case it is PFOA. The removal of only non-fluorinated radical to form the corresponding PFCA, in this case PFNA isminor. In another study, these compounds were not detected (Wang *et al.*, 2009). Degradation studies using radio labelled compounds [14C] on FTOH 8:2 molecules revealed a number of important results (Wang *et al.*, 2009). After seven months of incubation, 35% of the 14C molecules were irreversibly bound to the soil and couldonly be removed by combustion. This was confirmed by the fact that free fluoride (F)accounts for only a part of the mass loss (Dinglasan *et al.*, 2004). A number of metabolites were identified, including:

- 3-OH-acid 7-3 F (CF_2) $7CHOH\text{-}CH_2COOH$;
- 7-2 FT-ketone F (CF_2) $7COCH_3$;
- 7-3 acid F (CF_2) $7CH_2CH_2COOH$;
- 2H-PFOA F (CF_2) $6CH_2\text{-}COOH$ (11% after 7 days).

The formation of some of these metabolites and the fact that the 14C-labeling could be dismissed after the formation of $14CO_2$ (6.8%) shows that multiple CF_2-groups were reduced from FTOH 8:2. Three of the metabolites, PFOA (25%), 2H-PFOA (2%), and 7:3 acid (11%) were found to be stable. The remaining metabolites were detected only transiently. The ratio of PFOA to 7:3 acid (1.8 to 2.5) can be used as an indicator of the source of PFOS. PFOS was not observed as a transformation product from the degradation of FTOH 8:2 (Wang *et al.*, 2009). Results also showed that degradation of FTOH 8:2 was relatively fast, with a half-life of approximately seven days. Partialmineralization of FTOHs to carbon dioxide during the study also shows that microorganisms can derive energy and grow from the removal of the non-fluorinatedmoiety.Studies on the degradation of FTOH 8:2 in rat, mouse, trout, human hepatocytes, human liver microsomes and cytosol suggests that FTOH 8:2 in humans is converted slightly, and that FTOH 8:2 is not a significant source of the formation of PFOA or other PFCAs (Nabb *et al.,* 2007).

Microbial degradation of the polyfluorinated alkyl phosphates (PAPs) can occur by hydrolysis of the phospho-ester bond to form the respective FTOH as a by-product,which may then be converted according to further transformation processes (Lee *et al.,* 2010). Short-chain PAPs were fully converted within ten days, but complete transformation of 2-mono-PAP after 90 days was not observed. PAPs can also bebio-transformed in higher organisms as demonstrated by experimental results with rats (D'Eon and Mabury, 2007). To study the degradation of industrial polymers, a synthetic fluoroacrylate polymerwas synthesized with different FTOH side chain lengths and incubated aerobically in soil over a period of two years (Russel *et al.,* 2008). Terminal biotransformation byproducts detected included PFOA, PFNA, PFDA, and PFUNa. However, abiodegradation half-life of 1.200 to 1.700 years was determined for these biotransformations.Thus it is concluded that microbial degradation of fluoroacrylatepolymers hardly plays a role in the fate and transport of these compounds in the natural environment.

Biotic transformations of PFAS can be associated with substantial changes in the physicochemical properties of the compounds.

Chemical Transformations

PFCAs and PFSAs have shown to be very persistent in the environment (Wang *et al.,*2015). One study of Taniyasu *et al.* (2013) provided the first experimental evidence from field studies (at altitudes more than 2.500 m) that PFAS including PFOS can undergo photolysis. Taniyasu *et al.* (2013) states: "Long chain PFAS (PFCAs, PFSAs and FTOHs) can be successively dealkylated to short chain compounds such asperfluorobutanoic acid (PFBA) and perfluorobutane sulfonate (PFBS), but the shortchain compounds were relatively more resistant to photodegradation". However, Wang *et al.* (2015) clearly doubt these results looking at the lack of information provided in the research report no. 8/1620.

Prior to the above mentioned study, photolysis was already investigated by many scientists (e.g. Chen *et al.,* 2006, Hori *et al.,* 2007 and Giri *et al.,* 2011), demonstrating photolysis of PFCAs. These studies were mostly performed with relatively high concentrations of PFAS and partly under extreme reaction conditions (e.g. underpressure, in combination with photochemical oxidants), not representing natural environmental conditions. No other studies were found that showed photolytic degradation of PFOS and PFOA under natural circumstances. Regarding chemical degradation of precursors,volatile compounds such as FTOHs may react in the atmosphere and be oxidized by chlorine atoms, oxygen molecules,or photochemically generated OH radicals (Houtz *et al.*, 2012). These authors concluded that photo-oxidation of FTOHs with chlorine atoms mainly produces by-products including fluorotelomer carboxylic acids (FTCAs), fluorotelomer aldehydes (FTALs), perfluoraldehyde (PFAL), carbonyl, PFOA and PFNA. It was also concluded that photo-oxidation of FTOH with hydroxyl radicals leads to the production of FTAL, PFAL and carbonyl. Abiotic transformations of PFAS can also be associated with substantial changes in the physicochemical properties of the compounds.

PFAS EFFECTS AND ITS EXPOSURE TO HUMAN

Data on PFAS toxicity is dominated by PFOS, PFOA and also perfluorohexane sulfonate (PFHxS) due to the widespread detection of these compounds in humans and the environment, and concern that these could biomagnify to a level whereby humans consuming fish may be adversely affected. PFCAs and PFSAs can bioaccumulate in living organisms in the environment with the long-chained substances being more bioaccumulative than the short-chained. However, because these substances are both hydrophobic and lipophobic, they do not follow the typical pattern of partitioning into fatty tissues followed by accumulation but tends to bind to proteins and therefore are present rather in highly perfused tissues than in lipid tissue. Precursors such as fluorotelomers may be partially responsible for the observed bioaccumulation of the acids.

The shorter chain length acids tend to be more soluble in water and have a lower potential for sorption to particles than the long-chain analogues. Thereby, they have a higher potential for aqueous long-transport. Precursors like FTOHs, on the other hand, will mainly be transported over long distances via the atmosphere.

With regard to environmental effects, PFOS/PFOA and other long-chain PFAS are generally more toxic than the short-chain analogues and the sulfonic acids tend to be more toxic than the corresponding carboxylic acids. However, the toxicity of short chain PFAS is not thoroughly studied or well described, in particular with regard to log term effects, and there are examples of exceptions to the general picture. FTOHs have been shown to be xenoestrogens causing effects down to 0.03 mg/L, and 6:2 FTOH to be more potent than 8:2 FTOH.

There are a variety of ways that people can be exposed to these chemicals and at different levels of exposure. People can be exposed to PFAS in their workplace if they are involved in the manufacture or use of

PFAS. Outside the workplace, exposure to PFAS can occur from food, water (ground and surface water) and various consumer products by Australian government department of health. Primary exposure routes to PFAS include food and water (Haug, 2006). Human exposure to PFAS is mainly by ingestion of contaminated food or water. These compounds are not metabolised, bind to proteins (not to fats) and are mainly detected in blood, liver and kidneys. Elimination of PFOS, PFHxS and PFOA from the human body takes some years whereas elimination of shorter chain PFAS is in the range of days. The half-life of PFOS and PFOA in rodents is in the range of months which differs significantly from humans and can cause extrapolation issues in tests.There is significant data available on the impact of (sub) chronic PFOS and PFOA exposure on reproductive and/or developmental and other types of effects in both humans and animals. However, the results from epidemiological studies are not always consistent.

For example, people can be exposed to low levels of PFAS through *food,* which can become contaminated through:

- Contaminated soil and water used to grow the food
- Food packaging containing PFAS
- Equipment that uses PFAS during food processing.
- They are released during biodegradation, or disposal of consumer products that contain PFAS.
- PFAS used in commercially treated products to make them stain and water repellent or non-sticky goods include carpets, leather, textiles, paper and packaging materials, and non-stick cookware.
- Through contaminated air people may be exposed to PFAS at PFAS production or manufacture goods
- PFAS contamination in drinking water is typically localized with an industrial facility where PFAS were produced or used to manufacture other products or an oil refinery, airfield or other firefighting location.

Both in animals and humans, PFOS and PFOA cross the placenta, and are also excreted in breast milk (Stahl *et al.,* 2011). Gender dependent differences are as follows: men generally show higher concentrations of PFAS than women (Rylander *et al.,* 2009).

Distribution in Tissue

Perfluoroalkylated substances such as PFOS and PFOA have, contrary to most other persistent organic pollutants (POPs), a low affinity to lipids, but bind to proteins. PFOS is associated with cell membrane surfaces and accumulates in various, mainly high perfused, body tissues of exposed organisms. The highest concentrations are usually detected in blood, liver, kidneys, lung, spleen and bone marrow. Lower concentrations are detected in heart, testes, fat, brain and muscles. In general public, PFOS concentrations in the blood range between subppb levels up to the hundred ppb levels. PFOA levels in blood are generally lower (subppb)levels up to tens of ppb levels (Loganathan *et al.*, 2011).

The very low annual average Environmental Quality Standard (EQS) however is based upon consumption of fish by humans. Both in animals and humans, PFOS and PFOA cross the placenta, and are also excreted in breast milk (Stahl *et al.*, 2011).

An unequivocal correlation between age and blood PFAS concentrations is not evident. However, gender dependent differences are as follows: men generally show higher concentrations of PFAS than women (Rylander *et al.*, 2009).

This gender related difference in concentration levels was also detected during other studies, such as the study of Calafat *et al.* (2007), based on data of the U.S. population.

Effects on Aquatic SP

Seven types of seafood collected from fish markets in Guangzhou and Zhoushan were analysed by Gulkowska *et al.* (2006), including fish, molluscs, crabs, shrimp, oysters, mussels, and clams. PFOS has been categorised as moderately acute and slightly chronically toxic to aquatic organisms. Fluorochemicals were detectable in all the samples, and concentrations of PFOS in seafood samples ranged from 0.30-13.9 ng/g ww. The greatest concentration of PFOS was found in mantis shrimp, while the greatest concentration of PFOA was found in swimming crab (1.67 ng/g wet weight). PFOS and PFOA were detected in mussels and oysters from coastal waters of southern China (So *et al.*, 2006).

Effects on Organism

Animal studies show mainly effects from PFOS and PFOA on the liver, thegastrointestinal tract and the thyroid hormone levels. In general, PFOS is more toxiccompared to PFOA. Both PFOS and PFOA were detected in liver and muscle tissue, whereas concentrations of PFOS were significantly higher in organs and tissues. Considering the TDI for PFOS and PFOA, negative health effects from consumption of wild boar are not expected (Stahl *et al.*, 2012)

Concentrations of PFOS and PFOA in blood serum of giant pandas and red pandas housed in zoos and animal parks from six provinces in China were reported by Dai *et al.* (2006). The results showed that PFOS was the predominant PFC in pandas. Concentrations of PFOS in serum of red pandas was comparable to those observed in polar bears collected from Alaska Kannan *et al.*, 2001, while concentrations of PFOS in serum of giant pandas was one third of those observed in polar bear collected from Alaska (Kannan *et al.*, 2001).

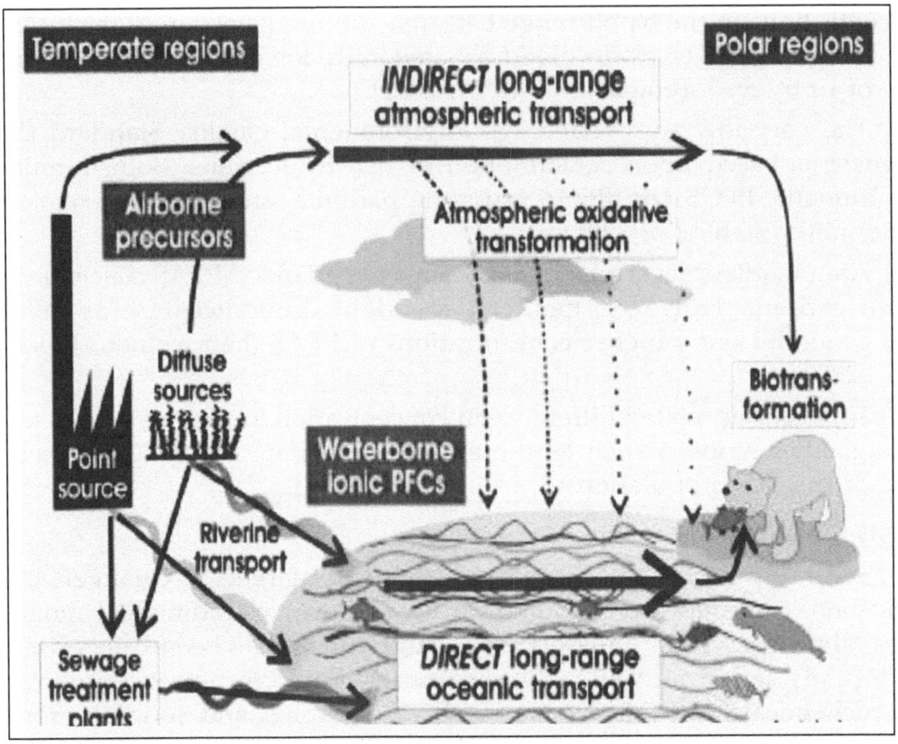

Fig. 5.1: Marine food web from the eastern Canadian arctic (Butt *et al.*, 2008)

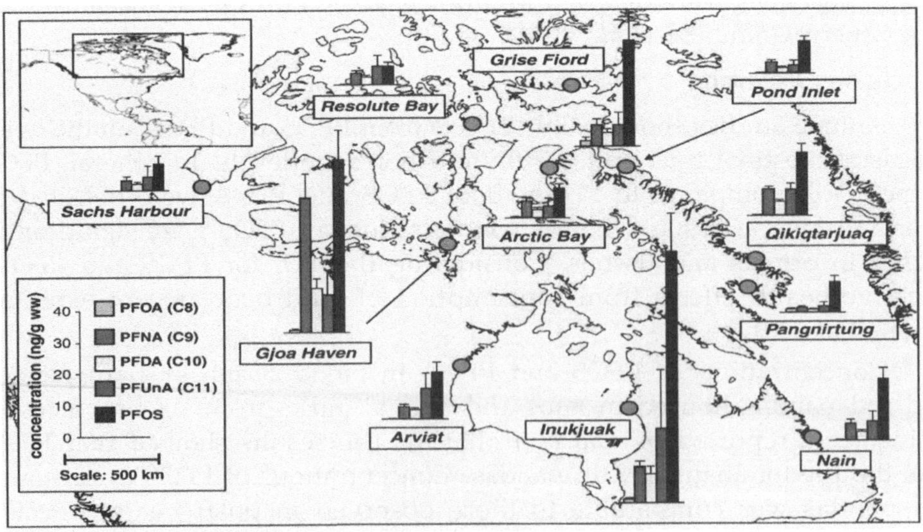

Table 5.4: Studies carried out to examine chronic exposure on Animals Klein & Brown (2016)

Animal	Injestion	NOEC/LOAEL mg/kg bw/d	Effects	References
PFOS				
Rats	Oral Diet, 14 weeks	NOEC: 0.4	Liver Effects	Seacat *et al.*, 2003
Rats	Oral Gavage	NOEC: 1	Developmental Effects	Lau *et al.*, 2003
Rats	Oral Diet, 90 days	LOAEL: 2	Liver Effects	Goldenthal, 1978
Cynomolgus Monkey	Oral Diet, 6 Months	NOEC: 0.03 LOAEL: 0.15	Effect on Thyroid hormone values	Seacat *et al.*, 2002
PFOA				
Mice	Oral Gavage, 14 days	LOAEL: 0.3	Liver Weight	Loveless *et al.*, 2006
Rats	Oral Gavage, 14 days	LOAEL :1NOEC: 0.3	Effect on hormone values	Loveless *et al.*, 2006
Rats	Oral Diet, 90 days	LOAEL: 0.6 NOEC: 0.06	Liver Effects	Perkins *et al.*, 2004
Mice	Oral Gavage	LOAEL: 1 (maternal)	Developmental Effects LOAEL: 3 (foetal) NOEC: 1 (foetal)	Lau *et al.*, 2006

FINDING ALTERNATIVES TO PFAS

- Alternatives to PFAS coated food packagingconcerns about their hazards are creating demand among grocery stores and government, health care, educational and other institutional purchasers for safer alternatives.
- Single use disposable food packaging and service ware are available without PFAS, including uncoated paper products, products made with materials other than paper, and paper products treated with coatings other than PFAS.
- Alternates to paper treatments bowls PLA (compostable plastic) are bamboo palm leaf (Uncoated), clay soak proof shieldplates, wrappers and liners such as muffin papers, cookie bags, hot or cold sandwich bags, parchment paper, self-serve sheets

Alternative Treatments: Paper coated with PLA, silicone, clay, and other proprietary-branded coatings and treatments are used to impart oil and grease resistance to disposable food ware.

PFAS LAWS AND REGULATIONS TO PROTECT PUBLIC HEALTH AND THE ENVIRONMENT

There are a variety of laws and regulations to protect public health and the environment. The following list relates to PFAS in the environment.

SAFE DRINKING WATER ACT

The Safe Drinking Water Act (SDWA) protects public drinking water supplies across the United States. Under the SDWA, EPA has regulated more than 90 drinking water contaminants. EPA has the authority to set enforceable Maximum Contaminant Levels (MCLs) for specific chemicals and can require monitoring of public water supplies. There are currently no MCLs established for PFAS chemicals. EPA initiated the steps to evaluate the need for an MCL for PFOA and PFOS. In addition, EPA is developing and updating toxicity values for two additional PFAS, GenX and PFBS.

Under the Third Unregulated Contaminant Monitoring Rule (UCMR3), EPA collected data for chemicals that are suspected contaminants in drinking water but do not have health-based standards set under the SDWA.

In the UCMR3, there were six PFAS included for monitoring including:

- perfluorooctanesulfonic acid (PFOS)
- perfluorooctanoic acid (PFOA)
- perfluorononanoic acid (PFNA)
- perfluorohexanesulfonic acid (PFHxS)
- perfluoroheptanoic acid (PFHpA)
- perfluorobutanesulfonic acid (PFBS)

Toxic Substances Control Act (TSCA)

On June 22, 2016, the Frank R. Lautenberg Chemical Safety for the 21st Century Act significantly amended the Toxic Substances Control Act (TSCA). EPA has issued three new rules to provide a framework for the implementation of the amended law. The rules outline EPA's path forward for prioritizing, evaluating and regulating chemicals and include a requirement for industry reporting of chemicals manufactured in the past 10 years.

Till date, 330 non Confidential Business Information (CBI) PFAS chemicals have been reported to EPA and are listed in the public interim report. EPA reviews new chemicals before they are allowed to commercialize. Since 2006, EPA has reviewed 294 new PFAS chemicals and has regulated 191 through a combination of orders and Significant New Use Rules (SNURs).

Additionally, on January 21, 2015 EPA proposed a Significant New Use Rule (SNUR) to manufacturer and processors of perfluorooctanoic acid (PFOA) and related chemicals to notify EPA. The notification required by SNURs obligates EPA to assess risks that may be associated with the significant new use, and regulate the proposed activity before it occurs.

Comprehensive Environmental Response, Compensation and Liability Act

The 1980 Comprehensive Environmental Response, Compensation, and Liability Act (CERCLA), provides the federal government with authority to address the threatened environmental releases and remedies to protect the environment in some circumstances. EPA is beginning the necessary steps to propose designating PFOA and PFOS as "hazardous substances" through one of the available statutory mechanisms, including potentially CERCLA Section 102.

Clean Air Act (1970)

The Clean Air Act requires us to regulate toxic air pollutants, also known as air toxics, from large industrial facilities in two phases. In addition, every eight years after setting the technology standards, it revises the standards for improvements in air pollution controls. As a result of these assessments, it removes the use of specific chemicals like PFAS, if effective and feasible alternatives exist.

New Federal Report

On June 20, ATSDR released a draft "Toxicological Profile for Perfluoroalkyls," which "characterizes the toxicologic and adverse health effects information for" 14 PFAS chemicals, including perfluorooctane-sulfonic acid ("PFOS") and perfluorooctanoic acid ("PFOA"). ASTDR calculated minimal risk level ("MRLs") for four such chemicals, which, according to the Association of State Drinking Water Administrators, equate to approximately 11 parts-pertrillion ("ppt") for PFOA and 7 ppt for PFOS. Those MRLs, which are "an estimate of the amount of a chemical a person can eat, drink, or breathe each day without a detectable risk to health," are substantially lower than the 70 ppt health advisory levels that EPA established for PFOA and PFOS in 2016. However, neither the MRLs nor EPA's health advisory levels are legally binding on drinking water suppliers.

The US Agency for Toxic Substances and Disease Registry has released a controversial draft toxicological profile on four per and polyfluoroalkyl substances (PFASs). The move comes amid uproar over allegations that other federal agencies were suppressing its release.

Environmental Working Group researchers tell Chemical Watch that using the EPA's methodology for translating these figures into drinking water advisory values results in the following levels:

- PFOS: approximately 7 parts per trillion (ppt);
- PFOA and PFNA: approximately 11 ppt; and
- PFHxS: approximately 74 ppt.

This contrasts with the EPA's non-enforceable lifetime health advisory level for PFOA and PFOS of 70ppt in drinking water. This makes its level seven to ten times higher than that recommended by the ATSDR, says the EWG.

REMEDIATION

The remedial options available to address PFAS contamination are limited by theunique physical and chemical properties of these compounds. Many remediation methods utilized to address hydrocarbon contamination, such as air stripping, sparging, soil vapour extraction and bioremediation, are ineffective due to the low volatility of these compounds and their resistance to microbial degradation. Technologies currently used for the remediation of PFAS in soil and groundwater include excavation to landfill for soil (where authorised), and abstraction combined with activated carbon or resin treatment for groundwater. Groundwater extraction volumes may be high if remediation is required to very low environmental quality standards (e.g. for PFOS). Current best practice disposal routes for spent PFAS adsorption media are high temperature incineration at >1000°C, or regeneration at a specialist facility. Possible alternative remedial techniques include soil washing, soil solidification and the use of *in-situ* permeable reactive barriers or funnel and gate systems. Emerging water treatment technologies for PFAS, such as photolysis/photocatalysis, reductive decomposition, advanced oxidation and sonolysis, require high energy input per unit water volume and long residence times. Careful monitoring of treatment performance is also required to ensure complete breakdown of the various PFAS substances that may be present. Consequently, these technologies are unlikely to be feasible for high flowrate, low concentration applications.

Conventional water treatment technologies, such as flocculation, are largely ineffective at removing PFASs. However, established methods exist that can reduce PFAS concentrations in drinking water to acceptable levels, including granular activated carbon (GAC), reverse osmosis, anion-exchange resin, nanofiltration, and electrochemical treatment (Appleman *et al.*, 2014; Schaefer *et al.*, 2015). However, the elimination behavior of many of these methods may be dependent on the carbon chain length of the respective PFAS compound. There are indications, for example, that GAC filtration is effective at removing long chained PFCA with eight or more carbons, including PFOA and PFSA with six or more carbons, including PFHxS, whereas short-chained PFASs cannot be removed as effectively (Eschauzier *et al.*, 2012). Electrochemical treatment avoids this problem by breaking down the perfluorinated compounds but this has thus far only been tested at lab scale (Schaefer *et al.*, 2015). Shorter chains have been reported to have a higher uptake in lettuce leaves, while longer chains PFASs are found primarily in the roots (Blaine *et al.* 2014). Furthermore, shorter chain PFASs has been shown to absorb into the liver more readily than those with longer ones which are concentrated in the blood proteins (Lau 2015).

CONCLUSION

The availability of PFAS as increased every day based on the usage of PFAS compound contained materials. PFAS has great environmental significance towards creating pollution, and ill effects to humans. Their transport generally depends on chemical structure and functional groups. They are generally non-volatile and mobile in groundwater, non-reactive, biotransform more rapidly under aerobic thananaerobic conditions and in wastewater treatment plants. Atmospheric deposition of PFAS can occur tens of miles away from the release location. Long chain PFAS retardation in subsurface is dominated by hydrophobic sorption. Electrostatic effects may be more significant for cationic precursors and short chain PFASs. PFAS in soil and ground water are currently difficult and expensive to remediate. Options include excavation to landfills for soil. Current best practice disposal routes for PFAS adsorption media are high temperature inceneration at >1000 degree celcius. Alternateive water treatment techniques such as sonolysis and advanced chemical oxidation, are being developed that may be more widely used in the future.

REFERENCES

1. Armitage, J., I.T. Cousins., R.C. Buck and K. Prevedouros. 2006. Modeling Global-scale Fate and Transport of Perfluorooctanoate Emitted from Direct Sources. *Environ. Sci. Technol,* 40, 6969-6975.
2. Buck, R.C., J. Franklin and U. Berger. 2011. Perfluoroalkyl and Polyfluoroalkyl Substances in the Environment: Terminology, Classification, and Origins. *Integrated Environmental Assessment and Management,* 7 (4), 513-541.
3. Busch, J., L. Ahrens., R. Sturm and R. Ebinghaus. 2010. Polyfluoroalkyl Compounds in Landfill Leachates. *Environmental Pollution,* 158, 1467-1471.
4. Butt, C.M., U. Berger., R. Bossi and G.T. Tomy. 2010. Levels and Trends of Poly- and Perfluorinated Compounds in the Arctic Environment. *Science of the Total Environment,* 408, 2936-2965.
5. Casal, P., B. Gonza., Y. Zhang., A.J.F. Reardon., J.W. Martin. 2017. Accumulation of Perfluoroalkylated Substances in Oceanic Plankton. *Environ. Sci. Technol.*
6. Dai, J.Y., N. Jin., M.Q. Xu and F.W. Wei. 2006. Perfluorooctanesulfonate and perfluorooctanoate in Red Panda and Giant Panda from China, *Environ. Sci. Technol,* 40, 5647-5652.
7. Eggen, T., M. Moeder and A. Arukwe. 2010. Municipal Landfill Leachates: A Significant Source for New and Emerging Pollutants. *Science of the Total Environment.*
8. Filipovic, M and U. Berger. 2015. Are perfluoroalkyl Acids in Waste Water Treatment Plant Effluents the Result of Primary Emissions from the Technosphere or of Environmental Recirculation? *Chemosphere,* 129, 74-80.
9. Gulkowska, Q.T., M.K. Jiang., S. Taniyasu., P.K.S. Lam and N. Yamashita. 2006. Persistent Perfluorinated Acids in Seafood Collected from Two Cities of China, *Environ. Sci. Technol,* 40, 3736-3741.
10. Haug, L.S., S. Huber., G. Becher and C. Thomsen. 2011. Characterisation of Human Exposure Pathways to Perfluorinated Compounds—Comparing Exposure Estimates with Biomarkers of Exposure. *Environ. Int.* 37, 687-693.
11. Houde, M. and A. De Silva. 2011. Monitoring of Perfluorinated Compounds in Aquatic Biota: An updated Review. *Environ. Sci. Technol,* 1(45), 7962-7973.
12. Huset, C.A., M.A. Barlaz., D.F. Barofsky and J.A. Field. 2011. Quantitative Determination of Fluorochemicals in Landfill Leachates. *Chemosphere,* 82, 1380-1386.
13. Kannan, K., J. Koistinen., K. Beckmen., T. Evans., J. F. Gorzelany., K.J. Hansen., P. D. Jones, E. Helle., M. Nyman., and J. P. Giesy. 2001. Accumulation of Perfluorooctane Sulfonate in Marine Mammals, *Environ. Sci. Technol.* 35, 1593-1598.
14. Kucharzyk, K.H., R. Darlington and M. Benotti. 2017. Novel Treatment Technologies for PFAS Compounds: A Critical Review. *Journal of Environmental Management.*
15. Lindstrom, A.B., M.J. Strynar and E.L. Libelo. 2011. Polyfluorinated Compounds: Past, Present, and Future. *Environ. Sci. Technol.,* 45, 7954-7961.
16. Muir, D.C.G., P. Kurt-Karakus., J. Stow., J. Blais and B. Braune. 2013. Occurrence and Trends in the Biological Environment. Chapter 4. In Persistent Organic Pollutants in Canada's North. Aboriginal Affairs and Northern Development Canada: Ottawa. 273-422.
17. Prevedouros, K., I.T. Cousins., R.C. Buck., S.H. Koreniowki. 2006. Source, Fate, and Transport of Perfluorocarboxylates. *Environ. Sci. Technol,* 40, 32-44.

18. Sharma, B.M., G. K. Bharat., S. Tayal., P.G. White and L. Nizzetto. 2016. Perfluoroalkyl Substances (PFAS) in River and Ground/Drinking Water of the Ganges River Basin: Emissions and Implications for Human Exposure. *Environmental Pollution,* 208.
19. Tang, C.Y., Q. Shiang., D. Gao.,C. S. Criddle and J.O. Leckie. 2010. Effect of Solution Chemistry on the Adsorption of Perfluoro Octane Sulfonate onto Mineral Surfaces. *Water Research,* 44, 2654-2662.
20. Taniyasu, S., P.K.S. Lam., G.J. Zheng., J.P. Giesy and N. Yamashita. 2006. Alkaline Digestion and Solid Phase Extraction method for Perfluorinated Compounds in Mussels and Oysters from South China and Japan, *Arch. Environ.Con. Tox,* 50, 240-248.
21. Wang, Z., J.C. DeWitt and C.P. Higgins. 2017. A Never-Ending Story of Per- and Polyfluoroalkyl Substances (PFASs)?. *Environ. Sci. Technol.*
22. Yan, H., I.T. Cousins and C. Zhang. 2015. Perfluoroalkyl Acids in Municipal Landfill Leachate from China: Occurrence, Fate during Leachate Treatment and Potential Impact on Groundwater. *Science of the Total Environment.,* 524, 23-31.
23. Yan, H., T. Cousins and C. Zhang. 2015. Perfluoroalkyl Acids in Municipal Landfill Leachates from China: Occurrence, fate during Leachate Treatment and Potential Impact on Groundwater. *Science of the Total Environment,* 23-31.
24. Yeung, L.W.Y., N. Yamashita., S. Taniyasu., P.K.S. Lam., R.K. Sinha and K.Kannan. 2009. A Survey of Perfluorinated Compounds in Surface Water and Biota including Dolphins from the Ganges River and in other Waterbodies in India. *Chemosphere,* 76, 55-62.
25. Zhang, W., Y. Zhang., S. Taniyasu., P.K.S. Lam., J. Wang and J. Dai. 2013. Distribution and Fate of Perfluoroalkyl Substances in Municipal Wastewater Treatment Plants in Economically Developed Areas of China. *Environmental Pollution,*176.
26. Zhang,T.,H.Sun., Y. Lin and K. Kannan. 2013. Distribution of Poly- and Perfluoroalkyl Substances in Matched Samples from Pregnant Women and Carbon Chain Length Related Maternal Transfer.*Environ. Sci. Technol.* 47, 7974-7981.
27. Zhaoyun, Z., T. Wang and J. Giesy. 2014. Perfluoroalkyl and polyfluoroalkyl Substances in Sediments from South Bohai Coastal Watersheds, China. *Marine Pollution Bulletin,* 85, 619-627.

Pages: 104-143

Research in Chemistry and Chemical Sciences
Edited by: Dr. Vijender Singh and Dr. Pawan Kumar 'Bharti'
ISBN: 978-93-88854-40-5
Edition: 2020
Published by: Discovery Publishing House Pvt. Ltd., New Delhi (India)

6

Binding and Interaction Studies of Metal ions with Protein by Spectrophotometric and Viscometric Methods

Shveta Acharya[1], Arun Kumar Sharma[2]

ABSTRACT

The present chapter consists of the following:

1. The interactions between triethanolamine, lauryl sulphate and albumin molecule.
2. The pH and diffusion current measurements on the binding of copper and mercury ions with albumin.
3. The effect of physico-chemical factors on interaction between divalent metal ions and albumin.
4. The interaction between cupric ionosed albumin molecule by physico-chemical method.
5. A polarographic study on the binding of mercury ions with albumin.
6. Physico-chemical studies on the binding of Hg(II) and molybdenum (VI) ions with ribonucleic acid.
7. The interaction between anionic surfactant TEALS and albumin.
8. Studies on the binding of Congo red with a collagen.

INTRODUCTION

The term biopolymer includes a variety of macromolecules including proteins, carbohydrates, nucleic acids, etc. for example, proteins are widely

[1] Department of Chemistry, Govt. College Kota - 324 010 Rajasthan, (India)
[2] Department of Chemistry, Govt. P.G. College Jhalawar - 326 001 Rajasthan, (India)

distributed in cells of plants, vertebrates, invertebrates and microorganisms. They have a variety of functions. The fertilizine, a protein, present at the surface of ova is responsible for reproduction. Some of them act as hormones, enzymes and as inhibitors. In almost every field of biology, bio polymers find remarkable applications. The uses of these proteins as lubricants, carriers and structural proteins, etc. are well known.

All molecules that are found in biological systems beginning with the low molecular weight compounds through proteins and coenzymes and up to organised phospholipid micelles are called biological regardless of their physio-chemical solution state. Complex bio aggregates such as membranes, body fluids, etc. provide distinct microenvironment for biological functions in which the macromolecules like proteins, Polynucleotides, carbohydrates. etc. are involved. Micellar systems are often used as models for such investigation. The static and dynamic of the membranes are responsible for the regulation of lipid medicated phenomenon.

The interactions between acidic and basic macromolecules in the living systems in the presence of micromolecule ions form the basis of the formation of biofluids and these combinations have been included under the trophic phase equilibria in systems of interacting polyelectrolytes. It has been assumed that the coacervationdemixing process represents the primary ordering process by which mixtures of randomly formed pre biologic polymers were condensed into preprotophasmic assemblies. Such studies on complex coacervation have thrown light on the development of living system via interactions between the random polymers produced in the atmosphere of the earth. The interactions between proteins and a variety of bio-acceptable compound/ion has been carried out for several reasons (Lundgren, 1941 and 1943; Hellerman, 1943; Nutting *et.al.*, 1945; Coleman and Howitt; 1945; Berger, 1946; Highberger and kersten, 1938; Whittier and Gould, 1940; Gurd and Wilcox, 1956). The most significant of these is to find out the effect of any particular compound for any specific system (Valee and Wacker, 1970) among the various bio active compounds. The metal ions play a vital role in a large number of widely differing biological processes. Some of these processes are quite specific in their metal ion requirements. In that only certain metal ions, in specific oxidation states, can fulfill the necessary catalytic or structural requirement, while other processes are much less specific. It is possible to replace one metal ion by another, although the activity may be reduced (Dennard and Williams, 1960). metals like Mg, Mn, Fe, Co, Cu, Mo and Zn are important catalysts of a variety of enzyme reactions such as group transfer, redox or hydrolytic processes. Some protein system are involved in strong and controlling the concentration of the metal ion and then in transporting it to the appropriate sites of the enzyme. Many of them are used in maintaining the structure and controlling the function of the cell wall. Not only the common metals but even the lanthanide find used as nuclear magnetic resonance shift probe in biological systems (Glasses, 1973). The physiological pH is limited to 7.0-7.5 while these lanthanide ions are reported not to be precipitated even up to pH 8.43, thus it is feasible to say that in this sense they are even superior then the well known biologically active ferric and chromic ions. These ions are reported to form complexes with adenosine mono phosphate (Barry *et. al.* 1972). The role of uranyl ions in enzymatic systems has recently been reported by several workers (Barry, *et. al.* 1972 and Feldman, 1968).

Characerization of Metal Protein Complex

Many complexities arise in the investigation of protein which are ascribed to the factors like uncertainty in molecular weights, variation in chemical behavior depending on the nature, origin, purity and their great sensitivity to denaturation. A large number of physico-chemical methods viz. Ultracentrifungation, ultrafiltration, magnetic susceptibility, light scattering solubility, precipitation, migration in electric field polarography, spectrophotometry, equilibrium dialysis, electrophoretic mobility, pH displacements, electron paramagenetic resonance (EPR), optical rotatory dispersion (ORD), circular dichroism (CD), Mossbauer spectroscopy etc. have been used in ascertaining the mode of binding and also in achieving greater success in quantitative aspects of metal protein problem besides these techniques the chemical testing of metalloenzyme and aproenzyme for the presence of specific groups has been of great value.

Literature on Metal-protein System

The studies on metal-protein system carried out so far may be divided under the following heads.

1. The evaluation of intrinsic association constants.
2. A comparison of association constants.
3. Experiments performed to show the absence or presence of the phenomenon of chelation.
4. The study of the system involving sluggish equilibria.

Transition metals (d-block element of all the three series) have unique efficacy in catalyzing various industrial reactions and also in living system, the redox reaction and redox changes in the metal ions catalyse valence chanes in the substrate molecule. The transition metal ions are involved in a wide range of catalytic function. The more important metals in biological redox processes are iron, copper, cobalt and molybdenum. Molybdenum is involved with several redox enzymes it is well known for its association with nitrate reduction in the nitrogen cycle. here it is thought that the metal change from oxidation V to oxidation state VI. It is also well known as being essential for nitrogen fixation in root nodules of leguminous plants.

The biological significance of molybdenum is well established (Riohert and Westerfeld, 1654; Berducou and Macha, 1963; Slesareva, 1962; Bray and Meriwether, 1966; Gut Freund and Sturtant, 1959; Handler and Rajgopalan, 1964; Beinert and Palmer, 1965), its interaction with auxine has been studied to suggest its role in xanthine oxidase. (Knowles and Lee, 1968). Similar model studies have been carried out with cystine (Spence and Lee, 1968), glutathione (Haung and Haight, 1971) and lumiflavn-3acetic (Spence, *et. al.* 1967) applying electron paramagnetic methods.

The unique biological role of molybdenum is due to its aspects of peculiar chemistry (Mitchell, 1966). Molybdenum is an element of the second transition series having a $4d^5$ $5s^1$ configuration. In its compounds it shows a range of oxidation states and stereo chemistry. The Biologically important oxidation states of molybdenum are Mo (V) (D^1) and Mo (VI) (d^0) but the lower ones particularly Mo (III) cannot be avoided completely. The preferred co-ordination numbers for Mo (V) and Mo (VI) are five and six and four and six respectively. Mo (V) complexes are usually anionic having oxygen halogen thiocyanate of cyanide as ligands. Mo (III) complexes are also anionic. the tetrahedral oxoanion is well known but in acid solution polymerisation occurs giving a range at polymolybdate ions of some complexity. It is to be expected that in biological system it will be bound though carboxyl and hydroxyl groups. Dennard and Williams (1966) have suggested that it might be possible to replace molybdenum in enzymes by niobium tantalum and tungsten. The first two will not undergo redox reactions but will give a stable complex.

Owing to the presence of molybdenum in several enzyme system attempts were made to determine its actual oxidation state in the specific molybdoenzymes. Some important molybdenum metalloenzymes are listed below (M.N. Hughes, 1972).

S.No.	Enzyme	Source	Mol.wt.	Stoichiometry	
				Metal	Co-enzyme
1.	Xanthane oxidase	Bovine Milk	300,000	8Fe2Mo	2FAD
2.	Xanthane oxidase	ChickenLiver	300,000	8Fe2Mo	2FAD
3.	Aldehyde oxidase	Hogliver	250,000	8Fe2Mo	2FAD
4.	Nitrate reductase	E.coli.		Mo	FAD
5.	Nitrate reductase	E.erass			

In all the above enzymes flavin adenine nucleotide (FAD) is a cofactor. The presence of this particular co-enzyme is a complicating factor in the study of the role of molybdenum as this is largely based on the EPR signals associated with Mo (V) species. The generation of free radical semiquinones and the presence of reduced non-hemetran, will result in a more complex spectra. Several studies of these molybdenum enzymes have been carried out using ERR technique, (R.c. Bray, G. Palmer and H. Beinert, 1964; R.C. Bray and D.C. Watt, 1966; H Beinert and G. Palmer; H. Blinert, 1964; H. Beinerl and G. Palmer, 1965; Ennard and Willams, 1966; P. Handler, Rajgopala and Aleman, 1964). In spite of its several biological and biochemical roles its interaction with proteins has not been investigated employing conventional binding methods. Verma *et. al.*, (1988) first time made a quantitative study on the binding of the molybdate ions with fibrillar and globular protein employing physio-chemical method (Malik and Arora, 1969, a, b) and observed studies that the binding was pH-dependent i.e. the binding sites(n) decreased with increasing pH but the association constant were found to be of the same order hence it was concluded that the reacting groups were of the same type of each pH value (Arora *et. al*, 1989). Arora, *et. al* (1984) have studied the interaction between gelatin molecule and molybdate ions using polarographic and equilibrium-dialysis methods and reported the involvement of cationic groups in the interaction process. Statistical effects seem to be more pronounced at low while electrostatic one at higher molybdate concentration. These workers investigated molybdate interaction with ovalbumin-S and denatured ovalbumin (Arora *et. al.*, 1984). ?H values were found to be – 238.2 and - 233.8 cal./mole for the native and denatured ovalbumin respectively. They have also investigated the effect of protein charge on molybdate binding by studying interaction between bovine serum albumin and molybdate ions and gelatin derivative (Arora *et. al.*, 1984). Recently Nayal and Cora, (1991) and Wilcox (1999), have studied the interaction between bovine serum albumin and molybdate ions employing and equilibrium-dialysis methods.

In the present investigation the author have studied the interaction between molybdate ions and egg albumin employing transmitance and pH measurements in the acid range. The stoichiometry of the combination between molybdate and protonated nitrogen groups of protein was found to be one to one. The pH-dependent binding result have been ascribed to the existence of anionic species of molybdenum (VI). The pH-metric titrations and ultraviolet absorption spectra of molybdenum (VI)-egg albumin mixtures also supported the existence of polymerisation and depolymerisation of molybdenum as well as deprotonation and conformational changes in the protein molecule. The free energy enthalpy and entropy of binding have been determined and the effect of molybdate ion on the heat of ionization and pK interaction of protein groups has been discussed.

It is well known that most metal ions will not specifically bind to transferrin in the absence of a synergistic anion which is concomitantly bound and is probably directly coordinated to the metal in the resulting metal-anion-protein ternary complex in biological systems, the anion is biocarbonate. The inter-locking site model for this ternary complex (Bates and Chlabach, 1973) is now generally accepted. In this model, the anion binds to cationic protein side groups in the immediate vicinity of the metal binding site. the carbonate anion shields the metal ion from the destabilizing positive charges on the protein and also provides one oxygen as a direct ligand to the metal. Arginine is frequently involved in the binding of anionic substrates (Riordan *et. al.* 1977) and indeed, chemical modification studies have shown that there is a one essential arginine residue per metal binding site in ovotransferrin (Pogers *et. al.*, 1978). The protonated amino groups of lysine and the imidazole group of histidine have also been suggested as possible anion binding groups. (Zweier and Aisen, 1977).

Although metal ion, protein and anion are all required for the formation a stable protein complex, the mechanism of formation does not involve a true third-order reaction. Kofima and Bates (1981) have studied the affects of bicarbonate concentration on the kinetics of the binding and oxidation of ferrous ion. Saturation kinetics with respect to the bicarbonate anion were observed and the results were interpreted in terms of the formation of a binary anion-protein intermediate species.

The biological significance of vanadium is well established as it effects the enzymatic activity of enzymes (Barron and Kalintsky, 1947; Takani *et. al.*, 1978; Courtois and Angstopoulour, 1948; Courtois and Anagstopoulour, 1949; Edlbacher and Ballor, 1983). enhances the oxidative power of certain tissue enzymes (Bernhim and Bernhin, 1938) and assists the metabolism of pyridoxal phosphate (Marcitelh, 1959). It reduces the cholesterol level in aorta (Rygh, 1951; Conandoli and citteria, 1959) affects lipid biosynthesis in man (Carron and Robert, 1967) and influences nitrogen fixation by azotobactor along with molybdenum (Horner *et. al*, 1942). Its presence in bean crop (Jormasova and Peterburgshu, 1968) the teeth of several mammals (Duerr, 1969) is also known. Although it is in the form of vanadium (III), forms and intergral part of haemovanadin (Bieling and Cmazplik, 1953), a metalloprotein, acting as oxygen carrier (Hughes, 1992) like iron in heamonglobin and copper in heamocyanin. The reaction of vanadyl ion with amino acids (Theriof *et. al.*, 1969 and Johnson, 1978), enzyme ATP (Waterman *et. al*, 1974), nucleic acid (Spinpes and Gordy, 1964) and with metal sites of a number of proteins (Chasteen *et. al.*, 1973; Fitzgerald and Chasteen, 1974; Dekoch *et. al* 1975; Canon and Chosteen, 1975) have been extensively investigated owing to its use as a probe in different systems. Johnson, (1974) in a study of vanadium toxicity and molybdenum utilization in rats found it as protein bound vanadyl ion. Chasteen *et. al* (1976) investigated vanadyl-serum albumin complexes employing EPR studied Lindquist *et. al.*, (1973) reported the potent inhibition of ribonuclease by complexes that the nucleoside uridine forms with oxovanadium (IV) and (V) ions. the involvement of the imidazole and amino groups of lysine in the enzyme has been suggested in binding with the nucleoside-vanadium complex. Daniel and Hewston, (1942) have shown that vanadium also functions in the normal nutrition of rat tissues and egg yolk in less then 1 to 5 ppm of the metal. Gericke (1940) has confirmed that vanadium supplied as anion to the soil is more useful than as cation in nitrogen fixation. It along with molybdenum also influences the nitrogen fixation by azotobactor.

Arora *et. al.* (1994) have studied the binding of oxovanadium (V) to ovalbumin-S (OAS), denatured ovalbumin (OAD), etc. by equilibrium-dialysis and pH-metric methods. The pH dependence of interaction between vanadium(V) and protein groups has been shown to be electrostatic in nature. The uniformity of association constants (log K) suggested the involvement of identical non-interacting groups in the binding process. The availability of the binding sites (n) has been shown to be dependent on pH and protein conformation. The pH-metric results also supported the pH dependence of oxovanadium (V)-ovalbumin interaction.

Recently, the effect of protein, oxovanadium (V) ion concentration and pH on the ratio of diffusion current $[Id/(Id)_0]$ was studied in vanadium (V) – ovalbumin-S and denatured ovalbumin systems by Arora *et. al.* (1987). In both the cases, marked decrease in diffusion current was observed at the respective pH values, indicating that the binding takes place with cationic groups of the proteins. the binding sites (n) were found to be pH-dependent. The uniformity of log K and G^0 values at all pH values indicated the involvement of same sites in interaction. Further more the linear scatchard plots in both the systems supported the involvement of single class of independent sites in oxovanadium (v) anion interaction. The difference in the binding sites (n) has been attributed to the folded structure of ovalbumin-S while unfolded one of the denatured ovalbumin.

The binding of vanadium (V) ion has also been studied with bovine serum albumin and bovine pancreatic trypsin (BPT) at different pH values and temperatures by the polarographic technique by Arora *et. al.* (1983). The binding data were found to be pH and temperature dependent. The intrinsic association constant (K) and the number of binding sites (n) were calculated from scatchard plots and found to be maximum at low pH and lower temperatures, The values of enthalpy change (C H^0) and entropy change (C S^0) at pH 7.50 have been found to be -2.090 K. cal $mole^{-1}$ and + 6.372 cal $mole^{-1,}$ $degree^{-1,}$ respectively for the vanadium (V) bovine serum albumin system. The free energy change (C G^0) of the combining sites were last at the higher pH and highest at the low pH; therefore, a lower temperature and lower pH offered more sites in the protein molecule for interaction with vanadium (V) ions. Statistical effect scan to be more significant at lower vanadium (V) ion concentrations, while at higher concentrations electrostatic effects and heterogencity of sites are more significant.

The binding of vanadium (V) to bovine serum albumin (BSA), human serum albumin (HAS) and bovine pancreatic tyrosine (BTP) in the absence and presence of urea as been studied at different pH values and temperatures by spectrophotometric and equilibrium-different pH values and temperatures by spectrophotometric and equilibrium-dialysis methods by Arora et.al. (1983). The binding data were found to be pH and temperature dependent. The binding data at pH 5.57, studied by absorbance methods at this pH.The enthaply change at pH 5.57 for vanadium (V)-protein was-368.4 cal $mole^{-1}$ for BSA. -328.8 cal $mole^{-1}$for HAS and -1372 cal $mole^{-1}$for BPT, respectively. the association constants and the number of binding sites were calculated form scatchard plots and found to be maximum at lower pH and at lower temperature. The free energy of the combining sites was lowest at higher pH and highest at low pH. Therefore, a lower temperature and lower pH offered more sites in the protein molecule for interaction with vanadium (V) ions. Statistical effects seem to be more significant at lower vanadium (V) ion concentrations, and electrostatic effects more significant at higher concentrations.

Recently, Keller and Sharma (1985) have reported in vitro and in vivo. The effects of vandate ions on the K-dependent phosphatase activities from subcellular fraction of brain, kidney and liver. Harris *et. al.* (1984) in previous studies have shown that vanadate binds to the phenolic oxygen of metal binding sites of human serum transferrin (Harris, 1985). The binding of phosphate, bicarbonate, sulphate and vanadate to human serum transferrin has been evaluated by two different ultraviolet spectroscopic techniques (1985).

The interaction of mercuric ions of methyl mercury salts with sulphydryl groups of many proteins has been reported (Hughes, 1950; Hughes, 1947 and Edel-roch, 1953). However, Malik *et. al.* (1987) reported the involvement of carboxyl and imidazole groups of casein in interaction with mercuric ions employing potentiometric method. Malik *et. al.* (1977) and Arora *et. al* (1979) have studied its binding with native and modified transfusion gelatin using pH-metric and equilibrium-dialysis methods and showed stronger binding with imidazole than the carboxyl groups. Arora *et. al.* (1984) have also reported the binding of mercuric ions to ovalbumins using physico-chemical methods.

The interaction of the metal ions to transfusion gelatin (TG) has been studied by Malik and Muzajriddin (1963, a, b, and c). They have determined the ionisable groups of TG and evaluated their intrinsic association constants and electrostatic interaction factors. (Salahuddin and Malik, 1963). A similar study with soybean protein gave 18 imidazoles, 46 amines, 42 guanido and 94 carboxyl groups. (Malik and Jindal, 1968) per 10^5 gram of the protein. The binding of Copper, Zinc, magnesium, Manganese and Strontium with case in has been studied pH-metrically Agarwal and Malik. A binding study of TG with Copper, Zinc and Cadmium has shown the involvement of its carboxyl groups in interaction (Malik and Muzajjriddin, 1965). The have also reported the binding of lead and manganese ions with TG (Malik and Jindal 1968).

Malik and Salahuddin (1963) studied the binding of cupric ion with transfusion gelatin employing polarographic method. Malik and Jindal (1968;) studied the interaction between Cu (II) and Cd (II) and ovalbumin with the help of polarographic measurements and found that Copper binds strongly then cadmium. Malik and Arora (1980) investigated the binding of lead and Zinc to ovalbumin by polarographic methods. Arora *et. al* (1979) have studied the interaction between ovalbumin and lead and zinc by pH-metric and equilibrium-dialysis method. The extent of binding (V_m) was calculated by the difference of hydrogen ions dissociated from protein in the presence and absence of metal ions. The values of log K for metal carboxyl systems were found to be 1.84 and 1.94 in case of Pb(II) and Zn(II). The thermodynamic of the binding of Pb(II) and Zn(II) with ovalbumin-S was studied by equilibrium dialysis method and the interaction was found to be pH and temperature dependent (Arora *et. al.* 1986). They have also determined the ionisable groups of ovalbumin-S and denatured ovalbumin employing pH-metric method. (Arora and Singh, 1981). They have also investigated the effect of salts on the isoionic protein and found the order as : MO(VI)>V(V)>Pb(II)>Zn(II) and I>Br>Cl, respectively. They have also studied the interaction of Pb(II) and Zn(II) with ovalbumin-S using polarographic method. (Arora *et. al.* 1983). The evaluation of intrinsic association constants (log K) by scatchard'sequation showed that binding with imidazole groups was stronger than with the carboxyl groups. The log K values for lead-carboxyl and zinc-carboxyl were found to be 1.84 and 1.81 while those of lead – imidaze and zinc-imidazole to be 2.27 and 2.57, respectively. The order of reactivity of metal ion binding to respective groups of ovalbumin-S was found to be Pb(II)>Zn(II). The thermodynamics of Pb(II) and Zn(II) with transfusion gelatin has been reported by equilibrium-dialysis method (Arora and Kumar, 1986). In recent years they have studied the binding of many transition metals to ovalbumin and modified ovalbumin employing Physico – chemical methods (Arora *et. al.* 1985, a, b).

Arora *et. al* (1983) have also studied the interaction of Ni(II) and Co(II) to ovalbumin by Physico-chemical methods. The log K values were found nearly the same by pH- metric and equilibrium dialysis methods. the thermodynamic constants revealed electrostatic bonding between metal ions and carboxyl groups. The cation-carboxyl interaction was also supported by the pH-titrations of these metals with this protein at pH 5.50. The involvement of carboxyl groups in cobalt interaction has also been obtained from spectrophotometric method.

Malik *et. al* (1980) studied the interaction of soybean protein with hydrous oxide solution of iron, aluminum and chromium by pH-metric method. The calculation of binding at different pH-values showed the order : Fe> Al > Cr in acid range, most probably through carboxyl groups whereas in the basic range Cr > Fe > Al, either through amino group or Phenolic groups of tyrosyl residues of the protein. Malik *et. al* (1980) have also applied pH-metric method to study the reaction of salicylic acid with proteins. A comparison of titration of proteins or KOH of the same pH with salicylic acid solution has shown that salicylic acid or initial pH range. The interaction has been shown to take place though the silanol and reactive groups of protein by hydrogen bond formation. The binding in higher pH followed by order,-casein >transfusion gelation > ovalbumin, which in acid pH it was found to be transfusion gelation >-casein>ovalbumin which has been ascribed to structural differences and biological specificity of proteins.

Mailk and Agrawal (1967) have studied binding of Mg(II) and Sr (II) with transfusion getatin (TG). Arora *et. al.* (1985 a and b) Cole *et. al.* (1998) Degtyarenko *et. al.* (1999) Roe and Pang (1999) YiZhang *et. al.* (2000) Harding (2000 and 2001) have studies the binding of these metal ions to different proteins. Arora *et. al.* (1986) have studied the effect of temperature and pH on the binding of Be(II) ions with TG employing pH metric and equilibrium dialysis methods. The binding of vanadium to ovalbumins (1992) has been reported by means of pH-metric and polarographic methods.

Detergent-protein Interaction

The interaction of synthetic detergents to proteins have been studied for several reasons. Putnam (1948) has reviewed the diverse effects of detergents on the structure of proteins. Depending on the nature of protein, association (Johnson and Juberi, 1951) or dissociation (Wolf and Briggs, 1958; Brand and Johnson, 1956; and Lundgren *et. al.*, 1943) Complexation (Putnam and Neurath, 1945; Neurath and Putnam, 1946) Denaturation (Lundgren, 1941; and Putham and neurath, 1944) precipitation (Rulisek and Vondrasek, 1998) etc. may occur. These have also been used to expose groups in proteins normally unavailable to specific reagents (Rathelot *et. al*, 1978). On many cases they are used for isolation of protein (Julien *et. al*, 1978. Vrijsen and Boeye, 1978; and Huppert, and Rebegrote, 1960). SDS has also been used for the extraction of transforming DNA (Israel and Winkle, 1955). Several workers have also shown protein precipitated by anionic detergent does not show any change in its viscosity after its recovery from the detergent protein complex (Sarkar and Dotty, 1966). Among anionic detergents used, the interaction of SDS with proteins, besides including anti-parallel sheet conformation. Morton (1955) has been undertaken mainly due to its two biochemical applications, firstly it solubilizes mitochondrial proteins (Ilsm, *et. al*, 1998) and secondly to gel electrophoresis of SDS-protein complexes for determining molecular weights (Vrijsen and Boeye, 1978; Huppert and Rebegro *et. al.* 1960; and Weber and Osborn, 1969; Edelhockandrew, 1978; Dean, 1989; Dean *et al,* 1990 and 1995; Fiendbeg *et. al.,* 1993; Albert, 1998) investigated the properties of thyroglobulin SDS solutions. Mosoro (1970) and Yin XV (1998) was able to isolate a calcium binding protein, employing the method which involved extracting a membrane fraction prepared from sarcoplasmic reticulum with buffer containing 10 mm SDS and following centrigugation to remove material not solubilized to remove the detergent by dialysis.

As extensive review of interaction of detergents with proteins has been given by Steinhardt and Reynolds (1969). There is also a more recent review on the same subject (Stern Hardt *et. al.* 1969). Theoretical aspects of these interactions have been treated by Tanford (1973). Karushand Sonenberg (1949) first attempted to determine the equilibrium isotherm between BSA and purified alkyl half-esters, 8,10,12 carbon compounds. On the basis of the binding data they estimated the thermodynamic parameters of the binding. yang and Faster (1953) studied the binding of sodium Dodecyl benzene sulphonate with BSA using equilibrium dialysis and electrophoresis methods. Deoker and Foster (1966) have re-examined the interaction of sodium dodecyl sulphate (SDS) with serum albumin. Three electrophoretic components have been distinguished at higher levels of binding at pH 6.50. The complexes have a constant composition throughout the range of their existence. formation of the higher complexes form AD_{11}proceeds with some los of helix content in the protein, as found by ORD measurements. Pollacesch and Briggs (1954) obtained results similar to those of Yang and Foster (1953) in experiments with 1% BSA and purified SDS at 22°C, and u =0.2. Their results led them to conclude that there two sets of groups, one containing 10d groups and the other 80 groups. Reynolds *et.al.* (1967) have determined values of V_m and K, the binding constant for octyl sulphate and dodecyl sulphate. Reynolds, herbert *et. al.* (1973) have given values for numerous other highly purified normal alkyl sulphates and sulphonatesand BSA. In these two studies, and attempt has been made to resolve the components of the binding energy by comparing the anion with one another and with the unchanged homologous. They have also noticed that only two of many unbranchedalophaticsulphates and sulfonates, namely, dodecyl sulphatte and tetradecyl sulphate, unfold serum albumin when amounts larger then 10 equivalents are bound. Subsequent work as shown that a 14-carbon sulphanate as well as a dodecylsulphate, at much higher concentrations then those used by Reynolds *et. al* (1967) also unfolds. Goodman (1958) examined the interaction of human serum albumin with six long chain fatty acid anions by the method of partition analysis in which varying amounts of each fatty acid were equilibrated between N-heptane and an aqueous solution of albumin in phosphate buffer with pH 7.45 and u=0.16 at 23°C. The data were analysed in terms of three classes of binding sites, 2,5 and 20 respectively. The values of binding constants wee also determined.

Reynolds *et. al* (1968) studied in detail the binding of three aliphatic long-chain carboxylates and a long chain alchohol to BSA. None of these ligands caused disruption of protein structure, such as is observed in case of alkhylsulphates. It has been concluded that the binding sites of carboxylates and sulphates / sulfonates are different. Spector *et. al.* (1971) also studied the binding of long chain fatty acids to BSA. The data have been analysed in terms of a model consisting of many classes of binding sites. The binding is assumed to proceed in a series of step-wise equilibrium reactions. The first binding constant, K_1 involving one site is considerably large than the other binding constants. With the help of detergent binding studies. Steinhardt *et. al.* (1971 and 1972) have disclosed the differences between BSA and HAS. Hill and Briggs (168) studied the binding of N-octyl benzene Sulfonate, which is more soluble then Dodecyl benzene sulfonate to B-lactoglobulin. They found it to behave similarly to SDS. At low detergent concentrations the protein molecule interacts with 2 or 3 molecules of detergents and than undergoes a change resulting in an increased ability of binding the detergent. Simultaneously, a third type of binding appears to take place that is "Micellar in nature" involving interaction between the molecules already bound to the protein and those in solution. The micellar binding is reversible and has a limit at CMC.

Edelhoch and Lippoldt (1960) observed that the interaction with SDS at low concentrations led to dissociation of thyroglobulin into two subunits without much change in shape. Jirgensons (1961 and 1962) has investigated the effect of several anionic detergents on the conformation of non-helical proteins. He has shown that the interaction with detergent results in a partial transition of the – helical folding. The change in the UV cotton effect of a group of proteins produced by treating the proteins with decyl and dodecyl sulphatesand acid were studied by Jirgensons (1962). The proteins having a high – helical content became slightly disorganized. The proteins that are largely disordered acquired a partial organised structure. Lee and Jirgensons (1971) studied the effect of alkyl sulphates of various chain length on the properties of certain proteins. They have observed that non-helical polypeptide chains were partly ordered. These conformational change were dependent on the lenght of hydrophobic tail. In acid solution, anionic detergents appeared not only to promote – helical formation, but also reduced the amount of unordered structure. The sequence of effectiveness of individual compounds is tetradecyl dodecyl, decyl, and octyl sulphate which indicates the importance of hydrophobic interactions.

Jirgensons (1973) using circular dichroism studies indicated an increase of helix contant by octyl, and dodecyl sulphates. Visser and Blout (1971) also observed that treatment of elastase, trypsin, chymotrypsin and pepsin with SDS caused a substantial change in their CD spectra, attributable to an apparent increase of – helix in their conformations. Darmall and Barela (1971) found that rabbit muscle glyceraldehyde-3phosphate dehydrogenase is denatured by SDS. It also undergoes dissociation into four sub-units. This results in the alteration of the CD spectrum from one that is typically of ???type spectrum to one characteristic of –helix.

Oakes (1973) studied the interaction between BSA and SDS using NMR and ESR techniques. Muller and Moad (1973) have studied the binding isotherms of the interaction of flourinated alkyl sulphates with BSA. They have disclosed initial interaction to be electrostatic while higher detergent caused denaturation. Verma *et. al* (1989) first performed a systematic comparative study of SDS binding to a number of proteins by equilibrium dialysis. They found that most of the proteins examined bound 90 to 100 percent of their weights of SDS. The glycoproteins bound 70 to 90 percent of their weight of SDS, considering only the polypeptide moiety of the molecule. Proteins not containing disulfide bonds bound about 140 percent of their weight and the same amount was found after reduction of four proteins (ovomucid, ovalbumin, lactoglobulin and ribonuclease) containing disulfide bonds.

Greenwell *et. al.* (1971) have studied the interaction of detergents with proteins employing sedimentation method. nelson (1971) has determined the maximum amount of SDS bound to a number of proteins at high SDS concentrations. The amount bound vary between 1.1 gm and 2.2 gm at SDS per gm of protein. The charge of the protein is also important since it causes a variation in amount bound by 20 to 50 percent. Allen (1974) investigated the extent at binding of SDS to BSA at high binding ratios by gel filtration and found that weight ratio of SDS bound to BSA increases with NaCI concentrations.

Wright *et. al* (1975) applied the method of transient-electric birefringencesto study the conformation of SDS-protein complexes. The model they proposed for the complex was a deformable prolate ellipsoid. Rowe and steinhardt (1976) also confirmed the findings of Wright *et. al.* (1975) using the same method. Mattice *et. al.* (1976) determined the CD spectra of several protein in the presence of SDS and dithiothreitol. All of the spectra have a shape anticipated for a mixture of random coil and helix, whereas the ellipticities differ markedly. They have emphasized the interaction of SDS with cationic amino acid residues of the protein. To elucidate the mode of interaction between SDS with special reference to SDS – polyacrylamide gel electrophoresis. Takagi *et. al.* (1975) have re-examined the binding of SDS to various reduced protein polypeptide by the equilibrium dialysis method. Each of the binding isotherm displace the occurrence of two phases, an initial gradual increase in the amount of binding to 0.3 to 0.6 g/g and subsequent steep increase up to 1.2 to 1.5 g/g of protein.

Oakes (1974) has made a systematic study of the interactions between BSA and SDS at pH 5.6 NMR spectroscopy. The binding isotherms has been also determined under the same conditions. In contrast to previous studies (Birdi and Stein Hardt, 1975) where the SDS. NMR spectrum was average of those for "Free" and 'Bound' molecules, in this study information has been obtained about the state of physically bound SDS in each of the binding isotherms. he has found that the SDS head groups and alkyl chains are associated with the protein at the initial 10 binding sides. At higher binding number the environment continuously changes united V_m about 50. At still higher value of V_m, all of SDS molecules have an methylene chemical shift equal to and an alkyl chain and head group mobility similar to those in simple SDS micelles. Interesting results have been obtained by studying the solubilization for water insoluble dye, dimethyl amino azobenzene by protein-SDS complexes (Steinhardt *et. al.*, 1974). Early study has shown that such complexes solubilize DMAB similarly as do micelles of the same detergent in the absence of protein (Steinhardt, 1967). This occurs at the SDS concentration far below the CMC with BSA, HAS and OA it is possible to show that the amount of DMAB dispersed is proportional to the amount of DMAB bound to the protein. Grourke and Gibbs (1967) investigated the interaction of SDS to poly-L-lysine in neutral solution and reported the coil-to-Binding- transition in the synthetic polypeptide. On the other hadn, SDS induced coil-to-helix transition in case of poly-L-ornithine. The only difference between the two polypeptides is that there is one methylene group less in ornithine than in lysine. Satake and Yang (1973) studied by means of CD the effect of N-alkyl- sulphates with 8 to 16 methylene groups on the coil-to binding-transition of poly-L-lysine. In sodium octyl sulphate solution the polypeptide is in a partly helical conformation, whereas in solution of decyl and higher alkyl sulphates it assumes the - form. Feldshtein and Zenin (1972) and Zenin, Feldshtein (1973) also studied the interaction of poly-L-lysine with SDS in aqueous solutions by means of CD and ORD at various pH values and by potentiometric titration at 20°C. They observed a reversible-to-helix transition at pH 11.6 to 11.9, which they explain in terms of destruction of the electrostatic polypepeptide-SDS complexes. Satake and Yang (1976) determined the binding isotherms of SDS complexes to poly-L_lysine, poly –L-ornithine and poly-D, L-ornithine at neutral pH potentiometrically. In all three cases, the binding was highly co-operative which suggests micelle like clustering of the detergent anions on to the polypeptide side groups.

There is a strong hydrophobic interaction between the non-polar groups of detergent molecules, where as the electrostatic that it is decisive for binding.

Jones *et. al.* (1973) established by UV difference spectroscopy that SDS unfolds an ribonuclease while cationic detergent do not.Tipping Jones *et.al.* (1974) have calculated the enthalpy of SDS binding to BSA., OA and ribonuclease by macrocalorimetry over the temperature range 18.5 to 32°C. The amount of SDS to the proteins at pH 7.0 or 7.3 determined by equilibrium dialysis, and changes in protein conformation were followed by viscometry. Jones, Skinner *et. al.* (1975) noticed that potassium n-decyl phosphate binds, exothermically to BSA at pH 7.0 with the formation of a specific complex containing about 60 phosphate anions. Studies of the binding of anionic, deoxycholate and a non-ionic, Trition X-100 detergent to BSA by equilibrium dialysis revealed that there were four main sites fo reach ligand 14 weaker sites for deoxycholate (Makino *et. al.* 1973). Co-operative binding of large amounts of ligand with accompanying unfolding does not take place with these two detergents. This is probably due to the fact that these two detergents have a relatively low CMC, and a monomeric concentration sufficient for the cooperative mode of binding cannot be attained.

Peterson and Strohman (1970) have found by using SDS polyacrylamide gel electrophoresis that myosin isolated from chicken or rabbit muscle extracted at low pH and high ionic strength in the absence of Mg^2 ions contains only two low molecular weight components. Several other workers such as Weeds and Lowey (1971), Lowey and Risby, 1971, Hayashi, 1972 Mani and Kay, 1972, Yazaki and Mochinaga, 1973 and Gilbert 1995, Mathew 1995, EvehinJabri 1995, Chakrabrati (1997), Degyarenko (1997) Yizhang *et. al.* 2000, Harding (2001) have made systematic studies on the myosin from different sources using SDS-polyacrylamide gel electrophoresis. Examination of the various data reveals that in some instances an agreement on the number and size of light chains in particular type of myosin does not exist. However, the differences undoubtedly reflect in part different producers used for sample preparation so that different products have been obtained and identical results cannot be expected.

Norde and Lyklema (1978) studies the adsorption of human serum albumin and bovine pancreas ribonuclease at negatively charged polystyrene surface by H^+ ion titration curves and suggested hydrophobic interaction between protein and polystyrene particles, resulting in partial unfolding of the part of the molecule attached to particle surface. However, the part of the molecule oriented to the solution remains in its native conformation since it has preserved immunological activity against specific antibodies. Fishman and Eirich (1975) investigated the interaction of aqueous poly-n-vinyl-pyrrolidone with SDS and correlated the equilibrium dialysis data with conductometric and viscometric results. Arora *et. al.* (1986) investigated flow properties of casein-SDS mixtures and observed structural change in its molecule with rising concetrations of SDS. They have shown that increase in intrinsic viscosity and hydrodynamic radius is due to rapid protein unfolding while at lower pH, the results are explained in terms of solvation and desolvationprocessess.

Arora *et. al.* (1984) have studied the gelation of modified ovalbumin employing viscometric method. The geletion of ovalbumin as modified by formaldehyde was studied in the presence of additives by employing a viscometric method. The gelation time of modified OA was found to be highly dependent on the concentration of all the components in the gelationmixture. All the gel forming mixtures exhibited thixotropic nature. The transformation of modified protein by sodium metasilicate has been shown to be two stage process. The order of reactivity of water structure breaking compound was found to be urea acetamideformamide, while those for electrolytes as K^{+}>, NA^{+}>, $Li^{+}$and CNS^{+}>, NO_3> C1.

Chatterjee *et. al.* (1979) studied the binding of SDS, Trition X-100 short chain fatty acids to DNA from equilibrium dialysis experiments. Binding ratio for anionic ligand SDS to DNA is observed to be negligibly small irrespective of the ligand concentration below CMC and the ionic strength of the medium. At 30°C the isotherms for binding neutral surfactant and fatty acids to DNA exhibit signs of co-operative interactions. Chatterjee and Chatterjee (1979) have also studied the thermal transition of DNA in the presence of long chain amines and concluded that a higher value of $V_{M'}$ the hydrocarbon groups of the bound ligand molecules, close to each other, begin to exhibit interaction lateral interaction as a result of the hydrophobic effect.

The interaction between triethanol amine lauryl sulphate (TEALS), an anionic tenside and three types of proteins, viz. Bovine serum, albumin, gelatin and casein was examined using equilibrium dialysis and viscosity measurements (Arora *et. al.*, 1985). The binding constants, viz association constants (log K) and number of binding sites (n), were determined in the lower limits of tenside concentration up to which statistical binding occurs. These were found to be 3.55, 3.35 and 3.25 and 19, 31, 40 at pH 5.57 at 25°C for BSA, G and C, respectively. The free energy changes were found to be -4.87 and -4.65 and -4.44 K cal./mole of the respective proteins. At higher tenside concentrations, a co-operative binding has been suggested due to the exposure of the masked groups of the proteins. Viscosity measurements have shown that C and G at lower TEALS concentration behaves like BSA at higher TEALS concentrations. Arora and Malik (1985) have reported the binding of anionic detergents by soluble ovalbumin with the help of viscometric method. Detergent with long hydrocarbon tail was found more effective than that with small tail.

Arora *et. al.* (1984) have reported the binding of catechin to native and modified bovine serum albumin using physico-chemical methods (Arora *et. al.* 1988, and 1989). They have also reported the binding of Ca(II) and Cd(II) to OA by pH and dialysis methods (Verma *et. al.* 1989). Arora *et. al.* (1991) have reported the interaction between TEALS and gelation by viscometric methods. Intrinsic viscosity(n) was used to explain the changes produced due to opening of gelatin molecule in the presence of TEALS. The higher viscosity in the presence of SLS than TEALS suggested the greater effect of the former. The interaction of surfactant anions with gelatin has shown to invole two modes of linkages, namely salt link and hydrophobic. The effect of OA and OAS on the CMC of ionic and non-ionic surfactants was studied by means of conductance measurements. The increase in conductance of detergent – protein mixtures was attributed to the change in the nature of solvent as the protein formed mixed micelles with the surfactants by the incorporation of the paraffin part of protein in the micelle (Arora *et. al.* 1992).

The interaction between TEALS and BSA and OA was examined viscometrically by Arora and Balyan (1992). Intrinsic viscosity values were used to explain the change produced as being due to unfolding of the protein molecule in the presence of the detergent. BSA was found to be more reactive then OA. Arora *et. al* (1992) have also studied the interaction between SDS and transfusion gelation (TG) by means of physico-chemical methods. The linkage was found to increase with decreasing pH of the reaction mixtures. the transmittance and viscosity results proved the existence of a complex of constant composition throughout the entrie pH range. The pH displacement measurements suggested the involvement of ionic linkage while equilibrium dialysis proved the ionic, hydrophobic and micellar nature of surfactant protein linking. The temperature dependent intrinsic viscosity values favoured either helix-coil transition or the increase in chains flexibility.

Arora *et. al* (1993) have also studied the effect of temperature, ionic strength, pH and protein charge in a TEALS-BSA system. The binding constants werre determined by equilibrium dialysis in the lower limits of surfactant concentrations up to which statistical linkage occurs, while the structural change were observed by flow mesurements. The results indicated electrostatic, micellar and co-operative types of linking. The linkage constants and isotherms for BSA and its derivatives in the statistical zone shows the linkage order as EBSA>FBSA>ABSA. This sequence showed that the bigger the positive charge on the protein, the greater will be its linking capacity. However, in the higher linkage region, the linkage character remained independent on protein charge, showing that hydrophobic linkage is more prominent on surfactant-protein systems.

It was thought of interest to sutdy the interaction between anionic surfactants and albumin molecule. Although several binding studies have been made between surfactants and proteins (FraenkalConrat 1949, Fraenkal *et. al.* 1947, Chatterjee 1979) but not work has been done on the binding of surfactants with albumin proteins. In the present investigation the binding of Triethanalamine lauryl sulphate (TEALS) to albumin is discussed in order to explain the nature of binding and the structural implications induced within the molecule. The chapter describes the thermodynamics of interaction using dialysis equibrium method. The importance protein charge, ionic effect, pH and protein concentration on binding, behavior has been discussed critically.

At the biochemical level, mercury and copper exert their toxicity by linking the essential e.g. to sulphydryl (SH) groups at the active sites of some enzymes. The biochemical and other importance of mercury and copper ions are well established (Taylor and Smith, 1950; Kolthoff and Lingane, 1952; Wieser 1942; Tanford, 1951 and 1952 Malik and Jindal, 1968; Malik and Arora, 1969; and Malik and Arora, 1968). The linkage of Cadmium to metalothion like proteins seems to be the reason for its long biological half life (Arora and Jadon, 1980; Arora *et. al.* 1983). In order to extend our existing knowledge of the metal ion binding sites in biological systems, their linking with model organic compounds is of great interest. After having established about their relative binding capacity with simple organic ligands, investigations are extended towards the study of biopolymers. Many workers have exensively investigated the linking of Cadmium and Zinc ions with Carboxyl and imidazole groups of many proteins and a few papers have appeared describing the binding of these ions to ovalbumin (Arora and Singh, 1981; Barry *et. al.* 1972; Chakrabarti; *et. al.*, 1981, Annm and Wilcox, 1989; Jon Kull, 1990; Vallie and Aurd, 1990; Dearfierd, 1991; Vallie and Auld, 1992; Shangk *et. al.* 1993; Gilbert, 1995; Dean, *et. al.* 1995; David Eidi, 1996; Nayal and Cera, 1996; Degtyarenko, 1997; Yin Xv, 1998; Dean, 1999; Yizhang *et. al.* 2000; Harding, 2001).

In the present investigation the binding of mercury and copper ions with albumin has been studied by polarographic and metric method. It is because the polarographic method has got numerous advantages over the conventional equilibrium dialysis method which entails errors due to the Donnaneffect and adsorption of ions on the dialysis membrane. Further more, this method can be most conveniently used in the higher as well as in the extremely low concentrations of the metal ions. Owing to these facts, Tanford (1951) for the first time applied this method for the investigation of metal-protein interactions. The main conclusions of his studies are:

1. For a given metal and protein concentration, the diffusion current ratio $[Id/Id_0]$should increase with increase in pH and attain a limiting value.

2. the diffusion current ratio at a fixed metal Ion concentration and the diffusion current ratio should decreased with decreasing concentration of metal ions.

Taking these facts into consideration, investigator have applied polarographic method to metal ion-albumin system. The results are also strengthened by pH measurements on protein sand metal protein mixtures. The binding capacity of mercury and copper ions to albumin have been compared on the basis of their periodic properties. The binding results are discussed in terms of the complexity of molecular organization of macromolecule of albumin (Arora and Singh 1981).

The energetic of binding between copper and albumin is reported using transmittance and pH measurements. However its literature survey revealed that no such studies between copper and albumin have been made so far using physico-chemical methods. In this investigation the energetic of binding between copper and albumin is reported using transaminase and pH measurements. The thermodynamic of the combination and structural implication for the albumin are critically discussed. The aim of the present investigation is to show that the pH metric method is of more general application than the other methods so far used in studying metal-protein interactions. This method not only provides a means of determing, the extent of binding, but also through light on the mechanism of interaction. Several workers have investigated the biochemical and biological significance of heavy metals (Bragdon and Havel, 1954; a, b, Rosoff and spencer 1964, Corner 1948, Michaels and Miekha 1961, 65 Mathews 1965, Goldsawar and Putman 1954, Monod *et. al.* 1963, Herang *et. al*, 1964, Olins *et. al.*, 1967, Liquori *et. al.* 1967, Leong and Felsen Feld 1966, Hummel and Witzel 1966, Lindskag 1966 and Coleman 1967; Chakrabarti 1990 a, b, anc, Vallie and Aurd 1990, Yamoshita *et. al.*, 1990, Cain *et. al.* 1990, Dearfierd *et. al.* 199, Fiendbeg *et. al.* 1993; Vallie and Aurd 1992; Shangkiwang *et. al.* 1994, Chakrabarti 1994, Gilbert 1995; David Eidi 1996, HarnietKruszyna *et. al.* 1998, Alber *et. al.* 1998; Hornischar and Blocker 1996, Karclin and Zhu 1996, Nayal and Cera 1990, Chakras Tipal 1997; Cde *et. al.* 1998, Goto *et. al.* 1998, Ruclisck and Vondrasck 1998; Degtyarenko *et. al.* 1999; Kleywegt 1999; Degtrygrenko 2000; Harding 2000; Yizhang *et. al.* 2000; Harding 2001, Benjamin *et. al.* 2001 yizhang and Wilcox 2001).

Polarographic maxima in the reduction wave of reducible species, protein about a marked decrease in the diffusion current. This decrease in diffusion current has been attributed to a number of physical factors (Zuman 1954, Tanford 1952, Weismen 1947, Kolthoff and Lingane 1952) but the most important cause of this decrease in diffusion current has been found in complex formation between the reducible species and the protein (Zuman 1954 and Tanford 1952) provided the studies are carried out in higher pH range so that the possibility of adsorption on mercury drop is also ruled out. Tanfer (1951 and 1952) and Epstein (1954) studied cadmium serum albumin reaction and the reaction of many other metals with protein. Rao and Lal (1954) investigated the complex formation of bovine serum albumin with copper and cadmium. Malik and Arora (1969) sutided the interaction of large number of metal ions with globular and fibrillar types of protein. Saroff and Mark (1953) investigated the Zinc and mercury complex of serum albumin while Lampanjee (1964) has reprted the binding of Cadmium ions and the thallous ions to pepsin in aqueous unbuffered medium. Lampanjee (1966), Heyrovskey (1929), Wills (1946) Pecok and Ligane (1950) Ababackar and Malik (1959); Holleck and Exner (1952) and Cambel (1954) was observed that the palarography has been used in the area of medical science as in biochemistry, immunological and enzymatic reaction.

According to LiandDoody (1954), Keefer (1946), Malik and Khan (1960) and Khan and Malik (1959), the polarographic method is best way of study on metal complexes of simple organic ligands, amino acid and peptides. Strick and Kolthoff (1949) evaluate the molecular weight of protein by this method and Li and Doody (1954) used to this method in the estimation of sulphydryl in many protein.

Scatchard (1946), Klotz and Urquahart (1948) Bleek (1949) and Steinhardt (1941) studied on anions binding have been carried out by other methods. In a few cases of anion binding where other electronic methods fail the polarographic method give the desired information. Filipovic *et. al.* (1954) made systematic polarographic studies on the binding of vanadate ion. Curren and Rober (1967), Jormasova and Peterburgshu (1968), Duerr (1969), have investigated the interaction of serum albumin and bovine pancreatic trypsin with vanadium. However the literature survey revealed that no interaction of mercury ion to egg albumin has been done so far. This part of research the results of polarographic study on the binding of mercury with albumin are reported.

The biochemical functions of Mo(v) i.e. enzymes in metabolism of xanthine sulphites, sulphureaminoacid and Hg i.e. lipid metabolism regulation of cholesterol, ATP-ase etc. are well established. Since they can form complexes with all functional groups which are present in nucleic acids, therefore was thought of interest to study their interaction with RNA employing physico-chemical methods. The present work reports the result of the polarographic study on the binding of Mo and Mercury to ribonucleic acid. The result of polarographic methods are also supported by spectrophotometric and pH metric result. Kruger and Yoshimura, (1970), Adamson, (1971), Mayer and Kruger (1970), Cavalieri and Angelos, (1950), Weissman, *et. al* (1952), Gupta, *et. al.* (1979), Muller and Carother, (1968), Behr, *et. al.* (1969), Fuwa *et. al.* (1960), Cohen and Hughes, (1962), Eisinger, *et. al.* (1966) and Rabinowitz, (1966) studied on the interactions of dye and heavy metal with protein ribonucleic acid in order to understand the molecular mechanism of their action in vivo. Eichhoran (1966) had shown that reaction with phosphate groups stabilizer order structure. Shack *et. al.* (1953), Thomas (1954) and Gold Berg and Friedman (1971) observed the reaction with bases detabilizes order structures.

A literature survey revealed that interaction of Mo (vi) and mercury with ribonucleic acid (RNA) are taking however, such interactions with protein have been extensively investigated (Arora *et. al.* (1987), Malik and Arora (1970) and Malik *et. al.* (1969). There are various techniques available for determining the structural organization but the viscometric method is superior due to simplicity. Morawetz, (1975) has been reviewed the extensive treatmetn of the polymers. Several notable workers have studied the diverse effects of surfactants on proteins using to this method (Holcomb and Van-Hold 1962, Bigelow, 1964, Jirgensons, 1952; Lapanje, 1969; Lovrein, 1963; Edelhoch, 1960 Tipping *et. al.* 1974)

However, a literature survey revealed that no such work has been done so far on the interaction of anionic surfactant like detergent and dye with protein (albunin). With a view to extend the existicknowledge of ecological nature of detergent-protein system, it was thoughts of interest to investigate of properties of TEALS-gulten mixture. The present chapter of the thesis reports the results of TEALS-albumin mixtures. The effect of pH and temperature on the flow behavior is discussed. A tentative mechanism of combination and unfolding is postulated.

The survey of the existing literature revealed that the binding of Molybdenum, Vanadium, Zinc, Cadmium, Copper, Nickel and Cobalt is lacking to egg albumin, similarly, no binding studies of molybdenum copper and mercury are made with nucleic acid and those of anionic surfactants with albumin. Investigations on the aspects of these binding problems were planned and their binding constant have been determined using suitable physico-chemical methods.

EXPERIMENTAL

pH Measurement

These were carried out with a digital Systronics pH meter using a wide range glass electrode. The instrument was calibrated against 0.05M potassium hydrogen phthalate (pH 4.0) and 0.05M sodium borate (pH 9.20) for acidic and alkaline ranges, respectively.

Diffusion Current Measurements

These measurements were carried out on a Toshniwalpolarograph Model Cl 02A in conjunction with an Osaw galvanometer in the external circuit. An H-shaped polarographic cell as recommended by Tanford was used. Nitrogen, purified by passing through a solution of chromous chloride and alkaline pyrogallol, was passed through the solution for producing an inert atmosphere. Triply distilled mercury was used for the D.M.E. The cell was immersed in water thermostat maintained at 25±0.1°C. The capillary used had a flow rate of about 2.2 mg/s with a drop time of 3.5 s. Since the capillary characteristics *(m, t)* have a marked effect on diffusion current (which is directly proportional to ($m^{2/3}$, $t^{1/6}$), *these* factors were therefore controlled carefully throughout these experiments.

RESULTS AND DISCUSSION

The binding of anionic surfactant to albumin have been observed that in each case of the mode of combination of the triethanolamine lauryl sulphate (TEALS) ions to albumin change in three distinct patterns of the free concentrations of surfactant is progressively raised. The patterns of linking have been roughly demarcated by dividing the logarithmic plots in to three areas A, B and C to understand the mechanism of TEALS albumin combination at different stages. In going from acetylated albumin, formylated albumin to estrified albumin the region 'A' goes on lengthening in area followed by vanishing the vertical shape. In a similar manner, the logarithmic plots incase of albumin at varying temperature indicated a nature lake those of protein derivatives i.e. resin 'A' increasing B decreasing and 'C' assuming vertical identify with raising temperature. The variation in the pattern of the length of different zones is indicative of the elimination of some intermediates is surfactant albumin interaction thus the effect of temperature on binding isotherms appears to follow the same course so the protein charge. Further the relative position and highly vertical shape of the isotherms in case of higher temperature and estrified protein indicates some structural changes in surfactant and protein or both proportion of albumin to surfactant. The plot or *Y* Vs log free surfactant concentration followed a liner course. The linearity of plots is in favour of more or less statistical distribution as the surfactant on the entire available albumin molecule in this region. The binding data in the statistical regin were determined by the application of scatchard equation in the form.

$$Y/D_F = K_n - K_r$$

Y and D_F have their usual meaning and K is the average apparent association constant for binding at each site and n is the average maximal number of binding sites on macromolecule with the same association constant K. The effect of temperature is highly interesting as is evident from the values of n and K. The hyperbolic character of plots increases with rising temperature. The linearity of region 'A' continuous to increase, region 'B' decreasing and the nature of region 'C' becoming more and more vertical in relation to Y/D_F axis. The elevated temperature thus vanishes the transition state of unfolding in region 'B' and causes its rapid unfolding as shown by the plots in region 'C'. The increasing values of binding sites(n) in the statistical region and increasing values of surfactant moles bound per mole of albumin (Y) in region 'C' suggest that conformational variations in the albumin molecule exposed more and more positive and apolar groups for linkage with the TEALS ions.

The intrinsic constant (log K) at all the reaction temperature appears to be almost the same. This is indicative for a single type of sites reacting with the TEALS molecule in the statistical zone. The occurrence of different number of sites (n) is therefore not responsible for enhanced linkage, which is probably due to the increased availability of the same type of sites. The increasing value of n as the temperature rises at pH 7.40 is indicative of this. The thermodynamic constant viz. free energy (DG^0) enthalpy (DH^0) and entropy (DS^0) also revealed the uniformity of log K and the involvement of single type of site in TEALS – Albumin combination. The free linkage energy is mostly due to changes in entropy, the apparent enthalpy contribution being small and some times close to zero. The entropy changes are in the range of 7.8 to 1.9 cal/mole with in which the entropy values of the TEALS albumin reaction lies.

From the data as unmodified and modified proteins, one can see the different in ionic and hydrophobic linkage of the straight line region (A) decrease from EA, A, FA and AA as well as the following sequence EA>A>FA>AA. This indicates that the larger the positive charge, the greater is the surfactant linkage. The higher linkage with EA is due to the fact that there is no electrostatic repulsion between surfactant anions and the protein because extension protected the carboxyl groups so that the negative charge which effected surfactant linkage line region. On the other hand formylation extracts albumino positive charge, there by resulting in a decreased surfactant linkage. However in the higher linkage in all cases the nature of linkage remained unaffected hence these linking parameters show that hydrophobic linkage is much more significant in surfactant-protein linking.

The pH titration of 0.05 percent albumin in absence and presence of 2.0×10^{-3} m Hg^{++} and Cu^{++} ions have also been observed. The titration curve of albumin alone lies above the similar curve of mercury-albumin page No. 124 type start mixtures through out the whole pH range. The decrease in pH by the addition of albumin to mercury ion solution indicates that hydrogen are displaced by mercury ions from reactive sites of albumin. This shift of titration curve towards more acidic side of the functional groups in indicative of interaction between mercury ions and the albumin. The pH titiration of copper is analogous with mercury curve. The pH displacements are larger in copper-albumin than in mercury-albumin.

The polarographic measurements on mercury-albumin system revealed that the presence of increasing amounts of albumin decreased the diffusion current of mercury ions. Assuming that the decreases in diffusion current in of metal ion is solely due to complex formation between metal and protein. The mercury and copper ions also give a reversible polarogram. The strength of respective linkage may be compared by a knowledge of formation constant and thermodynamic parameters. The formation constant (log K) for mercury-albumin was computed from classical scatchard's equation. These were found out to be 1.16, 2.69 and 3.38 for mercury-carboxyl, mercury-imidazol and mercury-amino linkage respectively the free energy change for the different linkage were found to be 1.619, 3.755 and 4.718 K cal/mole respectively. The comparison of log K and free energy values of different linkage justified a stronger combination with amino groups and weakest for carboxyl groups.

The addition of albumin to mercury ions solution caused a decrease in its current height, which continuously decreased with increasing concentration of protein and finally become more or less constant. This decrease in the current height could not be due to viscosity changes and absorption on the mercury drops since the studies were made in higher pH range. The result of mercury-albumin system may be explained as the similar date of copper-albumin.

The diffusion current of 0.833 molar buffered copper sulphate solution was depressed by the addition of 0.5 percent albumin. This depression was continuous by increasing the albumin concentration and it ultimately becomes constant at extremely higher concentration of albumin in a similar way. When 0.1 percent albumin was added to varying amounts of copper solution the diffusion current was depressed in proportions of the copper ions solution. The linking result can be calculated by taking diffusion current ratio of metal alone and when albumin is present in the mixtures.

For the study of pH displacement from ligand by the added metal cations albumin (A) alone and in the presence of 2.0 × 10.3 M. cobalt chloride, nickel chloride and manganese chloride was titrated against 0.10M. hydrochloric acid and 0.10 M. potassium hydroxide, respectively. Nickel and Manganese did not show any binding with the carboxyl groups from the nature of titration curves. It is because the drifts of titration curves above protein are indicative of the adsorption of hydrogen ions. It appears that these metal ions formed insoluble complexes with albumin in lower pH range and the precipitate adsorbs the added hydrogen ions. However in alkaline range both nickel and manganese displaced protons from immidazole and ammonium groups of albumin. This cobalt-manganese and nickel ions get co-ordinate with nitrogen atoms it histidyl and lysyl amino acid residues as protein.

The absorption spectra of nickel and manganese show maxima at 675 and 775 nm respectively. The presence of 0.15 to 0.08 percent albumin does not alter the position of maxima but the absorbance of nickel-albumin mixture is increased. this increased in absence by the addition of albumin is an indication of interaction between Ni (II) and reactive groups on albumin molecule. However the addition of 0.75 to 1.5 percent albumin at pH 5.0 caused a shift in maxima i.e. it change from 675 to 600. Such a characteristic shift is due to the chelation of nickel ions with carboxyl groups as protein. The increase in the absorbance by the addition of allbumin provides enough qualitative evidence for the linking of cobalt ions by the protein. The addition of gradually increasing amounts of the protein brings about a much marked increase in absorbance so that in the presence of 1.8 percent albumin the absorbance increases from 0.012 to 0.024. The fact was further supported by the results on mixtures having fixed amount of albumin and cobalt chloride at different pH values when the absorbance was found increasing order since in the pH range 3.25 to 5.30 the carboxylic groups lose their protons hence due to rising pH more carboxylic groups lose their protons hence due to rising pH more carboxyls become ionised for linking with the cobalt ions.

The metal oxide colloidal micelles are positively charged and there fore combination with anionic albumin may be affected either by means of mutual adsorption or through purely chemical forces where the metal ions forms the inner pant of the obuble layer make themselves available for reaction with the reactive sites of the albumin molecule. The titration curves of albumin metal oxide solution lie above the corresponding curves of solution and KOH in all the cases binding occurred above pH 10.50 where all the carboxyls and phenolic groups are anionic while the imidazole and amino groups are fully deprotonated. The extent with which solution alkali or electrolyte. May be assumed as a qualitative meoruse of the extent of metal albumin linking. In general the complexes are formed through chelation to carboxyls and co-ordination with nitrogen of imidazole and amino groups of albumin.

The viscosity data on the binding also favoured interaction of anionic albumin with metal oxide solution. The progressive addition of metal oxide solution to fixed amount of albumin caused regularly increased viscosity providing valuable informations about the mutual interaction of hydrophobic and hydrophilic solution. From viscosity solution concentration curves. it is evident that a sharp inflexion occurred in each curve which represented a new slate of aggregation in the collodial system it might be concluded that it was due to information of oxide solution protein curves may be due to the formation of absolutely, positive charge complexes.

In case of pH metry, no binding of nickel ions is indicated with carboxyl groups while spectrophotometry showed the linking of nickel ions with carboxylate residues of albumin. The pH metric as well as viscometric data provided sufficient evidence about the linking of cobalt, nickel and manganese ions with the nitrogen groups of albumin. From the nature and height of curves in the three cases it may be concluded that nickel ions bound strongly while the cobalt ions bound weakly 10.0 ml. 0.3 percent albumin solution of different pH as the protein. The pH values of the above mixtures were recorded immediately after mixing and after 24 hours. These measurement at pH 5.35, 9.85 and 11.50 were carried out at 25°C and 40°C respectively.

In the study of binding Cu ions to the albumin was calculated by carrying out direct and reserve titrations. The inflexion in the transmittance versus concentration curves indicates the point where the formation of the insoluble complex in complete. Furthermore, if this point does not indicate the completion of the formation of the insoluble complex, then with the addition of more Cu would be an even larger decrease in the percentage transmittance. Form the break in the curves, the number of moles of copper bound per mole of protein was found suing the relationship $V_M = C_B/P$ where P is mortality of protein and C_B the mortality of copper bound at the inflexion point. The anion or cation of Cu interact with albumin at different fixed pH values was studied between 5.35 to 11.50. At all pH values, the pH of protein was found to decrease by the addition of Cu of the same pH values. this decrease in pH was attributed to the preferential binding of Cu ions to the reactive sits of the protein. In such a case negative pH (pH protein-pH protein + Cu) indicates cation binding while a positive pH (pH protein + Cu - protein) is indicative of anion binding.

In the present investigation the negative pH values showed that Cu binds in the form of cation. In low pH there was perception, hence no significant changes in pH occurred. however above isoelectirc point of protein a regular small decrease in pH was observed. This has been assumed to the binding of Cu to the protein. The amount of ligand bound per mole of albumin (10^5g) was calculated by the method of Scatchard and Black (1949) from which the value of bound (C_B) and free (C_F) molar concentration of Cu was determined from the known molar concentration of albumin ($0.72{\times}10^{-2}$M). The binding was found to be sigmoidal at pH values 5.35, 7.50 and 9.50 since saturation is attained at higher free Cu concentration. The Cu_M values at saturation limit correspond the maximum number of binding sites occupied by ligand molecules on the protein molecule. At pH 9.85 and 11.50 the Cu_M rises linearly as the free ligand increased. this type of sigmoidal and linear binding isotherms are indicative of more than one class of sites and a single set of site involved in the binding process.

The Cu binding by albumin is observed to be modified by pH and temperature. The number of binding sites decreases with rising pH and temperature but log K remains nearly constant. The important of constant values of log K, almost independent of pH and temperature, is that only a single primary class of sites is reacting and the appearance of their different number is there fore not responsible for decreased binding which may than be due to decreased availability of the same class of sites owing to irreversible effects in the protein structure. The free energy (DG^0) enthalpy (DH^0) and entropy (DS^0) changes of the interaction were calculated using standard methods. The positive entropy (DS^0) were probably indicates that water of hydration is released both from the polar sites of protein and tetrahedral oxocopper species and that the configuration of the polypeptide is changing to a random coil as the complex formation occurs. The higher values of entropy and enthalpy change at pH 9.85 possibly indicates that all the above mentioned factors may be involved at this pH.

In experimental result showed that Cu interaction depends upon the pH of system. The anion is first attracted to the positive centers on the protein surface by coulombic forces and when it is sufficiently near water molecules are removed, making the lone electron pair on nitrogen available for co-ordination with the copper atom of copper ions. The shift of the titration curve of Cu-albumin complex to wards higher pH may perhaps be in line with the type of binding because H^+ reacts with $Cuso_4$ ion which inturn is removed as water molecule on reacting with albumin. In the lower pH range, the complex may be formed through co-ordination and hydrogen bonding with protonated nitrogen and undissociated carboxyl groups of albumin. However in the higher pH range the decreased binding can be explained on the basis of the following facts.

1. The number of –OH groups in the polyacid decreased and as a result the number of linkage also progressively decreases with the decreasing metaloxide.
2. Protein becomes either swollen or unfolded when the net negative charge increases. At the pH increases and the charge becomes more negative, electrostatic repulsion causes as even greater opening of the protein until a maximum is reached, as predicted by the diminished Cu binding results.
3. The progressive deprotonation of the nitrogen atoms would result in a smaller number of positive loci therefore, resulting in a decreased binding.
4. Protein becomes swollen or unfolded when the net negative charge increases. As the pH increases and the charge becomes more negative electrostatic repulsion causes an even greater opening up of the protein until a maximum is reached as predicted by the diminished anion binding results.

Table 6.1: Binding constants of albumin – Cu (II) system by pH displacement method

pH	n	log k	G^0 (Kcal/mole)	S^0 (cal $mole^{-1}$ deg^{-1})	H^0 (Kcal/mole)
25°C					
5.34	11	3.95	-5415	+5.0	
7.50	9	3.78	-5.182	-	
9.50	8	3.61	-4.949	-	
9.85	7	3.60	-4.835	+14.0	
11.50	3	3.60	-4.835	+8.6	
40°C					
5.34	9	3.81	-5.486	+4.7	+4.000
9.85	6	3.58	-5.155	+14.6	-0.572
11.50	2	3.52	-5.068	+6.0	-2.266

The polarographic behavior of mercuric chloride ion is interesting due to the fact that the polarograms in lower potential range possesses a small maxima. Addition of even a smaller amount of albumin suppressed the maxima as well as decreased the current height. The abstraction of maxima from polargram by the presence of albumin is a direct indication of combination between albumin and mercury (Hg) ions. Furthermore the addition of more and more amounts of albumin caused progressive decrease in the current height. This reduction in current height may be due to successive removal of Hg ions from the systemic increasing amounts of albumin react with more and more Hg. Which is a cause of the depression in the current height of axometal ion.

The polarographic data viz. Hgm and Hgf can be analysed in many ways. for qualitative representation, these are plotted in the from of logarithmic plots i.e. Hgm is plotted against log free equilibrium concentration of Hg ions these isotherms at 25°C indicate the extant of binding increases progressively as the log free concentration rises and ultimately assumes S-shape. this indicates the saturation of binding sites in both cases i.e. at and 0.5 percent albumin concentrations. The binding data were also explained in terms by a protein, the first bound ion tends to reduce the affinity of the protein for the second oncoming ion because of the electrostatic factor in protein the binding constants n (binging sites) and K (association constant) may be calculated by the following relation.

Where, K is the average apparent association constant for the binding at each site and n is the average maximum number of binding sits on protein with the same association constant K. If all the protein sites are equivalent and independent a plot of Hg m/Hg F as a function of Hg m would reveal a linear nature such that the intercept on the Hg m/Hg F axis is Kn x as Hg m approaches zero as a limit and the intercept on the Hg m axis is n as Hg m/Hg F approaches zero as a limit deviation from linearity may occur when linking takes places at more than one set of site with different values of the association constant. The contribution of the electrostatic factors may also produce deviation from the liner nature of the plot. A linear relationship is found to exist between Hg m/Hg F and Hg m at both the albumin concentrations, Which is an indication of the involvement of only one classes of sites which are equivalent and independent. A slight curvature in lower limit of scatchard plot may be due to change in the structure of interacting mercury species as its nature is concentration depended the binding sites for 0.5 and 0.2 percent albumin were found to be 33 and 50, respectively. While the association constant for single site being 303 and 140 respectively corresponding to log K value of 2.481 and 2.146 respectively. The free energy changes of the combining sites are found to be only 4.6458 and 4.1852 K cal./mole.

The difference in number of binding sites (n) association constant (log) and free energy at two-protein concentration reveled that the protein molecule possess different structural organizations in its dilute and concentrated solution. This is reflection of the availability of different ligand binding sites is less than the total of 53 cationic groups on albumin molecule but the increased Hg m at pH 9.5 than at 7.50 creates some ambiguity of the mercury ions binding sites. Furthermore, at pH 7.50 the 15 imidazolium would be unprotonated i.e. out of the 53 cationic groups only 38 groups remained protonated. On the other hand at pH 9.50 both imidazolium and ammonium groups get deprotonated and thus only 24 albuminium group remain protonated. As Hg binding is found more at pH 9.50 than at 7.50 hence the ionized carboxyl and phenolic groups have participated in interaction with oxo-mercury (Hg) albumin linkage. The albumin constrain carboxyl group and mercury is known bind with phenolic oxygens of the metal binding sites of human serum transferring (harries and Carranno, 1984). Thus in case of albumin the anionic carboxyls and phenolic group are bound to oxo-mercury rather than the nitrogen containing groups.

Kustein *et. al.* (1973) have reported the linking of vanadate ions to ethylenediamine tetra acetate and alizarine both having donor atoms and the anionic oxogen atoms and they have shown the existance of one-to-one complex between vanadate ions has been predicted in this complexation reactions. In case of albumin the unprotonated nitrogen atoms from amino and imidazole nitrogen served as electron donors while the ionize carboxyl as anions for binding the oxy (Hg O_2) species of the mercury.

CONCLUSION

The results obtained from the binding of Congo red (dye) with the collagen the following points can be summarised:

1. Diffusion current ratio id/id_0 (dye) decreased with increase in pH levels.
2. The values of Congo red (dye) is higher at low concentration of protein. the relatively higher Congo red at lower protein concentration may be due to :
   (i) Some loosening of protein structure favored by large nte charge, on the protein resulting in to a greater binding.
   (ii) Some saturation effect on the binding sites owing to relatively higher concentration of anion in comparison to the protein.
   (iii) At lower protein concentration higher Congo red may also be due to second order electrostatic effect in which protein molecules swells and becomes penetrated with solvents and ions.

REFERENCES

1. A. Gornall, C. Bardawill and N. David, *J. Biol. Chem.*, 177, 751 (1949).
2. A. Ray, J.a. Reynolds, H. Polet and J. Steinhardt, *Biochemistry*, 5, 2006 (1966).
3. Ray, J.A. Reynolds, H. Polet and J. Steinhardt, *Biochemistry*, 6, 937 (1967).
4. A. Spector, J.E. Fletcher and J. DouglesAshbrook, *Biochemistry*, 10, 3229 (1971).
5. A.B. Zenin, M.M. Feldshtein, V.P. Merzlov and J.J. Maletina, *Molecul. Bio.*, 7, 174 (1973)
6. A.E. Dennand and R.J.P. Williams in 'Transition Metal Chemistry', (Ed.) R.L. Carlin, 2, 158 (1966).
7. A.E. Dennard and R.J.P. Williams, in 'Transition Metal Chem'. R.L. Carlin (Ed.), 2, 158 (1966).
8. A.G. Weeds and S. Lowery, *J. Mole. Biol.*, 61, 701 (1971)
9. A.K. Wright. M.R. Thompson and R.L. Miller, *Biochemistry*, 14, 3224 (1975)
10. A.T. Andrews, Eur. *J. Biochem.*, 70, 59 (1978)
11. Arora, J.P.S. and Singh, R.P.: *Studia Biophysica*, 83, 181 (1981).
12. Arora, J.P.S., jadon, D.S., Singh, R.P. and Mittal, S.K.: *J. Ind. Chem. Soc.* 57, 180 (1980).
13. Arora, J.P.S., Singh, R.P., Soam, D. and Sharma, R.: *Bioelectro Chemistry and Bioenergetics*, 10, 57, (1983a).
14. Arora, J.P.S. Singh. R.P., Soam, D., Singh. S.P. and Kumar, R.: *Bioelectrochem. and Bioenergetics*. 10, 289 (1983b).
15. Ashraf, S.M.: Ph.D Thesis Submitted in University of Roorkee, Roorkee, India (1969).
16. S. Lowey and D. Risby, *Nature*, 234, 81 (1971).
17. A. Gornall, C. Bardawill and N. David, J. *Biol. Chem.*, 177, 751 (1949).
18. A. Ray, J.A. Reynolds, H. Polet and J. Steinhardt, *Biochemistry*, 5, 2606 (1966).
19. A. Ray, J.A. Reynolds, H. Polet and J. Steinhardt, *Biochemistry*, 6, 937 (1967).

20. A. Spector, J.E. Fletcher and J. DouglesAshbrook, *Biochemisry*, 10, 3229 (1971).
21. A.B. Zenin, M.m.Feldshtein, V.P. Merzlov and J.J. Maletina, Molekul, Biol. 7, 174 (1973).
22. B. Jirgensions, Biochim. Biophys. *Acta*, 317, 131 (1973).
23. B. Jirgension, Arch. Biochem. Biophys., 94, 59 (1961).
24. B. Jirgenson, *J. Biol. Chem.*, 241, 4855 (1966).
25. B. Jirgenson, *Makromol. Chem.*, 51, 137 (1962).
26. B.L. Valee and W.E. Wacker, in 'The Proteins,' 2nd edn., Vol. V, 1970, Academic Press.
27. B.P. Brand and P. Johnson, Trans. Faraday Soc., 52, 438 (1956).
28. B.P. Maliwal and M.S. Narsinga Ra, *Ind. J. Biochem. Biophys.*, 14, 108 (1976).
29. B.R. Puri and Neelam Bala Indian J. Chem., 13, 149 (1975).
30. Belman, S.: J. Am. *Chem., Soc.* 85, 2154 (1963).
31. Benjam in D. Malkin, Karen R. Thickman, Chrisopher, J. Markworth, Dean E. Wilcox, Frederick J. Kull, "Inhibition of Potato Polyphenol Oxidase (Tyrosinase) by Anions and Activity in Various Carboxylate Buffers (pH 4.8) at Constant Ionic Strenght", Journal of Enzyme Inhibition, in press.
32. C. Botre and M. Solmase, *J. Phys. Chem.*, 68, 3624 (1964).
33. C.K. Horner, D. Buck, F.F. Allisonn, M.S. Sherman, *J. Agri. Res.*, 65, 173 (1942).
34. C. Tanford, *J. Am. Chem. Soc.*, 73, 2066 (1951).
35. C. Tanford, *J. Am. Chem. Soc.*, 74, 211 (1952).
36. C. Tanford, *J. Am. Chem. Soc.*, 74, 271 (1952).
37. C. Tanford, *J. Phys. Chem.*, 59, 788 (1955).
38. C.A. Nelson, *J. Biol. Chem.*, 246, 3895 (1971).
39. C.D. Barry, A.C.T. North, J.A. Glasel, R.J.P. Wiliams and A.V. Yavier, Nature, 232, 236 (1972); Biochem. Biophy. Res. Commun. 47, 166 (1972); *Biochem. Biophys. Acta*, 262, 101 (1972).
40. C.H. Grogen and H. Oppenheirmer, *Arch. Biochem. Biophys.*, 56, 204 (1955).
41. Chakrabarti, P. (1990a) Systematics in the Interaction of Metal ions with the main-chain Carbonyl Group in Protein Structures. *Biochemistry* 29, 651-658.
42. Chakrabarti, P. (1990b) Interaction of Metal ions with Carboxylic and Carboxamide Groups in Protein Structures. *Protein engineering* 4, 49-56.
43. Chakrabarti, P. (1990c) Geometry of Interaction of Metal ions with Histidine Residues in Protein Structures. *Protein Engineering* 4, 57-63.
44. Chakrabarti, P. (1994) Conformational Analysis of Carboxylate and Carboxamide Side-chains bound to cations. *J. Mol. Bio 1.* 239, 306-314.
45. Chakrabarti, P., Venkatesan, K., Singh, U.C. and Rao., C.N. (1981). Systematic variation in bond Lengths of Peptides. Biochim. *Biophys. Acta* 670, 134-137.
46. Chatterjee and D.K. Chattoraj, *Ind. J. biochem. Biophys.*,16, 236 (1979).
47. Chatterjee, R., Mitra, S.P. and Chattoraj, D.K.: Indian J. biochem. *Biophys*. 16, 22-27 (1979). Binding SDS, Trition and Short Chain Fatty Acids to DNA.
48. D. Coleman and F.O. Howitt, *Nature*, 155, 78 (1945).
49. D.A. Riohert and W.W. Westerfeld, *J. Biol. Chem.*, 209, 179 (1954).
50. D.N. Hocomb and K.E. Van Holde, *J. Phys. Chem.*, 66, 1999 (1962).

51. D.S. Goodman, *J. Am. Chem. Soc.*, 80, 3892 (1958).
52. D.W. Darnall and T.w. Barela, Biochim. *Biophys. Acta*, 236, 593 (1971).
53. David Eide, Margaret Broderius, JanetteeFett, Mary Lou Guerionot, "A Novel Iron-Regulated Metal Transporter from Plants Identified by Functional Expression in Yeast", proceedings of the National Academy of Sciences, USA, 1996, 93, 5624-5628.
54. Dean E. Wilcox, Laura L. Bennett, Elizageth H. Cox, George Haleblian, Brain T. Hill, Eric P. Kowack, Xiaoyan Liu, Jane S. Merkel, Amy e. Palmer, Matthew C. Poswwitz, Joann E. roy, Karen E. Wetterhahn, "Interaction of Metallothionein with the Carcinogenic Metals Ni (II), Cr (VI) and As (III)", Metallothionein IV, C.D. Klaassen (Ed.); Birkhauser, Basel, 1999; pp. 585-594.
55. Dean E. Wilcox and Roger P. Smith, "Detection and Quantification of Nitric Oxide Using Electron Magenetic Resonance Spectroscopy", Methods 1995, 59-70.
56. Degtyarenko, K.N., North, A.C.T. and Findlay, J.B.C. (1997) PROMISE: A New Database of Information on Prosthetic Centres and Metal ions in Protein Active Sites. Protein Engineering 10, 183-186.
57. E.E. Jormasova and A.V. Peterburgshu, *DobalTskha*, 133, 259 (1968).
58. E. Edelhoch, *J. Phys. Chem.*, 64, 1771 (1960).
59. E. Edelthoch and R.E. Lippoldt, *J. Biol. Chem.*, 235, 1335 (1960).
60. E. Marcitelli, E.M. Coriandoili and C. Chitteria, *Nature*, 184 (Suppl. 21), 1641 (1959).
61. E. Tipping, M.N., Jones and H.A. Skinner, *J. Chem. Soc. Faraday Trans*. I., 70, 1306 (1974).
62. E.J. Masora and B.P. Yu, *Biochemistry*, 9, 2909 (1970).
63. E.M. Coriandoli and C. Chitteria, *Nature*, 193, 1527 (1959).
64. E.N. Slesareva, *DokiMosk. Sel. Akad.*, 78, 320 (1962).
65. E.O. Whittier and S.P. Gould, 'Making Casein Fibres'. Ind. Eng. Chem., 38 906 (1940).
66. E.P. Daniel and E.M. Hewston, *Am. J. Physiol.*, 136, 772 (1942).
67. E.S. Rowe and Steinhardt, *Biochemistry*, 15, 2579 (1976).
68. E.S.G. Barron and G. Kalintsky, *Biochem. J.*, *41*, 346 (1947).
69. F. Bernhein and M.L.C. Bernhein, *Science*, 88, 481 (1938).
70. F. Frits, N. Ingri and L.G. Sillen, *Acta, Chem. Scand.*, 8, 1557 (1964).
71. F. Jon Kull, Michael F. Reed Timoghy E. Elgren, Thomas L. Ciardelli, Dean E. Wilcox, "Solid Phase Peptide Synthesis of the a and Domains of Human Liver Metallothionein and the Nurosporacrassa Metellothionein", *Journal of the American Chemical Society* 1990, 112, 2291-2298.
72. F. Karush and M. Sonenberg, *J. Am. Chem. Soc.*, 71, 1369 (1949).
73. F. Karush, *J. Am. Chem. Soc.*, 73, 1246 (1951).
74. F.W. Putnam and H. Neurath, *J. biol. Chem.*, 149, 183 (1943).
75. F.R.N. Gurd and G.R. Murray, *J. Am. Chem. Soc.*, 76, 187-190 (1954).
76. F.R.N. Gurd and P.E. Wilcox, Wilcox, *Advances in Protein Chem.*, 11, 311 (1956).
77. F.W. Putnam and H. Neurath, *J. Biol. Chem.*, 159, 195 (1945).
78. F.W. Putnam,*Advances in Protein Chem.*, 64, 79 (1978).
79. Fajans, K. and Schwartz, E.: *Electrochemie*, Vol. II. Akademische Verlaggesellschaft, M.B.N. Leipzing, 397 (1933).

80. Filivporic, I., Hahl. Z. Casparal, Z. and Klemencie, V.: *J. Am. Chem. Soc.* 76, 2074 (1954).
81. Frito, F., Inori, N. and Sillen, L.G.: Acta Chem. *Scand.*, 18, 1577 (1964).
82. G. Allen, *Biochem. J.* 137, 575 (1974).
83. G. Scatchard and E.S. Black, *J. Phys. Chem.*, 53 (1949) 88.
84. G. Scatchard, Ann. N.Y. *Acad. Soc.*, 51, 660 (1949).
85. G. Scatchard, J.S. Coleman and A.L. Shen, *J. Am. Chem., Soc.*, 79, 19 (1957).
86. G. Scatchared, W.L. Hughes, F.R.N. Gurd and P.E. Wilcox, in Memories of the University Laboratory of Physical Chemistry, Harvard Univ., No. 3, Academic Press, New York (1954).
87. G. Strauss and U.P. Strauss, *J. Phys. Chem.*, 62, 132 (1958).
88. G. Tanford, K.C. Aune and A. Ikai, *J. Mole Biol.*, 73, 185 (1973).
89. G.B. Perlmann, *J. Biol. Chem.*, 127, 707 (1941).
90. G.C. Nutting, F.R. Senti and Copley, *J. Phys. Chem.*, 49, 192 (1945).
91. G.E. Perlmann, *J. Biol. Chem.*, 127, 707 (1941).
92. G.M. Waterman, R.A. Scot and G.P. Haight, *J. Am. Chem. Soc.*, 96, 7569 (1974).
93. G.R. Johnson and R.E. Spendherd, *Bioinorg. Chem.*, 8 (2), 115 (1978).
94. G.W. Bates and M.R. Schlabach, *FEBS Lett.*,33, 289 (1973).
95. Gericke, *Umschau*, 44, 597 (1940).
96. Goto, S., Nishioka, t. and Kaneshisa, M. (1998) LIGAND: Chemical Database for Enzyme Reactions. *BioinformAtics* 14, 591-599.
97. H. Beinert and G. Palmer, *Adv.Enzymol.*, 27, 105 (1965).
98. H. Edelhoch, E. Katchaiski, R.H. Maybury, W.L. Hughes (Jr.) and J.t. Edsall, *J. Am. Chem. Soc.*, 75, 5058 (1953).
99. H. Fraenkel-Conrat, B.A. Brandon and H.S. Olcott, *J. Biol. Chem.*, 168, 99 (1947).
100. H. Gutfreund and J.M. Sturtevant, *Biochem.* J., 73, 1 (1959).

H. Irving and R.J.P. Williams, Order of Stability of Metal Complexes

101. *Nature*, 162, 746-747 (1948).
102. H. Lal and M.N.S. Rao, *J. Am. Chem. Soc.*, 79, 3050 (1957); 80; 3222 (1958).
103. H. Lal and M.N.S. Rao, *J. Am. Chem.*, Soc., 79, 3050 (1957); 80; 3222 (1958).
104. H. Neurath and F.W. Putnam, *J. Biol. Chem.*, 160, 397 (1946).
105. H.A. Fiess, *J. Am. Chem. Soc.*, 74, 1539 (1952).
106. H.A. Fraenkel – Conrat and H.S. Olcott, *J. biol. Chem.*, 161, 259 (1945).
107. H.A. Fraenkel-Conrat, R.S. and H. Lineweaver, *J. biol. Chem.*, 177, 38 (1949)
108. H.P. Lundgren, D.W. Elam and R.A. O' Connell, *J. Biol. Chem.*, 149, 183 (1943).
109. H.P. Lundgren J. Am. Chem. Soc., 63, 2856 (1941).
110. H.P. Lundgren, 'The Vortex' Bull of the California Section of the American Chemical Society, IV, 231 (1943).
111. H.P. Lundgun, *J. Am. Chem. Soc.*, 63, 2854 (1941).
112. H.t. Bieling and B. Cmazplik, Ann., 580, 135 (1953).
113. Harding, M.M. (2000) The Geometry of Metal-ligand Interactions Relevant to Proteins. II. Angles at the Metal Atom, Additional Weak Metal-donor Interactions. Acta Crystallor. D 56, 857-867.

114. Harding, M.M. (2001) Geometry of Metal-ligand Interactions in Proteins. Acta Crystallogr. D Biolcrystallogr 57, 401-411.

115. Hemm, K., Aberer, K. and Hendlich, M. (1995) Constituting a Receptor-ligand Information base from Quality-enriched Data. *ISMB* 3, 170-178.

116. Hornischer, K. and Blocker, H. (1996) Grafting of Discontinuous Sites: A Protein Modeling Strategy. *Protein Engineering* 9, 931-939.

117. I. Feldman, J. Jones and R. Cross, J. Am. Chem. Soc., 89, 49 (1947); R.P. Agrawal and I. Feldman, *J. AM,. Chem. Soc.*, 90, 6636 (1968).

118. I. Hellerman, *J. Biochem.*, 147, 443 (1943).

119. I. Maruta, *J. Chem. Soc. Japan*, 83 782 (1962).

120 I. Satake and J.T. Yang, *Biopolymers*,15, 2263 (1976).

121. I. Satakeand J.T. Yang, Biochem. Biophys. Res. Commun., 54, 930 (1973).

122. I.M. Klotz and J.M. Urquhart, J. Am. Chem. Soc., 71, 1577 (1948).

123. I.M. Klotz and J.M. Urquhart, J. Phys. Colloid Chem., 53, 100 (1949).

124. I.M. Klotz, in The Proteins. H. Neurath and K. Bailey (eds.) Academic Press, New York, P. 727 (1953).

125. I.M. Kolthoff and J.J. Lingane, in Polarography, Interscience Publishers, New York, P. 398 (1952).

126. In 'The Inorganic Chemistry of Biolocgical Processes', (Ed.) M.N. Hughes, P. 189 (1972), A Wiley Interscience Publication.

127. J. Berducou and R. Macha, *Compt. Rend.*, 257, 229 (1963).

128. J. Courtois and C. Anagstopoulour, *Comp. Red.*,226, 523 (1948).

129. J. Courtois and C. Anagstopoulour, *Enzymologia*, 13, 183 (1949).

130. J. Huppert and N. Rebegrolte, Biochim. *Biophys. Acta*, 45, 189 (1960).

131. J. Inezedy, in 'Analytical Application of Complex Equilibria', Wiley, New York (1976) P. 182.

132. J. Oakes, *Eur. J. Biochem.*, 36, 533 (1973).

133. J. Oakes, *J. Chem. Soc.* 70, 2200 (1974).

134. J. Rathelot, P. Canioni, L. Sharda, J.G. Gregios and H. Rochat, *Biochimie*, 60, 103 (1978).

135. J. Reynolds, S. herbert, H. Polet ad J. Steinhardt, *Biochemistry*, 6, 397 (1967).

136. J. Steinhardt and C.H. Fugett. J. Res. Natl. Bur. Standard, 29 (1942) 315.

137. J. Steinhardt and J.A. Reynolds, Multiple Equilirbia, in "Proteins'. Academic Press, New York (1969).

138. J. Steinhardt, in 'Protein-Ligand Interactions', H.S. Sund and G. Blauer (Eds.) De Gruyter, Berlin, p. 412 (1957).

139. J. Steinhardt, J. Krifin and J.G. Leidg, Biochemistry, 10, 4065 (19).

140. J. Steinhardt, N. Stocker, O. Carroll and K.S. birdi, Biochemistry, 13, 4461 (1974).

141. J. A. Glasses, In 'Current Research Topics in Bioinorgaic Chemistry, Progress in Inorganic Chemistry', Vol. 18, J. LippardStepha (Ed.), An Interscriennce Publication, John Wiley and Sons, New York, P. 383 (1973).

142. J.A. Reynolds, S. Herbert and J. Steinhardt, Biochemistry, 7, 2606 (1968).

143. J.B. Niederl and V. Niederl, Micromethods of Quantitative Organic Analysis, New York (1942).

144. J.C. Canon and N.D. Chasteen, *Biochemistry*, 14, 4375 (1975).
145. J.D. Tersi, *J : Am. Chem. Soc.* 72, 3972 (1950).
146. J.F. Riordan, K.D. McElyaly and C.L. Borders, *Science*, Washington, DC, 195, 884 (1977).
147. J.H. Highberger and H.J. Kersten, *J. Am. Chem. Leather Chem. Assn.* 33, 16 (1938).
148. J.H. Israel and O.V. Winkle, *J. Phys. Chem.*, 59, 944 (1955).
149. J.J. Fitzgerald and N.D. Chasteen, *Anal. Biochem.*, 60, 170 (1974)
150. J.J. Fitzgerald and N.D. Chasteen, *Biochemistry*, 13, 4338 (1974).
151. J.J. Johnson, J.H. Cohen and K.V. Rajgopalan, Biochem. *Biophys. Res. Commun.* 56, 940 (1974).
152. J.K. Taylor and R.E. Smith, *Anal. Chem.*, 22, 495 (1950).
153. J.L. Lidquist, N. Robert and E. Gustev, *J. Am. Chem., Soc.*, 8, 762 (1973).
154. J.L. Zweier and P. Aisen, *J. Biol. Chem.* 252, 6090 (1977).
155. J.P. Hummel and W. Witzel, *J. biol. Chem.*, 241 (1966) 1023.
156. J.P.S. Arora and A. Kumar, *Egypt. J. Chem.*, 29, 153 (1986).
157. J.P.S. Arora and D. Soan,. *Cur. Sci.*, (1984).
158. J.P.S. Arora and Km. K.L. Balyan, *Tenside Surfact. Det.*, 29(1), 48 (1992).
159. J.P.S. Arora and Km. V. Verma, B.B.E. (1986).
160. J.P.S. Arora and R.P. Singh, *Stud., Biophys.*, 83 (1981) 181.
161. J.P.S. Arora and S.P. Malik, *Studia Biophysica,* 0, 183 (1985).
162. J.P.S. Arora and S.P. Singh, *Egypt. J. Chem.*, 28, 189 (1985).
163. J.P.S. Arora R.P., Singh, S. Soam, R. Sharma, *Bioelectrochem. Bioenerg.*, 10, 157 (1983).
164. J.P.S. Arora, A. Kumar, R.P. Singh and S.P. Singh, *StudiaBiophysica*, 100, 121 (1985).
165. J.P.S. Arora, C. Pal and D. Dutt, T*enside Surface. Det.*, 28 (3), 215 (1991).
166. ...
167. J.P.S. Arora, C. Pal and P.B. Jain, *Studia Biophysica,* 126, 61 (1988).
168. J.P.S. Arora, D. Soam and A. Kumar, *Studia Biophysica*, 120, 189 (1984).
169. J.P.S. Arora, D. Soam, S.P. Singh and R. Kumar, *Tenside Detergent,* 21, 87 (1984).
170. J.P.S. Arora, D.S. Jadon and R.P. Singh, *J. Ind. Chem. Soc.*, 56, 1189 (1979).
171. J.P.S. Arora, D.S. Jadon and R.P. Singh, *J. Ind. Chem., Soc.*, 56, 1189 (1979).
172. J.P.S. Arora, D.S. Jadon and R.P. Singh, *J. Ind. Chem. Soc.*, 83, 181 (1981).
173. J.P.S. Arora, D.S. Jadon, R.P. Singh and S.K. Mittal, *J. Ind. Chem. Soc.*, 57. 180 (1980).
174. J.P.S. Arora, J.S. Shankar and R. Chand, *WASP*, 36, 247 (1987).
175. J.P.S. Arora, Km. V. Verma and Km. K.L. Balyan, *Tenside Surface, Det.* 29(2), 124 (1992).
176. J.P.S. Arora, Km. V. Verma and S. Kumr, *Cur. Sci.*, 55, 717 (1986).
177. J.P.S. Arora, Km. V. Verma and S.R. Verma, *Environ, Sci.*, Communicated (1994).
178. J.P.S. Arora, Km. Vinita and M. Chand, *Tenside Surfact. Detergent,* 30(2), 136 (1993).
179. J.P.S. Arora, Km. Vinita and R.P. Singh, *Tenside Surfact. Det.*, 29(6), 418 (1992).
180. J.P.S. Arora, R.P. Singh and S.P. Singh, *Studia Biophysica*, Communicated (1994).
181. J.P.S. Arora, R.P. Singh D. Soam, S.P. Singh and R. Kumar, *Bioelectrochem. Bioenerg.*, 10, 441 (1983).

182. J.P.S. Arora, R.P. Singh, D. Soam and r. Sharma, *Bioelectrochem. Bioenerg.*, 10, 133 (1983).
183. J.P.S. Arora, R.P. Singh, D. Soam and S.P. Singh, *France Chem. Soc.*, 1, (2), 19 (1983).
184. J.P.S. Arora, R.P. Singh, D. Soam, S.P. Singh and R. Kumar, *Bioelectrochem. Bioenerg.*,10, 157 (1983).
185. J.P.S. Arora, R.P. Singh, D. Soam, S.P. Singh and R. Kumar, *Bioelectrochem, Bioererg.*,10, 289 (1983).
186. J.P.S. Arora, R.P. Singh, D. Soam, S.P. Singh and R. Kumar, *Bioelectrochem, Bioenerget.*, 10, 441 (1983).
187. J.P.S. Arora, R.P. Singh D. Soam, S.P. Singh, S.P. Malik and A. Kumar, *Egypt. J. Chem.*, 28, 57 (1985).
188. J.P.S. Arora, R.P. Singh, D.s.Jadon and S.K. Mittal, *J. Ind. Chem. Soc.*, 57 (1980) 180.
189. J.P.S. Arora, R.P. Singh, S. Kumar and V.K. Singhal, *J. Pract. Chem.*, 321, 164 (1979).
190. J.P.S. Arora, R.P. Singh, S.P. Malik and Smt. S. Jain, *Tenside Detergents*, TS 904, Vol. 23 (1986).
191. J.P.S. Arora, R.P. singh, S.P. Singh and S.P. Malik, *Stud. Biophys.*,29(2) (1984) 97.
192. J.P.S. Arora, R.P. Singh, S.P. Singh and S.P. Malik, *Studia Biophysica*, 99, 97 (1984).
193. J.P.S. Arora, R.P. Singh, Smt. S. Jain, S.P. Singh and A. Kumar, Bioelectiochem, *Bio Enegy*;13, 329 (1984).
194. J.P.S. Arora, R.P. Singh, V.K. Singhal and S.P. Singh, *Studia Biophysica*, 97, 213 (1983).
195. J.P.S. Arora, R.P. Singh V.K. Singhal and S.P. Singh, *Tenside Detergent*, 22, 123 (1985).
196. J.P.S. Arora, S.P. Malik and A. Kumar, *StudiaBiophysica*, 102, 189 (1984).
197. J.P.S. Arora, S.P. Singh and S.P. Malik, *France Chem. Soc.*, 2, 167 (1985).
198. J.P.S. Arora, S.P. Singh V.K. Singhal, *Tenside Detergent*, 21, 197 (1984).
199. J.P.S. Arora, S.P. Singh, D. Soam and R. Kumar, *Egypt, J. Chem.*, 27, 823 (1985).
200. J.P.S. Arora, S.R. Verma, J.S. Shankar and R. Chand, *Water, Air and Soil Pollution*, 36, 247 (1987).
201. J.P.S. Arora, S.r. Verma, D. Dutt and C. Pal, *WASP*, 43, 53 (1989).
202. J.P.S. Arora, Smt. S. Jain, C. Pal, Km. Laxmi and M. Chand, *France Chem. Soc.*,1, 58 (1989).
203. J.P.S. Arora, V.K. Singhal, M. Kumar, Km. Luxmi and C. Pal, Ind. *J. Biochem. Biophys.*, 26, 14 (1989).
204. J.P.S. Arora, D. Soam, S.P. Malik and A. Kumar, *Studia Biophysica*, 102, 182 (1984).
205. J.P.S. Arora, R.P. Singh and C. Pal, *Studia Biophysica*, 114, 191 (1986).
206. J.P.S. Arora, R.P. Singh, V.K. Singal and S.P. Singh, *Studia Biophysica*, 97 (3), 213 (1983).
207. J. Steinhardt, Ann, *Rev. Biochem.*, 14, 145 (1945).
208. J.t. Haung and G.P. Haight, *J.A., Chem. Soc.*, 93, 611 (1971).
209. J.t. Spence and J.Y. Lee, *Inorgan. Chem.*,4, 977 (1968); 6, 998 (1967); 7, 2510 (1968).
210. J.t. Spence, M. Heydanek and P. Hemmerich, in 'Magnetic Resonance in Biological Systems', 269 Pergamon (1967).
211. J.T. Yang and J.F. Foster, *J. Am. Chem. Soc.*, 75, 5560 (1953).

212. J.V. Gilbert, J. Ramakrishna, F.W. Sonderman, Jr. A. Wright, A.G. Plant, "Protein Hpn: Cloning and Characterization of a Histidine-Rich Metal-binding Polypeptide in Helicobacter Pylori and Helicobatermustelae", Infection and Immunity 1995, 63, 2682-2688.
213. K. Fajans and E. Schwartz, *Electrochemie,* Vol. II, Akademische, Verlag, Leipzing, p. 397 (1933).
214. K. Kustin and D.L. Toppen, *J. Am. Chem. Soc.*, 95, 3564 (1973).
215. K. Takaai, Martensen, Todd, N, Jayarree and F. Martin, *Biochem. Biophys. Res. Commun.*, 81 (4), 1313 (1978).
216. K. Weber and M. Osborn, *J. Biol. Chem.*, 24, 4406 (1969).
217. K. Wiesner, Collection Czechoslov. *Chem. Commun.*, 12, 594 (1947).
218. K.G.A. Pankhurst and R.C.M. Smith, *Trans. Faraday Soc.*, 40, 565 (1945); 43, 506 (1947).
219. K.G.A. Pankhurst and R.C.M. Smith, *Trans. Faraday Soc.*, 43, 511 (1947).
220. K.S. Birdi and J. Steinhardt, *Fed, Proc.*, 34, 598 (1975).
221. K.S. Kanwan, *Indian J. Ag.*, 7, 112 (1962).
222. K.V. Rajgopalan, I. Fudovich and P. Handler, *J. Biol. Chem.*, 237, 922 (1962).
223. Karlin, S. and Zhu, Z-Y. (1996) Characterizations of Diverse Residue Clusters in Protein Three-dimensional Structures. *Proc. Natl. Acad. Sci. USA* 93, 8344-8349.
224. Kleywegt, G.J. (1999) Recognition of Spatial Motial Motifs in Protein Structures. *J. Mol. Biol.* 285, 1887-1897.
225. Klotz, I.M. : Arches, *Biochem*. 9, 109 (1946).
226. L. Berger, *J. Gen. Physiol.*, 29, 379 (1946).
227. L. Visser and E.R. Blout, *Biochemistry*, 10, 741 (1971).
228. L.G. Longsworth and C.F. Jacobson, *J. Phys. Colloid. Chem*; 53, 126, (1949).
229. L.J. Theriot, G.O. Carbisle and J.H. Hug, *J. Inorg. Nucl*, 31, 284 (1969).
230. L.M. Klotz and J.M. Urquhart; *J. Phys. Coll. Chem.*, 53, 100 (1949).
231. Lindquist, R.N. Lynn, J.L. (Jr.) and Lienhard, G.L.: *J. Am. Chem. Soc.*, 95, 8762 (1973).
232. M. Kolthoff and J.J. Lingane, Polarography, New York, N.Y., P. 397 (1952).
233. M. Nakagki, *Bull. Chem. Soc.*, 37, 812 (1964).
234. M.J. Grouke and J.H. Gibbs, *Biopolymer*, 5, 586 (1967).
235. M.J. Pallansch and D.r. Briggs. *J. Am. Chem. Socl*, 76, 1396 (1954).
236. M.L. Fishman and F.R. Eirich, *J. Phys.* 79, 2740 (1975).
237. M.L. Fishman and F.R. Eirich, *J. Phys. Chem.*,75, 3135 (1971).
238. M.L. Fishman and F.R. Eirich, *J. Phys. Chem.*, 79, 2740 (1975).
239. M.M. Feldshein, A.B. Zenin and J.J. Gragerova, *Biokhimia*, 37, 305 (1972).
240. M.N. Hughes (Ed.). 'Inorganic Chemistry of Biological Process', A. Wiley Interscience Publication, Chapt, VII, P. 230 (1972).
241. M.N. Jomes, H.A. Skinner and E. Tipping, *Biochem. J.*147, 329 (1975).
242. M.N. Jones, H.A. Skinner, E. Tipping and A. Wilkinson, *Biochem. J.*, 135, 231 (1973).
243. M.N. Jones, *J. Colloid. Sci.* 23, 36, (1967).
244. M.S.N. Rao and H. Lal, *J. Am. Chem. Soc.*, 76, 4867 (1954).

245. M.S.N. Rao and H. Lal, *J. Am. Chem. Soc.*, 80, 3226 (1958).

246. makino, J.A. Reynolds and C. Tanford, *J. Biol. Chem.*, 238, 4926 (1973).

247. Malik, W.U. and Arora, J.P.S.: *J. Electroanal. Chem.*, 22, 359 (1969).

248. Matthew C. Posewitz and Dean E. Wilcox, "Properties of the Spl Zinc Finger #3 Peptide : Coordination Chemistry, Redox Reactions and Metal Binding Competition with Metallothionein", *Chemical Research in Toxicology* 1995, 8, 1020-1028.

N. Kofima and G.W. Bates, The formation of Fe3+-transferrin-CO3(2-) via the binding and oxidation of Fe2+*J. Biol. Chem.*, 256, 12034-12039 (1981).

249. N. Muller and R.J. Mead, *Biochemistry*, 12, 3831 (1973).

250. N. Paternson and R.c. Strohman, *Biochemistry*, 9, 4094 (1970).

251. N.D. Chasteen and J. Francavilla, *J. Phys. Chem.*, 80 (1976) 867.

252. N.D. Chasteen, R.J. Dekoch, B.L. Rogers and M.W. Hanna, *J. Am. Chem. Soc.*, 95, 1301 (1973).

253. Nalal, M. and Di Cera, E. (1996) Valence Screening of Water in Protein Crystals Reveals Potential Na+binding sites. *J. Mol. Bio* 1 256, 228-234.

254. O. Rygh, Bull. *Soc., Chem. Biol.*, 33, 133 (1951).

255. P. Handler and K.V. Rajgopalan, *J. Biol. Chem.*, 239, 2027 (1964).

256. P. Johson and F.J. Jubert, *J. Polymer Sci.*, 7, 605 (1951).

257. P. Souchary and G. Carperi, *Bull. Chem.,Soc., France,* 13m 160 (1946).

258. P.C.H. Mitchell, Quart, *Rev. Chem. Soc.*, 20, 103 (1966).

259. P.F. Knowles and H. Deilber, *Trans. Faraday Soc.*, 64, 977 (1968).

260. P.K. Sarkar and P. Dotty, *Proc. Natl. Acad. Sci.*, USA, 55, 981 (1966).

261. P.K.J. Lee and B. Jirgenson, *Biochim. Biophys. Acta*, 229, 631 (1971).

262. P.W. Boyer, G.a. Ballou and J.M. Luck, *J. Biol. Chem.*,162, 199 (1946).

263. Pope, M.t. and Dale, W.B.: *Quart. Rev. Chem. Soc.* 22, 527 (1968).

264. R. Bais, P. Greenwell, J.C. Wallace and D. Brucekeech, *FEBS Lett.*, 41, 53 (1974).

265. R. Chatterjee, S.P. Mitra and D.K. Chattoraj, Ind., *J. Biochem. Biophys.*, 16, 22 (1976).

266. R. Pitt-Rivers and F.S.A. Impiombato, *Biochem. J.*, 109, 825 (1968).

267. R. Vrijsen and A. Boeye, *Anal. Biochem.*, 85, 355 (1978).

268. R.A. Fineberg and M.W. Loewus, *Biochem. Biophys. Acta*, 26, 441 (1957).

269. R.C. Bray and D.C. Watts, Biochem. J., 98, 142 (1966).

270. R.C. Bray and L.S. Meriwether, Nature, 212, 467 (1966).

271. R.C. Bray, G. Palmer and H. Beinert, *J. Biol. Chem.*, 239, 2667 (1964).

272. R.J. Dekoch, D.J. West, J.C. Canon and N.D. Chasteau, *Biochemistry*, 13, 4347 (1974); 14, 196 (1975).

273. R.J. Kaller and R.P. Sharma, *Toxi Lett.*, 269 (1985).

274. R.K. Morton, *Method Enzymol*, 1, 25 (1955).

275. R.N. Lindquist, J.L. Lynn (Jr.) and G.L. Linhard, *J. Am. Chem*. Soc., 95, 8762 (1973).

276. R.S. Mani and C.M. Key, Can, *J. Biochem.*, 51, 178 (1972).

277. R.V. Deoker and J.F. Foster, *Biochemistry*, 5, 1242 (1966).

278. R.W. Green and K.P. Ang, *J. Am. Chem. Soc.*, 77, 5482 (1955).

279. R.W. Hills and D.R. Briggs, *J. Am. Chem. Soc.*, 78, 1590 (1956).

280. S. Barkin, H.P. Frank and F.H. Eirich, *Ric. Sci. Srz. A.*, 25, 844 (1955).
281. S. Edlbacher and H. Baur, *Z. Physiol. Chem.*, 254, 275 (1983).
282. S. Granick and P.F. Hahn, *J. Biol. Chem.*, 155, 661 (1944).
283. S. Saito, *Colloid, Z.*, 158, 12 (1958).
284. S. Saito, *Colloid, Z.*, 154, 19 (1957).
285. S.F. Sun, N.O. Del-Rosario and L.A. Goldstein, *Int. J. peptide Protein Res.*, 5 (1973) 337.
286. S.F. Sun, N.O.D. Rosairo and L.A. goldstein, *Int. J. Peptide Protein Res.*, 5, 337 (1973).
287. S.K. Agarwal and W.U. Malik, *J. Ind. Chem. Soc.*, 43, 11 (1968).
288. S.R. Verma, J.P.S. Arora, J.S. Shankar, D. Dutt and C. Pal, *WASP*, 43, 53 (1989).
289. Souchay, P. and Carperi, G.: *Bull. Chim. Fr.* 13, 160 (1646).
290. Sterling, K. and Tabachnick, M.: *J. Biol. Chem.*, 236 (1961).
291. T. Takagi, K. Tsufii and K. Shriahama, *J. Biochem. (Tokyo)*, 77, 936 (1975).
292. V. Duerr, *Borlin Muenchir Tieraerztl Wochenschr.*, 82 (7), 326 (1969).
293. Vallee, B.L. and Auld, D.S. (1990) *Active-site Zinc Ligands and Activated H2O of Zinc Enzymes. Proc. Natl. Acad. Sci. USA* 87, 220-224.
294. Vallee, B.L. and Auld, D.S. (1992) Cocatalytic Zinc Motifs in Conzymeclatalysis. proc. Natl. Acad. Sci. USA 90, 2715-2718.
295. W. Kauzman, *Adv. Protein Chem.*,14, 1 (1959).
296. W. Kauzmann, *Adv. Protein Chem.*, 14 (1959b) 1.
297. W. Norde and J. Lyklema, *J. colloid and Interface Soc.*, 66, 266 (1978).
298. W. Schottan, *Macromolecule Chem.*, 11, 131 (1954).
299. W. Spinpes and W. Gordy, *J. Chem. Phys.*, 41, 3661 (1964).
300. W.J. Ray and J.S. Multani, *Biochemistry*, 11, 2805 (1972).
301. W.J. Wolf and D.R. Briggs: *Arch, Biochem, Biophys.*, 36, 377 (1958).
302. W.L. Hughes (Jr.) *Cold Spring Harbor Symposia Quard, Biol.*, 14, 179 (1950).
303. W.L. Hughes (Jr.), *J. Am. Chem. Soc.*, 69, 1836 (1947).
304. W.L. Mattice, J.M. Riser and D.S. Clark, *Biochemistry*, 15, 4262 (1976).
305. W.R. Harris and C.J. Carrano, Binding of Vanadate to Human Serum Transferrin. *J. Inorg. Biochem.*, 22, 201-218 (1984).
306. W.R. Harris, *Biochemistry*, 24, 7412 (1985).
307. W.U. Malik and J.P.S. Arora, *Ind. J. Biochem. Biophys.*,6, 142 (1969).
308. W.U. Malik and J.P.S. Arora, *J. Elecrtroanal. Chem.*, 22, 359 (1968).
309. W.U. Malik and J.P.S. Arora, *J. Electroanal Chem.*, 26 (1970) 414.
310. W.U. Malik and J.P.S. Arora, *J. Electroanal Chem.*, 22 (1969) 539.
311. W.U. Malik and M. Muzaffruddin, *Aust. J. Chem.*, 18, 1397 (1965).
312. W.U. Malik and M. Muzaffrudin, *J. Elecroanal. Chem.*, 6, 214 (1963).
313. W.U. Malik and M.R. Jindal, *Chemistry and Industry*,1401 (1968).
314. W.U. Malik and M.R. Jindal, *J. Electroanal Chem.*, 19, 436 (1968).
315. W.U. Malik and M.R. Jindal, *J. Phys. Chem.*, 72, 3612 (1968).
316. W.U. Malik and S.K. Agrawal, *Ind. Chem.*, 5, 1 (1967).

317. W.U. Malik and S.M. Ashraf, *Colloid-Z.*, 237, 309 (1970).
318. W.U. Malik and Ashraf, *Lipids*, 5, 793 (1969).
319. W.U. Malik and Salahuddin, *J. Electroanal. Chem.*,5, 147 (1963).
320. W.U. Malik and Salahuddin, *J. Electroanal. Chem.*,5, 68 (1963).
321. W.U. Malik, A.K. Jain and A.P. Mittal, *J. Ind. Che., Soc.*, 59, 545 (1977).
322. W.U. Malik J.P.S. Arora, D.S. Jadon and R.P. Singh, *Egypt. J. Chem.*, 23, 223 (1980).
323. Y in Xu and Dean E. Wilcox, "Oxidation of Zinc Finger Cysteines to Thiolsulfinate", *Journal of the American Chemical Society* 1998, 120, 7375-7376.
324. Y. Yazaki, S. Mochinagu and M.S. Raben, Biochim. *Biophys. Acta*, 328, 464 (1973).
325. G.L. Carron and E.b. Robert, Proc. Univ. Mo. Anna. Cong. Tranc. Subst. Environ. health, 96 (1967). Yi Zhang, ShreeramAkilesh, Dean E. Wilcox, "Isothermal Titration Calorimery Measuraments of Ni (II) and Cu (II) Binding to His, GlyGly His, His Gly His and Boving Serum Albumin : A Critical Evaluation", Inorganic Chemistry 2000, 39, 3057-3064.
326. W.U. Malik, J.P.S. Arora, D.s.Jadon and R.P. Singh, *Egypt. J. Chem.*, 23, 229 (1980).

Pages: 144-168

Research in Chemistry and Chemical Sciences
Edited by: **Dr. Vijender Singh and Dr. Pawan Kumar 'Bharti'**
ISBN: 978-93-88854-40-5
Edition: **2020**
Published by: **Discovery Publishing House Pvt. Ltd., New Delhi (India)**

7

New Method and Machine for Manufacturing of Laser Irradiated Nano and Micro Composite with Graphene Filler

Hebatalrahman, A.*

ABSTRACT

Method and machine for manufacturing of micro and nano composite material with graphene filler, the new composite prevent the risk resulting from dissociation of graphite in water resources, the new composite have superior resistance to water absorption and dissociation beside high biocompatibility. The graphene is prepared from graphite industrial and household wastes.

The machine has peeling surface move in front of graphite rod, the graphite is collected by suction and collected in mold with movable base. The composite material is manufactured in closed mold. The manufacturing parameters such as temperature and pressure depend mainly on the matrix type and graphene volume percent.

Smart mold was designed, the mold absorb energy and return to it s original shape after extraction of the sample, the inner surface was machined and polished. The inner surface is treated by irradiation to change the microstructure of the inner surface without any change in external surfaces, the oils is used in lubrication is analyzed into gases and contain airbag system. it help the sample to extracted easily with very smooth surface.

Graphene is exposed to laser irradiation for drying, microstructure change and redistribution of atoms without any significant effect on matrix, The method is physical without any chemicals or harmful reactions.

The interaction of laser radiation with matter leads to the absorption of electromagnetic energy in a thin film10^{-5}:10^{-6}cm thick the absorbed energy rises the

Dr. Eng. Consultant in Materials Sciences & Material, Cairo, Egypt*

temperature of the surface at this initial stage of interaction, the processes of heating and phase transition play the main rule. The dynamic of laser heating depends on the laser parameters (wavelength, beam energy, density, and temporal and spatial distribution of energy and on the temperature dependence of the thermal and optical parameters of the target such as the specific heat, thermal diffusivity, phase transition energy and reflectivity all parameters was optimized for best quality and lower cost. The method and machine are registered as patent in the Egyptian patent office. it has different applications in different fields such as electronic industries, sensors, spare parts, solar cells, building and construction.

Keywords: *Nano-Composite, graphene, filler, laser irradiation.*

INTRODUCTION

Diamond and graphite are both pure carbon, They are called allotropes, The electronic configuration of carbon is $1s^2 2s^2 2p^2$, i.e. with four valence electrons spread in the *s* and *p* orbitals. In order to create covalent bonds in diamond, the *s* orbital mixes with the three *p* orbitals to form sp^3 hybridization. The four valence electrons are thus equally distributed among the sp^3 orbitals, while each orbital points to one of the four corners of a tetrahedron. The tetrahedral structure, with the highly directed charge density give strength and stability to the bonds. Diamond is a three-dimensional structure. Each carbon is connected to four other carbons in three-dimensional space as a tetrahedron. Every atom is locked down tight. Consequently, all the bonds in diamond are of the same length (1.54 Å), with the same bond angle (109.47°). Diamond is incredibly strong, and one of the hardest materials we know. Figure 7.1 shows The transformation diagram of graphite and diamond.

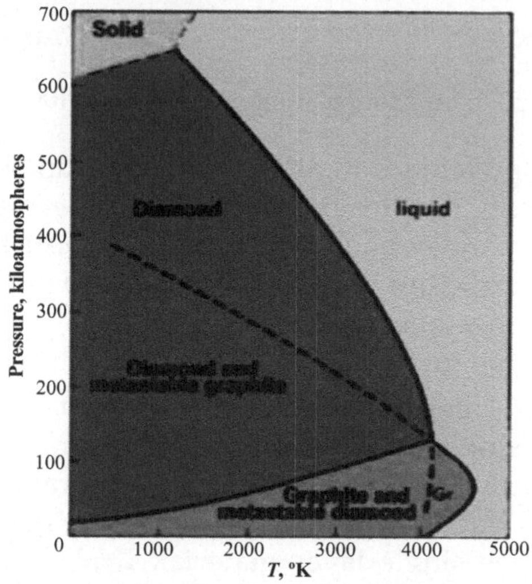

Fig. 7.1: Shows The transformation diagram of graphite and diamond

In graphite, each carbon is linked to three other carbon atoms in hexagonal arrays on a plane. There is little connectivity between the planes, so graphite is made up of flat surfaces that slide easily. The atoms on the planes are locked together, so the flat surface holds together. Figure 7.2 shows the structure of diamond and graphite. In the graphite crystal, the *s* orbital mixes with two *p* orbitals only, and each of the new three sp^2 orbitals points to one of the three vertices of a triangle which lies in the *x-y* plane (for instance). Three electrons occupy these orbitals and one electron stays in the p_z orbital which is directed perpendicular to the *x-y* plane. Hence, the carbon atoms are bonded by three σ bonds (the charge density lies between two atoms) and one Π bond (the charge density is concentrated above and under the *x-y* plane, perpendicular to the atomic bond).

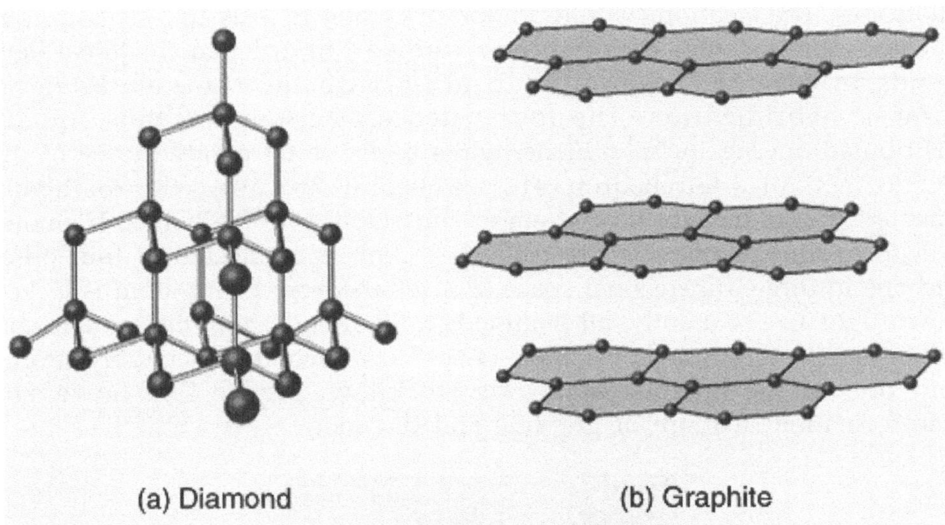

Fig. 7.2: Structure of diamond and graphite

Since there is no preference to atom the p_z-electron should bond to the bond formed (bond) with all three neighbors is weaker than the bonds, this electron is more free to move and contributes to conduction. Furthermore, the bond stabilizes the structure and "locks" it in the plane. The whole crystal is made of sheets held together by weak Van der Waals forces, separated by a distance of 3.40 Å. This gives softness to the structure [1,2].

Graphene is a two-dimensional matrix of carbon atoms, arranged in a honeycomb lattice. A single square-meter sheet of graphene would weigh just 0.0077 grams but could support up to four kilograms. That means it is thin and lightweight but also incredibly strong. Figure 7.3 shows the structure of graphene as single layer material. It also has a large surface area, great heat and electrical conductivity and a variety of additional incredible traits. This is probably why scientists and researchers call it "a miracle material" and predict it will revolutionize just about every industry known to man.

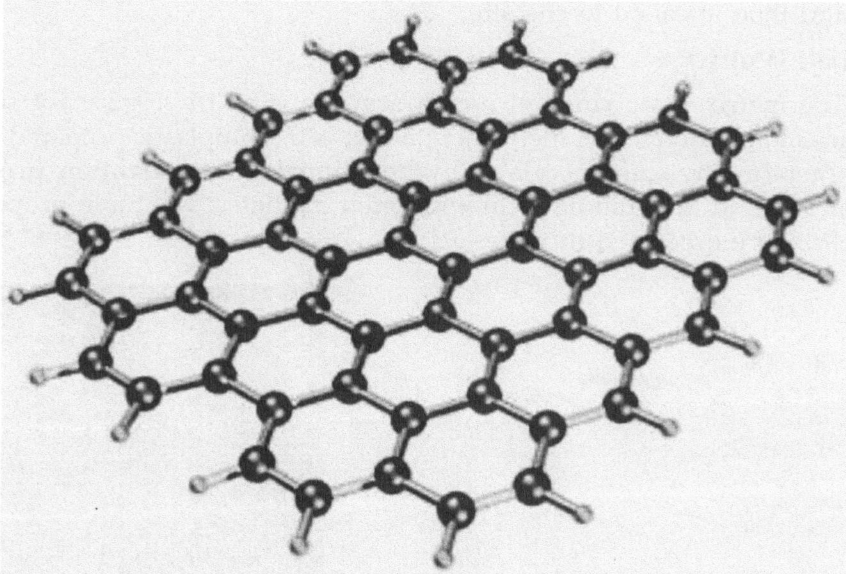

Fig. 7.3: The structure of graphene as single layer

COMPOSITE MATERIAL MANUFACTURING

The three main factors that help mold the composite material are the matrix, reinforcement and manufacturing process. As matrix, many composites use resins, which are thermosetting, thermoplastic or thermosoftening plastics (hence the name 'reinforced plastics' often given to them). These are polymers that hold the reinforcement together and help determine the physical properties of the end composite. Thermoplastic matrix is used in these work while micro and nano graphene are the reinforcement.

New method for preparation of new version of reinforced polymer for different applications. The new method overcomes the disadvantages in old materials such as low ductility, high corrosion rate, relatively high prices and fast crack propagation rate. with following modifications

1. Randomly distributed graphene are used to prevent crack propagation to critical size which leads to failure.
2. Additives are added to improve ductility and resistance to vibration and sudden actions.
3. New materials are manufactured in closed molds under temperature and pressure to reduce micro voids and external cracks.

4. The internal surface of mold has certain degree of roughness according to standard specifications.
5. The new composite material is completely prepared in the factory and then installed in the site

Materials (Matrix)

The matrix is polymethyl metha acrylate (PMMA. Figure 7.4 shows preparation of Polymethyl metha acrylate. It is thermoplastic prepared from monomer (methyl methacrylate) by additional polymerization process; polymer was in the granule form with 5mm diameter. The main properties of PMMA are explained in tables 7.1, 7.2, 7.3, 7.4 and 7.5.

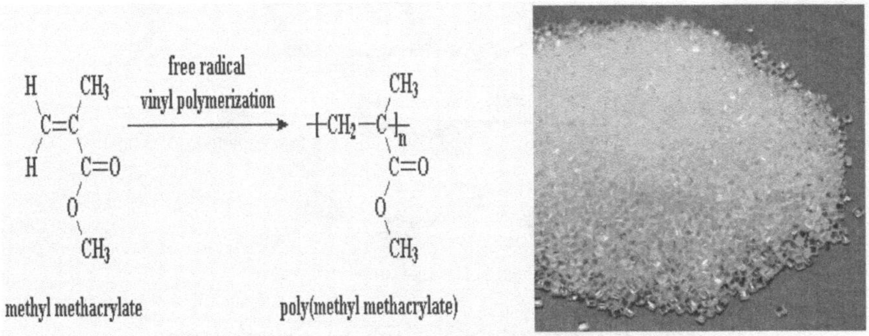

Fig. 7.4: Preparation of Polymethyl metha acrylate

Table 7.1: Typical physical properties of Poly (methyl methacrylate)

Physical Properties	Value
Density	1.15-1.19 g/cm^3
Water Absorption	0.3-2 %
Moisture Absorption at Equilibrium	0.3-0.33 %
Linear Mould Shrinkage	0.003-0.0065 cm/cm
Melt Flow	0.9-27 g/10 min

Table 7.2: Mechanical characteristics of Polymethyl methacrylate

Mechanical Properties	Value
Hardness Rockwell M	63-97
Tensil Strength Ultimate	47-79 MPa
Elongation at Break	1-30 %
Tensil Modulus	2.2-3.8 GPa
Flexural Modulus	3-3.5 GPa
Izod Impact, Notched	1.2-20k J/m^2
Izod Impact, Unnotched	11kJ/m^2
Tensil Creep Modulus, 1 h	1800-2700 MPa
Tensil Creep Modulus, 1000 h	1200-1800 MPa

Table 7.3: Electrical properties of Poly (methyl methacrylate)

Electrical Properties	Value
Electrical Resistivity	10^{14}-10^{15} Ωcm
Surface Resistance	10^{14}-10^{16} Ω
Loss factor 20° C, 1000 Hz, 60% humidity	0.04
Dielectric Constant	2.8-4
Dielectric Constant, Low Frequency	3-4
Dielectric Strength	17.7-60 kV/mm
Dissipation Factor	0.03-0.55
Arc Resistance	100-180s

Table 7.4: Thermal properties of Poly (methyl methacrylate)

Thermal Properties	Value
CTE, linear 20°C	60-130 μm/m, °C
CTE, linear 20°C Transverse to Flow	70-90 μm/m, °C
Specific Heat Capacity	1.46-1.47 J/g, °C
Thermal Conductivity	0.19-0.24 W/m.K
Maximum service Temperature, Air	41-103°C
Melting Point	130°C
Vicat Softening Point	47-117°C
Glass Temperature	100-105°C

Table 7.5: Optical properties of Poly (methyl methacrylate)

Optical Properties	Value
Haze	1-96%
Transmission, Visible	80-93%
Refractive Index	1.49-1.498

FILLER

Nano Graphene Inc,USA has developed a proprietary production process to manufacture a unique quality of Nano Graphene™ Graphene powder/dispersion from selected high purity graphite.The graphene powder can be dispersed in different solvent depending upon application. Tables 7.6, 7.7 show graphene characteristics from Nano Graphene Inc,USA.

In order to achieve maximum performance from graphene add required amount of graphene powder in desired solvent or solvent mixture and sonicate or shear mix for at least 30 min. Untrasonication or shear mixing will separate the graphene sheets and create homogeneous dispersion. If the graphene prepared in powder form or the product already dispersed there is no need for sonication or shear mixing.

Table 7.6: The main characteristics of graphene

Characteristics	Value
Form	Power
Purity	99.8%
Colour	Gray-black
Average particle size	Thickness <3 nm, Flake size: 1, 3-2,3 microns
Solubility	Standard
Number of layer	1-10
Electrical conductivity	80000 S/m
Density	130 Kg/m^3
Impurity	<0.003%

Table 7.7: Properties of graphene

Characteristics	Value
Appearance	Black-gray
Solubility	Standard
Elemental Analysis	C>99.5% O~0.05%
Thickness	<3 nm
Surface area	536 m^2/g (agglomerate)
Pore volume	0.25 cm^3/g (agglomerate)
Electrical conductivity	80000 S/m
Moisture Content:	>0.001%
Density:	130 Kg/m^3
Flake Size:	1.3-2.3 microns
Impurities:	>0.003%
SEM Image:	Attached
TEM Images	Attached
XRD Analysis	Attached
Raman Analysis	Attached
FTIR Analysis	Attached
BET Analysis	Attached

Grinding

A blinder with variable speeds is used to change the pieces of thermoplastics into powder form, The blinder speed is about 15,500 rpm, work at 200 volt - 50 Hz, and the grinding time is about 90 sec. Switch off for cooling is lasted about 180 sec to prevent the agglomeration of the particles and achieve reasonable degree of quality in grinding. The retained granules after sieving will be returned to blinder.

Preparation of Material

(A) *Mixing & Sieving*

The outcome of the two materials graphene and PMMA after grinding are collected the automatic sieve. Automatic mixing for thermoplastic in the powder form with different aspects ratio was done. The amount of material required was calculated. The mixture moves to the final drying and mixing phase by laser irradiation. This is for guaranteeing the final drying of the two mixtures.

(B) *Manufacturing process*

Plastic powders and treated graphene were mixed together in the solid state. The mixture is heated at the required temperature, according to its components. The heating rate depends on the type of the joining material, compression and cooling were done for heated mixture. Figure 7.5 and figure 7.6 show The manufacturing steps and parameters respectively.

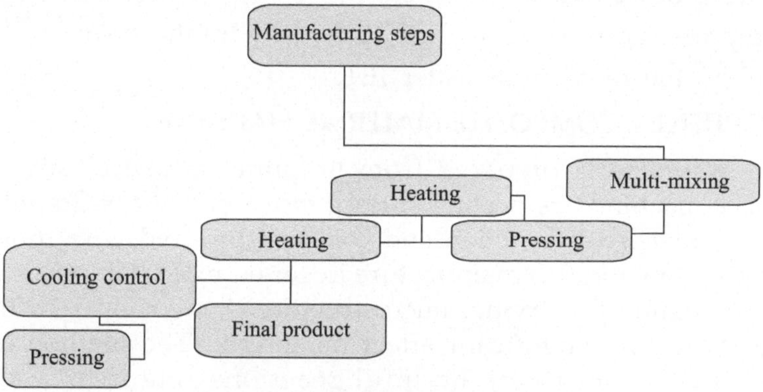

Fig. 7.5: The manufacturing steps

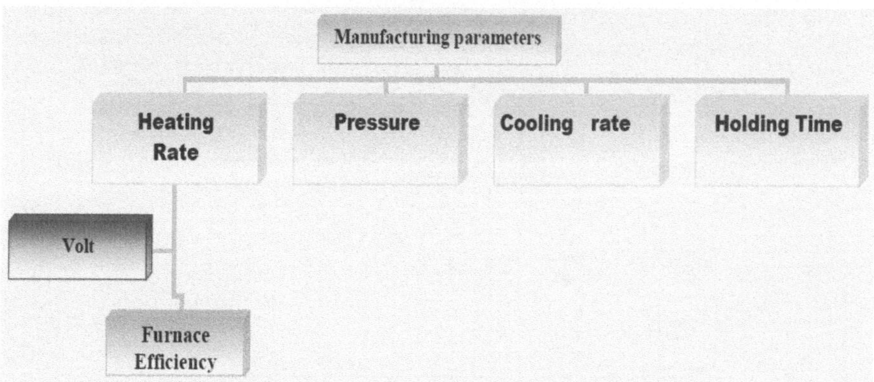

Fig. 7.6: The manufacturing parameters

Nano composite material is fabricated, the new composite material is distinguished with the light weight and the ability to endure scratch and damping capacity comparing with the natural graphene. It is also liable for the easy formation and distinctive with different colors and shapes.

THE MANUFACTURING QUALITY PARAMETERS

The manufacturing parameters were adjusted and the effect of temperature, pressure and cooling rates were recorded. Design and test of the new system were evaluated. The nano-composite material consists of poly methyl metha acrylate as matrix reinforced with graphene as filler The manufacturing steps may be summarized in the following steps:

1. Grinding of PMMA by electrical blinder-and control the grinding time to be less than 1.5 min to avoid temperature rise and agglomeration of particles after that use mesh < 300ìm diameter for sieving.
2. Graphene have used in powder form.
3. Mixing of the two powders.
4. Heating the mold.
5. Compress the mixture with (5:10 ton) hydraulic system.
6. Cooling the mold with water JET.

THE GRAPHENE - COMPOSITE MATERIAL MACHINE

The graphene is prepared from graphite industrial and household wastes. The machine has peeling surface move in front of graphite rod, the graphite is collected by suction and collected in mold with movable base. The composite material is manufacture in closed mold. Graphene is exposed to laser irradiation for drying, microstructure change and redistribution of atoms without any significant effect on matrix, The method is physical without any chemicals or harmful reactions. Figure 7.7 shows The manufacturing machine of composite with graphene filler.

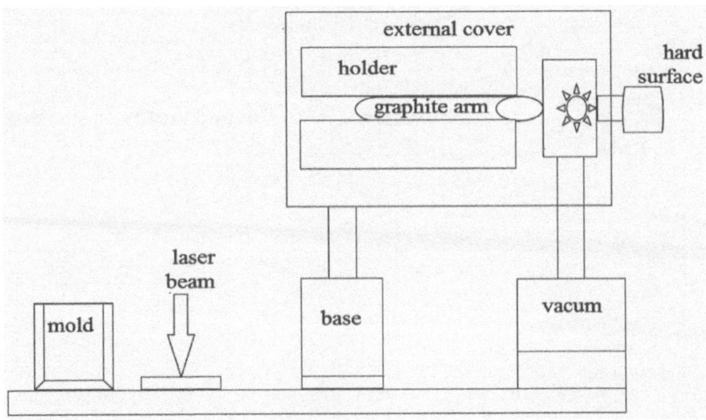

Fig. 7.7: The manufacturing machine of composite with graphene filler

The main parts of the machine

1. Metal body of peeling element
2. Rotating column with motor
3. Circular Knives
4. Coarse (rough) surface
5. Movable arm
6. Motor
7. Thick metal casing
8. Unpack
9. Graphite rod
10. Pull hose
11. Collection mold with mobile base
12. Laser beam
13. Closed mold for composite material

Steps of operation

1. The graphite rods is fixed between two arms
2. Sand paper is fixed in front of graphite rod
3. both graphite rod and sand paper inside metallic shell to allow cooling
4. mechanical peeling is done and powder material is collected under vacuum
5. The powder collected in mold with movable base
6. The base move in front of the laser beam
7. The graphene is dried due to laser irradiation action
8. The composite material manufacturing begin under certain conditions

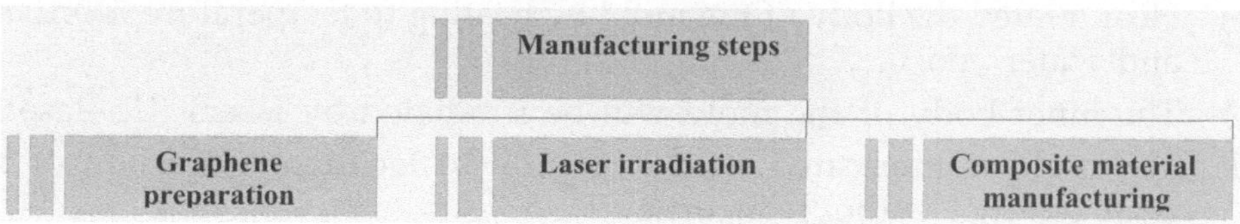

Fig. 7.8: The machine operation steps

Characteristics of new process

1. The manufacturing of composite material from graphene prevents its analysis and interaction with water and environment, while retain its properties.
2. Economic process depends on preparation of graphene from industrial and household waste.

3. The preparation of the composite material is controled and efficient process.
4. Treatment of graphene by laser irradiation without any harm effect up onPMMA matrix which is not affected by laser radiation.
5. The lasers irradation is affect the microscopic structure of graphene, rearrange, redistribute the atoms and improve its properties and structure without affecting its chemical composition.
6. The method is physical and does not contain any chemicals or reactions that harm graphene.
7. Graphene works very efficiently and can control the proportion of graphene added.

MOLD MANUFACTURING

Smart mold was designed, the mold absorb energy and return to its original shape after extraction of the sample, the inner surface was machined and polished. The inner surface is treated by irradiation to change the microstructure of the inner surface without any change in external surfaces, the oils is used in lubrication is analyzed into gases and contain airbag system. It help the sample to extracted easily with very smooth surface.The invention has been transferred to industry successfully in manufacturing of composite materials. Composite materials are considered as one of the most important industries in 21th century. The cost of that industry is concentrated on mold manufacturing. It is expensive relative to its low lifetime. The mold design and quality affects the size, shape, surface finish and amount of losses in the final product. The above disadvantages may be overcome by manufacturing a new type of mold.

Advantages of the new techniques

(a) The mold is made from iron with 2% carbon.
(b) Heat treated the body of the mold by heating to temperature 700:1000C and water cool
(c) The inner body of the mold will be irradiated by lasers (IR –lasers)
(d) The mold is lubricated with heavy oil to facilitate extraction of the final product without distortion.
(e) The system reduces the machining process to the minimum level, improve surface finish and reduce losses.

New topics in new mold technique

1. Manufacturing of new composite material with graphene filler to prevent reaction and dissociation of graphene with water
2. Preparation of graphene from industrial wastes
3. Treatment of graphene by laser without any significant effect up on the matrix

4. Laser irradiation change the microstructure and characteristics of graphene without any change in chemical composition
5. Laser irradiation is physical method without any chemicals may affect graphene characteristics
6. The method depends on mechanical peeling

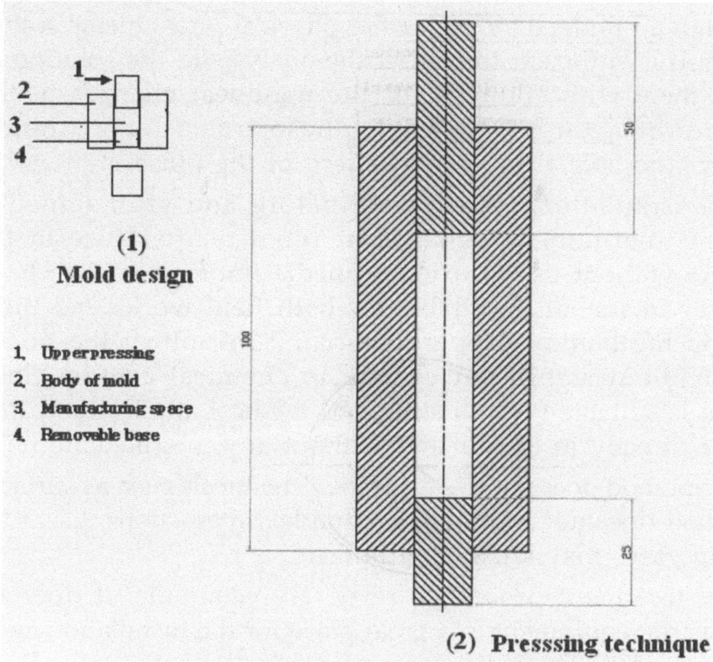

Fig. 7.9: The manufacturing closed mold

Fig. 7.10: Molds with external heaters

Laser irradiation process

The processes of laser interaction with materials generally involve either:

1. Heating of target surface
2. laser absorption during irradiation process and microstructure changer

To gain an understanding of the physical phenomena in the first type of process. It is sufficient to restrict the analysis to the solution of the heat problems there with allowing for the nonlinear changes in the thermal parameters of a target material, phase transition without melting, reflectivity, and spatial temporal pattern of the pulse.

Laser irradiation of graphene before and after impeding it into transparent thermoplastic matrix at room temperature in the normal atmosphere without use of external media improve surface hardness and wear. Laser treatment is suitable for both field works and industry. The improve in mechanical properties occur as result of the microstructure changes without significant change in chemical composition, so laser irradiation is suitable for industrial and medical applications. Processing is performed directly in the air and without any intermediate liquid or gas.

New method does not use expensive chemicals such as surface coverage. New method does not include any complex interactions, hazardous wastes or harmful gases may affect environment.

Laser treatment process is relatively economic. It does not need a huge industrial equipment in a great place for the installation and operation of such equipment.The main components in the new method are only the laser source and optical parts,it is considered as the only surface treatment method can be done in the field.

Method to improve the mechanical properties of nano materials, micromaterials and short fibers by indirect exposure to laser irradiations. The method was done by dipping powder materials in transparent plastics to allow the passage of a laser beam through it without being absorbed or interact with transparent material

The laser affect the structure of powder and improve properties, the treated nanomaterials or powder were collected. The method is a physical process free of pollutants and exhaust, it do not cause economic losses in the amount of material treated

The range of laser power density for the process of laser irradiation without melting and/or evaporation does not exceed a threshold value of 10^6w/cm^2. This region of small power densities is useful for heat treating of material in the range of moderate power densities from 10^6:10^8 w/cm^2. The second type of process employed, in laser irradiation, becomes dominant. The analysis of this process considers both the heat and the problems of target vaporization, plasma wave excitation and plasma effect during and after laser beam interaction.

The interaction of laser radiation with metals leads to the absorption of electromagnetic energy in a thin film10^{-5}:10^{-6}cm thick the absorbed energy rises the temperature of the surface which began to melt and vaporize at this initial stage of interaction, the processes of heating and phase transition play the main rule. The dynamic of laser heating depends on the laser parameters (wavelength, beam energy, density, and temporal and spatial distribution of energy and on the temperature dependence of the thermal and optical parameters of the metal target such as the specific heat, thermal diffusivity, phase transition, energy and reflectivity all parameters was optimized for best quality and lower cost.

ADDITIONAL PART: INTELLECTUAL PROPERTY ASSESSMENT

CREATION OF INDUSTRIAL CYCLE

This work is a complete industrial cycle done by individual efforts. The initiative have a lot of aims, and success to achieve almost all aims the first aim is the production of new composite material which have superior properties, this initiative produce more than 40 compound suitable for more than 120 industry. Second aim is the development of a new method of manufacturing, which is cheap, economic and suitable for our society. Our society is interested in small industries, this initiative transfer the up to date technology to Egypt, develop and simplify this technology. The third aim of the initiative are suitable to be separated initiative is the recycling of the industrial wastes. This part of the initiative is catch two apples with the same arrow because it makes the composite material industry get red of its wastes by mixing these wastes with the metal industries wastes this mixture is treated and used in production of building materials to complete this initiative different organizations work together as teamwork. Initiative uses the laser irradiation in surface treatment of the composite materials for the first time these consider as scientific contribution and help in research and development. To solve the problems have appeared during first steps, new aims such as material treatment, using local raw materials, and design of automatic industrial unit. New unit gives us the ability to transfer the project all over the world. Women begin the initiative and push it forward in all stages; she was the leader of the initiative that achieves gender equality and proves the abilities of women to deal with heavy industries

We can summarize the results of the initiative in Income generation, job creation, and vocational training. These beside the scientific and research contributions. We still have more steps and aims. Figure 7.11 shows the manufacturing cycle.

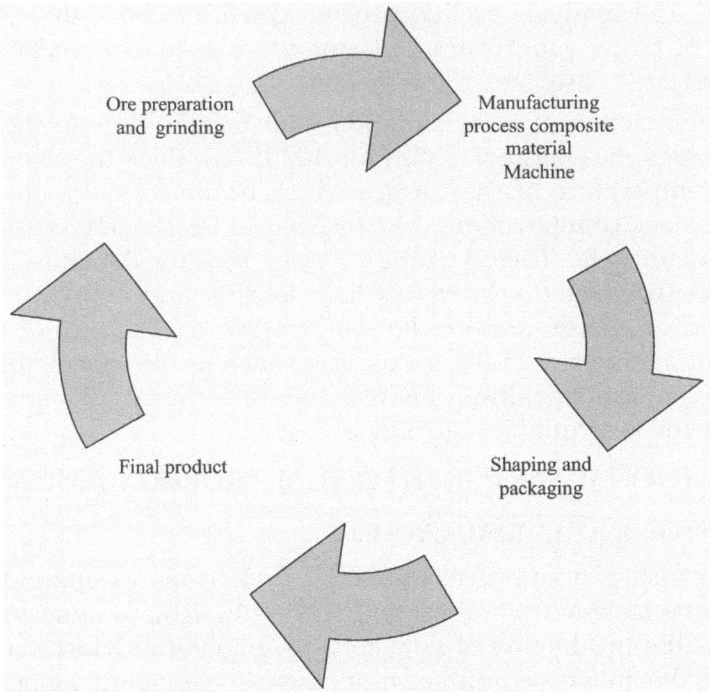

Fig. 7.11: The manufacturing cycle

The complete industrial cycle work in three directions the first direction is the production of new composite material with a new properties and new methods of treatment, the second direction is to develop a new method of manufacturing suitable for the society nature and economic, the third direction is the recycling of wastes by safe and valuable method. The initiative is main objectives are the technology transfer and technology development to our country, any initiative of this type have a lot of obstacles. The obstacles have been overcome step by step till success. The first obstacle we have not any financial support from any external sources. The initiative leader produce alone all the financial support required for this project to be completed. The technology of production of composite material especially the thermoplastic based is new and stranger technology not only in the Egyptian industry but also in the research field. No previous experience from any kind was found, and also this mean that there is a shortage of equipment, information, and technical support one of the important problems is the transfer of the project to industry economically to meet the requirements of the society. All of these obstacles have been overcome by plan of works according to timetable. First a lot of experiments were done to reach the most economical method of manufacturing. We developed the material's composition, manufacturing method, and method of treatment. In other words we now have our own technology in manufacturing of composite material and the treatment of composite material by laser irradiation are our invent. After the initiative obtains a group of patents all of the people become sure that our initiative have a really scientific contributions.

Co-operation with different organization help us some private sectors give us technical support about the raw materials properties and method of manufacturing. Non-government Organization pays attention to the recycling of wastes. Figure 7.12 shows The main features of the project.

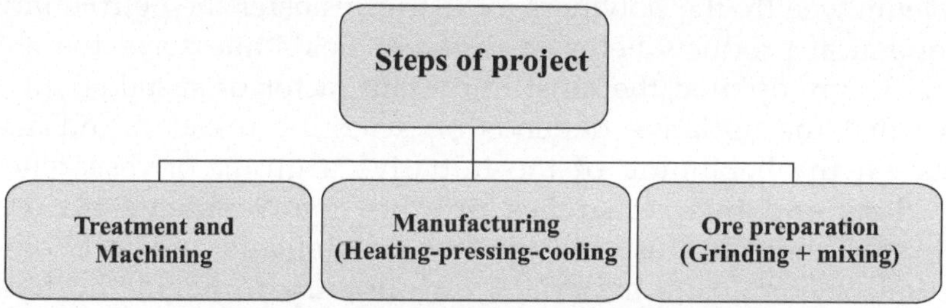

Fig. 7.12: The main features of the project

The greatest development in the history of the initiative was occurred by co-operation with factories. The first automatic unit was manufactured, and the products meet the requirements of the society. The continuity and sustainability of the initiative is related to the continuity in research and development and related mainly to the ability of our initiative to solve some of the Egyptian problems.

UNIQUE AND INNOVATIVE FEATURES

The composite material industry is a very complicated technology. Our project changes these concepts completely. The project makes the composite material manufacturing economic and suitable for small industries scale. The patents are transferred to industry, new technology is created. All steps of the project are done in Egypt without any foreign experience. The future developments in the project will try to replace imported raw materials with Egyptian ores.

The technology is unique in all steps. Our technology depends on a group of patents. First patent is related to new composite materials, second patent is related to moulds design and manufacturing techniques, third patent is related to design of full automated production line, fourth patent is related to new method of graphene treatment and preparation, fifth patent is related to using laser technology in composite material production and treatment of composites, sixth patent is related to the preparation of nano-materials necessary for nano-composites. Our technology is first production line depends on Egyptian patents all over the world.

SUSTAINABILITY

It is the main feature of the initiative. The initiative as we mentioned above will establish a small units for production of composite materials. The units can achieve a reasonable range of profit capable to produce continuity of the operation of the units, and these units can cover the establishment cost and initial costs from 5 to 10 years maximum, that depends on the size of the unit and the production rate. The initiative helps in solving the problems of the society such as Income generation, job creation, and vocational training. The initiative produces a good conservation of petroleum wealth; the polymers industries transfer the petroleum wealth into economical products helps in different fields and have the ability of recycling. In my opinion the most important factor of sustainability of the initiative that the initiative depends on scientific research and academic concepts. At the beginning of the initiative a group of researches have already done and this researches produce many patents till now, the research work not only use the up to date methods and technologies in production of composite materials, but also try to begin the tomorrow technology by using laser techniques in part of the initiative. The researches are followed by economical studies about the project's cost and profits. All of the above studies give the initiative the strong base of sustainability. The continuity in research and development of the final products is one of the most important factors of sustainability; Method is compatible with the environments and capable of applicability in a big cities or small towns. Both girls and boys can contribute in the initiative. Gender equality is achieved In other words we can say the welfare in society as a result of the initiative will produce strong push toward multilateral cooperation and assistance to sustainability.

TRANSFERABILITY

Transferability have considered as the main feature of the initiative. The initiative transfer first from scientific research to applied research, the transfer applied research and patents to experimental unit suitable for small industries. The manual experimental unit has transferred to industry and full automated. The automatic industrial unit become production line. The position of the initiative also transfers from Cairo (capital) to the industrial zones around Cairo. Transferability of the initiative is related strongly with the continuous research and development in the work conditions and requirements. Different parts all over the world have different customs and habits, this besides difference in climate, resources, and wealth. In Egypt Cairo, Delta, and Upper Egypt have different cultures and habits, some villages depends on the Agriculture completely while other towns have industrial Areas. When transferring our initiative to any position inside and outside Egypt there is some consideration and requirements that must be taken into account. First we must prepare heavy training courses to all the people work in the initiative transfer, Network of strong communications must be held between the original initiative leaders in Cairo and new position. The fast and strong communications will unable the new initiative to exchange data and information, the new initiative must be aware of any research and developments done in the original initiatives. The outputs of the initiatives I mean the type of composite material produced and their applications must be compatible with the needs of the people in that area. Marketing of the products results from the new projects must be managed by the original one to avoid any collapse may have bad effects on both of them. In agricultural area there are extra air filters and water treatments must be installed in the unit to avoid any contamination to the atmosphere. Using local products should solve the problems of transportation of the raw materials. Using final products in local market. Using cheaper method of transportation to avoid any extra costs may affect on the economic of the process. The numbers and sizes of the new units must be compatible with the population density in that area. Finally we can emphasis that our initiative has a strong transferability because it does not depend on certain climate and help in Income generation and job creation. The initiative has no disagreements with the customs and habits of the people anywhere.

SITUATION BEFORE THE INITIATIVE BEGAN

The world has a great revolution in the fields of new materials and laser applications. Egypt and poor countries are still away from modern technology, and try to solve the problems of poverty and unemployment. Our initiative begins to solve the social problems by using new methods of modern technologies

ESTABLISHMENT OF PRIORITIES

we establishes priorities of the initiative. The priorities were arranged according to their importance and according to the timetable The first priorities is the achievement of scientific contribution, development of research tools, and technology transfer to industry through the social needs. The initiative directs the scientific researches toward Income generation, job creation, and vocational training. One of the most important priorities of the initiative is the recycling of the wastes resulting from composite material industries. Conservation of petroleum resources by directs it toward petrochemical industries. Gender equality and social inclusions have been considered as one of the most important priorities.

FORMULATION OF OBJECTIVES AND STRATEGIES

The initiative has objectives such as scientific objectives, social objectives, industrial objectives, and environmental objectives. Gender equality and women role in leadership of new technology. The conservation of resources specially the petroleum resources is one of the important objectives of the initiatives. So this initiative direct petroleum resources toward the petrochemicals and polymers industries. The second objective is the help in solving the social problems by income generation from small industries this will reduce imports, increase exports, and create jobs chances for women in the new fields. The protection of environment by recycling of wastes in safe and economic way.

MOBILIZATION OF RESOURCES

The co-operation between different organizations is necessary for this practice to be completed. The first financial support comes from the women who begin this initiative for the first time. This individual effort needs a help from the private sector factories, the university and from the public sector factories. All of these organizations help in technology transfer and scientific research by allowing us to use the facilities and equipments; the help is summarized in testing and primary experiments of the project. After the project have a group of patents for the composite materials, the new method of manufacturing, treatment process, and design of new industrial unit. Establishment of a new lab for future developments is necessary. Design center and their factories help in the industrial execution, production and marketing of the project. Non-Governmental Organizations help also in this initiative they help in the publish of papers and introduce our initiatives in many conferences and work shops. The radio, television, and newspapers play a very important role to support the initiative.

RESULTS ACHIEVED

The initiative consider as an example of the successful projects. Women play a significant role from design to marketing. The initiative produce scientific contribution in a very specific field, the production of thermoplastic based composite material is a new trend all over the world and with these patents Egypt consider as one of the countries all over the world build and transfer new technology. Now we have shafts, gears, rods, chairs, tables, and electrical equipment made from composite. We will establish very small units for production of the parts mentioned above this small unit will manage by youth. We not only transfer the modern technology but also we develop it and make it suitable for our country.

The government studies a project for production of polymers. The initiative achieves co-operation between different organizations. The organizations have different objectives and different categories, all of these organizations include governments, universities, non government organizations, private sector factories, institutes, and pubic sector factories work as a team work and each of which help by their equipments and experiences. The initiative deals with the industrial wastes from a new point of view, transfer the industrial wastes to a new materials have insulation characteristics and resistance to environmental conditions. The initiative produces a complete industrial cycle and helps the metal industries to get red from wastes and achieve profit. In near future the initiative produces about 300-employment chance. Now the initiative transfer to other countries.

LESSONS LEARNED

Before beginning of the practice, we do survey for the published data about similar initiatives inside and out side, the United Nation programs for development was also studied. The study of the international projects gives us a clear fact that all of the industrial countries begin with small industries, China for example begins with very small industries, and now the Chinese products are every where with competitive prices. But there are some initiatives which give us a strong push such as Elbasisa Elgedida the project success in reclamation of 300,000 km^2 in the east desert in Egypt, the work is done by youth without any external funds or assistance from the government or any external sources. This project gives us the green light to begin our initiative with individual efforts, and without outside external support from any source. The second project was Elbragil project, Elbragil is a small village in Giza near Cairo, some people in the village began a project to collect and recycles of wastes from fields and houses the project is grow day after day and have been funded from the government. These projects encourage me to add a branch to my initiative deal with recycling of the composite material wastes and the metal industries wastes. There is also another initiative is done by (Future Generation Foundation). In this initiative a training course in computer software, English language, computer science, and management are learned to groups of youth. The youth have different qualifications and different cultures and almost all of them path the exams. So we are sure that the Egyptian youth especially girls have the ability to deal with the up to date technology from any kind easily, and they can deals with the modern equipments and modern methods of manufacturing after a very short training.

MARKET ASSESSMENT

A. Market Need

The customers used composite to achieve high strength, light weight and good corrosion resistance in other world to achieve superior properties for specific applications.

- automotive industries, medical applications, marine application, construction and airplanes industries.
- The market needs the products to avoid the disadvantages in normal material such as alloys and plastics.

- Our technology transfer the high technology to a simple and abundant technology.

  Composite technology now is available small industrial units suitable for youth projects.

B. Market demand

Prices and cost influence demand in the market, the demand is relatively week because the price is high. Demand will rise when the price become suitable.

C. Market size

The Egyptian market import similar products with about 700 million dollar every year. This data was calculated from the available data in the information center and decision making center.

- Suitable price and good quality are the main requirements to enter and capture the market
- The source of information in the web site

D. Market research information

E. Competing products

- Plastic machine manufacturing, spare parts suppliers
- The alloyed polymers companies are the alternative but quality is limited
- Chinese companies are the potential competitions (very low prices)

F. New developments and circumvention

New types of composite are developed and nanotechnology is the future.

My technology was developed in the same way but I invent a new technique for treatment of composites by laser irradiation. In the near future new techniques will developed to prepare raw material such as fibers and nanoparticles.

G. Suppliers

- The main supplier is the Chinese and French companies. All of them use the same technology so considered as one competitor.
- From the above data the market is relatively limited but our products are very specific and competitive because it is suitable for small industries scale.
- Most of these suppliers are potential licensees.

H. Competitive advantages

The composite material industry is a very complicated technology. Our project changes these concepts completely. The project makes the composite material manufacturing economic and suitable for small industries scale. The patents are transferred to industry, new technology is created. All steps of the project are done in Egypt without any foreign experience. The future developments in the project will try to replace imported raw materials with Egyptian one.

Our products have good quality and low cost. Our product is really competitive. We can say that, the products meet the customer needs. The competition with foreign product depends mainly on prices and competition with local products depends mainly on quality. The products have a wide range of applications.

I. Regulatory issues

- Now the Egyptian market is open, our product is competitive in price and quality. No real competition exists.
- Hard sale and soft sale advertising procedure will be arranged, and these will take from 6 months to 18 month
    - *(a)* The technology is protected by two ways. First, know how is registered as a group of patents in the Egyptian academy of science and technology (patent office). Patents protect the scientific idea, methodology, scientific contributions, modifications and theory of operation. Second, the technology is protected by industrial registration in the ministry of industry and trade, industrial registration protect morphology, colors, appearance and internal shape of the moulds and manufacturing machines. In the near future, industrial registration will be done.
    - (b) Technology is unique and completely different from similar techniques.

REFERENCES

1. Bovenkerk, H.P., Bundy, F.P., Hall, H.T., Strong, H.M. & Wentorf, R.H. Preparation of Diamond. Nature 184, 1094-1098 (1959).
2. Hall, D.R., Russell, M.E. & Hall, H.T.J. Composite Polycrystalline Diamond cmpact. USA Patent 4604106 (1986).
3. Hebatalrahman, Composite Material from Graphene, Egyptian Patent Office Registered in Sep. 2017.
4. Lai, A.J.D. Diamond Compact Abrasive. USA Patent 3141746 (1964).
5. Mao, W.L. *et al.* Bonding Changes in Compressed Superhard Graphite. Science 302, 425-427 (2003).
6. Yagi, T., Utsumi, W., Yamakata, M., Kikegawa, T. & Shimomura, O. Highpressure in situ x-ray-diffraction Study of the Phase Transfromation from Graphite to Hexagonal Diamond at Room Temperature. Phys. Rev. B 46, 6031-6039 (1992).
7. Kim, Y. & Na, K. High pressure X-ray Diffraction Study on a Graphite using Synchrotron Radiation. J. Petrol. Soc. Korea 3, 34-40 (1994).

8. Zhao, Y.X. & Spain, I.L. X-ray Diffraction Data for Graphite to 20 GPa. Phys. Rev. B 40, 993-997 (1989).
9. Lynch, R.W. & Drickamer, H.G. Effect of High Pressure on the Lattice Parameters of Diamond, Graphite, and Hexagonal Boron Nitride J.Chem. Phys. 44, 181-184 (1966).
10. Hanfland, M., Beister, H.& Syassen, K. Graphite under Pressure: Equation of State and First-order Raman modes. Phys. Rev. B 39, 12598-12603 (1989).
11. Goncharov, A.F., Makarenko, I.N. & Stishov, S.M. Graphite at Pressures up to 55 GPa: Optical Properties and Raman Spectra. High Press. Res. 4, 345-347 (1990).
12. Liu, Z., Wang, L., Zhao, Y., Cui, Q. & Zou, G. High-pressure Raman Studies of Graphite and Ferric Chloride-graphite. J. Phys.: Condens. Matter 2, 8083-8088 (1990).
13. Schindler, T. & Vohra, Y.K. A Micro-Raman Investigation of High-pressure Quenched Graphite. I. Phys.: Condens. Matter 7, L637-L642 (1995).
14. Miller, E.D., Nesting, D. C. & Badding, J.V. Quenchable Transparent Phase of Carbon. Chem. Mater. 9, 18-22 (1997).
15. Fayos, J. Possible 3D Carbon Structures as Progressive Intermediates in Graphite to Diamond Phase Transition. J. Solid State Chem. 148, 278-285 (1999).
16. Nakayama, A. *et al*. Compression of Polyhedral Graphite up to 43 GPa and x-ray diffraction Study on Elasticity and Stability of the Graphite Phase. Appl. Phys. Lett. 84, 5112-5114 (2004).
17. Reich, S. & Thomsen, C. Raman Spectroscopy of Graphite. Phil. Trans. R. Soc. Lond. A 362, 2271-2288 (2004).
18. Aust, R.B. & Drickamer, H.G. Carbon: A New Crystalline Phase. Science 140, 817-819 (1963).
19. Bundy, F. P. & Kasper, J.S. Hexagonal Diamond - A New form of Carbon. J. Chem.Phys. 46, 3437-3446 (1967).
20. Xu, J., Mao, H. & Hemley, R. The Gem Anvil Cell: High-pressure Behavior of Diamond and related Materials. J. Phys: Condens. Matter 14, 11549-11552 (2002).
21. Hanfland, M., Syassen, K. & Sonnenschein, R. Optical Reflectivity of Graphite under Pressure. Phys. Rev. B 40, 1951-1954 (1989).
22. Goncharov, A.F., Makarenko, I.N. & Stishov, S.M. Sov. Phys. JETP 69, 380 (1989).
23. Utsumi, W. & Yagi, T. Light-Transparent Phase Formed by Room-Temperature Compression of Graphite. Science 252, 1542 (1991).
24. Oganov, A.R. & Glass, C.W. Crystal Structure Prediction using ab initio Evolutionary Techniques: Principles and Applications. J. Chem. Phys. 124, 244704 (2006).
25. Li, Q. *et al*. Superhard Monoclinic Ploymorph of Carbon. Phys. Rev. Lett. 102, 175506-175509 (2009).
26. Umemoto, K., Wentzcovitch, R.M., Saito, S. & Miyake, T. Body-Centered Tetragonal C4 : A Viable sp3 Carbon Allotrope. Phys. Rev. Lett. 104, 125504 (2010).
27. Itoh, M. *et al*. New Metallic Carbon Crystal. Phys. Rev. Lett. 102, 055703 (2009).
28. Zhou, R. & Zeng, X. Polymorphic Phases of sp3-Hybridized Carbon under Cold Compression. J. Am. Chem. Soc. 134, 7530-7538 (2012).
29. Li, D. *et al*. Lowest Enthalpy Polymorph of Cold-compressed Graphite Phase. Phys. Chem. Chem. Phys. 14, 4347-4350 (2012).
30. Amsler, M. *et al*. Crystal Structure of Cold Compressed Graphite. Physical Review Letters 108, 065501, doi:10.1103/PhysRevLett.108.065501 (2012).

31. Niu, H. *et al*. Families of Superhard Crystalline Carbon Allotropes Constructed via Cold Compression of Graphite and Nanotubes. Physical Review Letters 108, 135501, doi:10.1103/PhysRevLett.108.135501 (2012).
32. Wang, J.T., Chen, C. & Kawazoe, Y. Low-Temperature Phase Transformation from Graphite to sp3 Orthorhombic Carbon. Phys. Rev. Lett. 106, 075501 (2011).
33. He, C. *et al*. New Superhard Carbon Phases between Graphite and Diamond. Solid State Comm. In press (2012).
34. He, C. *et al*. Four Superhard Carbon Allotropes: A First-principles Study. Phys. Chem. 14, 8410-8414 (2012).
35. Sheng, X.L., Yan, Q.B., Ye, F., Zheng, Q.R. & Su, G. T-Carbon: A Novel Carbon Allotrope. Phys. Rev. Lett. 106, 155703 (2011).
36. Yao, Y. *et al*. Comment on "New Metallic Carbon Crystal". Phy. Rev. Lett. 102, 229601 (2009).
37. Montgomery, J.M., Kiefer, B. & Lee, K.K.M. Determining the High-pressure Phase Transition in Highly-ordered Pyrolitic Graphite with Time-dependent Resistance Measurements. J. Appl. Phys. 110, 043725 (2011).
38. Loa, I. *et al*. Novel Graphitic Spheres : Raman Spectroscopy at High Pressures. Phys. Stat. Sol. (b) 223, 293-298 (2001).
39. Pocsik, I., Hundhausen, M., Koos, M. & Ley, L. Origin of the D Peak in the Raman spectrum of Microcrystalline Graphite. J. Non-cryst. Solids 227-230, 1083-1086 (1998).
40. Patterson, J.R., Kudryavtsev, A. & Vohra, Y.K. X-ray Diffraction and Nanoindentation Studies of Nanocrystalline Graphite at High Pressures. Appl. Phys. Lett. 81, 2073-2075 (2002).
41. Birch, F. Finite Strain Isotherm and Velocities for Single-crystal and Polycrystalline NaC1 at High Pressures and 300K. J. Geophys. Res. 83, 1257-1268 (1978).
42. Jeanloz, R. Finite-strain Equation of State for High-pressure Phases. Geophys. Res. Lett. 8, 1219-1222 (1981).
43. Liang, Y., Zhang, W. & Chen, L. Phase Stabilities and Mechanical Properties of Two New Carbon Crystals. EPL 87, 56003-56008 (2009).
44. Goncharov, A. F. *et al*. Thermal Equation of State of Cubic Boron Nitride: Implications for a High-temperature Pressure Scale. Phys. Rev. B 75, 224114 (2007).
45. Solozhenko, V.L., Ha¨usermann, D., Mezouar, M. & Kunz, M. Equation of State of Wurtzitic Boron Nitride to 66 GPa. Appl. Phys. Lett. 72, 1691 (1998).
46. Boulfelfel, S.E.,Oganov, A. R. & Leoni, S. Understanding the Nature of "Superhard Graphite". Scientific Reports in Press (2012).
47. Angel, R.J., Bujak, M., Zhao, J., Gatta, G.D. & Jacobsen, S.D. Effective Hydrostatic Limits of Pressure Media for High-pressure Crystallographic Studies. Journal of Applied Crystallography 40, 26-32, doi:10.1107/S0021889806045523 (2007).
48. Hammersley, A.P., Svensson, S.O., Hanfland, M. & Fitch, A.N. Two-dimensional Detector Software: From Real Detector to Idealised Image or Two-theta Scan. High Press. Res. 14, 235 (1996).
49. Xu, H. *et al*. Anisotropic Elasticity of Jarosite: A High-P synchrotron XRD Study. American Mineralogist 95, 19-23 (2010).

Patents

1. Hebatalrahman.A, "Design & Manufacturing of Lubricated and Treated Molds for Powder Metallurgy and Thermoplastic Composites", Patent Office magazine, Feb, 2004, No. 23021.
2. Hebatalrahman.A, "Effect of Laser Irradiation on the Composite Material Manufactured from Poly-Methyl Metha Acrylate by Nd-YAG and Argon Lasers", Patent Office magazine, June 2000, No. 20841.
3. Hebatalrahman. A, "New Treatment Method for Synthetic Fibers by Laser Irradiation", Patent Applications Bulletin, Issue No. 61, November, 2004, No. 428.
4. Hebatalrahman.A, "System for Manufacturing Composite Material Machine have Four Strokes", Patent Applications Bulletin, Issue No. 60, October, 2004, No. 399.
5. Hebatalrahman.A, "The Design and Manufacturing of Laser Unit for Treatment, Sterilization, and Melting", Patent Applications Bulletin, Issue No. 56, June, 2004, No. 227.
6. Hebatalrahman. A, "Laser Treated Hybrid Composite Material for Fire Resistance Applications", Patent Applications Bulletin, Issue No. 73, November, 2005, No. 452.
7. Hebatalrahman. A, "Industrial Unit for Nano-Materials Preparation by Magnetic Fields and Laser Beam", Patent Applications Bulletin, Issue No. 73, November, 2005, No. 442.

Commercial Literature

1. Algoumhouria Newspaper, No. 18169, Friday, 26 September 2003, pp. 9.
2. Algoumhouria Newspaper, No. 17642, Wednesday, 17 April 2002, pp. 16.
3. Algoumhouria Newspaper, No. 17967, Saturday, 8 March 2003, pp. 15.
4. Alakhbar Newspaper, No. 15693, Tuesday, 13 August 2002, pp. 2.
5. Alouma Alarabia weekly Newspaper No. 4, Monday, 23 January, 2006, pp. 7.
6. Alahram Newspaper, No. 43412, Saturday, 15 October, 2005, pp. 18.
7. Alakhbar Newspaper, No. 16522, Wednesday, 6 April, 2005, pp. 11.
8. Middle East Newspaper, No. 9288, Monday, 3 May, 2004, pp. 10.
9. Eltahdy, Electronic Magazine, June 2000.
10. www.idsc.gov.eg/customer/SiteLoginDetails.asp
11. www.idsc.gov.eg/ContactDirectory/Minist.

Index

❑ ❑ ❑ ❑ ❑